How to Use the Internet to Advertise, Promote, and Market Your Business or Web Site—With Little or No Money

Bruce C. Brown

How to Use the Internet to Advertise, Promote, and Market Your Business or Web Site—With Little or No Money

Copyright © 2006 by Atlantic Publishing Group, Inc.

1210 SW 23rd Place • Ocala, Florida 34474 • 800-814-1132 • 352-622-5836–Fax
Web site: www.atlantic-pub.com • E-mail sales@atlantic-pub.com
SAN Number: 268-1250

ISBN-10: 0-910627-57-6
ISBN-13: 978-0-910627-57-3

Library of Congress Cataloging-in-Publication Data

Brown, Bruce Cameron, 1965-
How to Use the Internet to Advertise, Promote, and Market Your Business or Web Site—With Little or No Money / Bruce C. Brown.
    p. cm.
Includes bibliographical references and index.
ISBN-13: 978-0-910627-57-3 (alk. paper)
ISBN-10: 0-910627-57-6 (alk. paper)
1. Internet marketing—Handbooks, manuals, etc. 2. Internet advertising—Handbooks, manuals, etc. 3. Web site—Design—Handbooks, manuals, etc. 4. Electronic commerce—Handbooks, manuals, etc. I. Title.

HF5415.1265.B765 2006
658.8'72--dc22   2006000621

EDITOR: Jackie Ness • jackie_ness@charter.net
FRONT COVER DESIGN: Lisa Peterson • Studio 6 Sense • www.6sense.net
ART DIRECTION & INTERIOR DESIGN: Meg Buchner • megadesn@mchsi.com
BOOK PRODUCTION DESIGN: Laura Siitari of Siitari by Design • www.siitaribydesign.com
Printed in the United States

CONTENTS

Introduction

Chapter 1   E-Commerce and Web Sites

Chapter 2   Starting Your Business

Chapter 3   The Importance of Internet Advertising

Chapter 4
Generating More Traffic to Your Web Site

Chapter 5   Branding

Chapter 6   Automation of Your Web Site

Chapter 7   E-Zines and Newsletters

Chapter 8   Using a Successful Auto-Responder

Chapter 9   Search Engine Optimization

Chapter 10 Banner Advertising

Chapter 11 Business Directories

Chapter 12 B2B Web Communities and Portals

Chapter 13 Google, Yahoo!, Overture, and Froogle Advertising

Chapter 14 Affiliate Programs

Chapter 15 Promoting Your Business Offline

Chapter 16 Unlocking the Secrets of EBay

Summary

Glossary of Terms

Additional Case Studies

Resources

Index

Introduction

To retain the competitive edge and marketing advantage in today's business environment, you must incorporate Internet marketing, Web presence, e-mail advertising, and other forms of e-commerce-driven marketing and sales campaigns. The Internet is a great tool to use if you have either a brick-and-mortar business or an online business, and a Web site for your business is almost a requirement. The Internet allows you to promote, advertise, and market your business in a cost-efficient manner so that you can focus your costs on other areas of your business. What other marketing tool do you have at your disposal where billions of people have the ability to reach out directly to your business or organization from anywhere in the world, and you have the capability of advertising to all of these potential clients for practically no cost or capital investment? You don't need to be a "techno guru," "Webmaster," or even possess a great deal of Web design knowledge or online experience to use the Internet in an effective manner that is going to push your business forward, increase sales, and promote your business and products to a new global customer base. After reading this book and applying the principles and techniques contained within, you will empower your brick-and-mortar business and Web site business to be leaders in the world of online marketing and promotion. We clearly and simply lay out all the steps that you need to take to maximize and harness the power of the Internet to promote and market your business and products at little or no cost. Over the past five years, there has been a boom in Web design firms and businesses trying to move their products and services to the World Wide Web. We reveal the simple steps, give you systematic Web site design knowledge, and arm you to compete with any professionally marketed Web site. The concepts and steps outlined in this book are easy to implement and can be managed at the small-business-owner level.

The bottom line is that you don't need a professional marketing firm to promote and market your online business! We tell you the secrets, time-tested methodology, and tricks of the trade to ensure that your site ranks at the top of the search engines. By implementing these procedures, you will reduce costs while increasing your online business sales and profits dramatically!

The concepts in this book are simple and will help you reach your existing and potential customers in a way that you previously couldn't. We designed this book for the small business that does not have an information technology or Web design staff and is limited on technology budget and knowledge. You'll be able to communicate with customers so that they can easily find you through a variety of methods and know exactly what you're selling and what your company and products stand for. Many of the advertising concepts outlined in this book will cost you little or nothing to implement, and in many cases you'll see immediate and substantial results. In addition, we provide you with additional tools, marketing suggestions, and other venues with which you can inexpensively expand your online business and increase customer visibility and profitability.

If you are the owner, proprietor, or manager of a traditional brick-and-mortar business, you need to tap into the power and potential of the Internet to reach your existing and potential customers so that you can communicate with them easily, so they can buy products direct without visiting your brick-and-mortar storefront, and so you can dramatically expand your customer sales base. You'll be saving the thousands of dollars in costs that you usually spend sending out flyers, postcards, and/or other forms of offline or postal advertising. These antiquated methods only reach a small customer base, are costly to produce and distribute, and typically fail to generate the return to break even. We will explain and show you how you can use your Web site to advertise current specials; let customers know what products or services are new and hot; let your customers know how to find you by providing contact information and directions to your business; provide your customers with additional information about your business, your products, and your services; how to use your products; and how to reach a potentially unlimited customer base at little or no cost!

If you have an online business, you'll discover that you can use the Internet in much the same way as if you were using the Internet to promote your brick-and-mortar business. We will take a look at several case studies of traditional brick-and-mortar businesses that have dramatically increased sales through establishment of an online sales and promotions division as well as many corporations that are strictly online and how they compete and thrive in a cutthroat marketplace. We'll arm you with the tools to ensure that your online business is ready to meet the potential onslaught of search engines, site visitors, and an expanding customer base.

No matter what type of business you have, the possibilities are endless when it comes to what you can do with Internet advertising and online business promotion solutions. It is critical that you understand the concepts, rationale, and procedures for each solution or suggestion that we provide. After reading this book, you will have learned the following Internet advertising concepts:

- What e-commerce means to your business, including e-commerce terms and definitions.

- The importance of using the Internet to advertise your business.

- How to come up with a successful marketing campaign.

- How to develop a Web site that will increase your profits.

- How to generate more site visitors and traffic to your Web site.

- What branding is all about and why it's important.

- How to efficiently automate your Web site.

- How to use an auto-responder effectively.

- How to launch a successful e-mail marketing campaign.

- Techniques for successful search engine optimization and submission.

- Effective ways to use banner ads for your Web site advertising.

- What affiliate programs are and how to use them successfully.

- The importance of business directories and Web communities.

- How to promote your business offline.

- The advantages of advertising with Yahoo! and Google.

- The benefits of using eBay storefronts and other eBay sales secrets.

- Other advertising strategies that can be successful in expanding and increasing the profitability of your business.

- A list of helpful resources and their Web sites.

Foreword

A classic American philosopher, George Santayana, once said, "Those who cannot remember the past are condemned to repeat it" (The Life of Reason, Volume 1, 1905). This concept doesn't just apply to history and cycles of life; it is a prominent theme in marketing.

Marketing on the Internet is not wholly distinct from traditional marketing. To qualify this, I simply intend to state that the "Four Ps" need to be maintained: product, place, price, and promotion. Far too often e-commerce businesses and brick-and-mortar companies moving toward the Web simply expect to succeed due to being there. It is the "If you build it, they will come" belief. Unfortunately, the Web is not the "Field of Dreams." Instead, the Internet is a global medium that serves its patrons as a commerce, research, contact, and entertainment platform. The key for businesses is determining how to best position themselves on the Internet to be found by those who can best use their site and monetize the experience.

Understanding all the nuances of Internet marketing does not have to be an overly daunting task. Though there isn't a shortcut method to achieving top search engine placements and prominent image branding worldwide, there is a method that companies can follow to ensure that their Internet marketing campaigns have a solid foundation and the potential for success. However, it is not simply the creation of the best Web site or loading content with a string of keywords, nor is it simply spamming the Internet with a product or service. Internet marketing is a fundamental understanding of marketing with a tool that can extend a company's reach. It is still a focused endeavor to reach a target audience and demographic with the ability to circumvent physical boundaries. Due to the seemingly endless methods of establishing one's presence on the Internet, it proves the strongest tool available for mass and targeted marketing.

Internet marketing allows companies to create additional presence anywhere that the Internet is accessed. Companies can start small with local directories and Internet Yellow Pages (IYPs). They may choose free listings, paid listings, enhanced listings, or paid performance. As well, businesses may choose to optimize their Web sites through search engine optimization (SEO) and other page rank building endeavors. The possibilities are endless. With the onset and probable domination of Internet television, companies can affordably compete on the Web with streaming video and audio, truly utilizing the high susceptibility to visual and aural stimulation of consumers. With so many possibilities of marketing on the Internet, the first step is to do some research and decide how to target an audience and which platform or tool to use to get there.

Bruce C. Brown's book, *How to Use the Internet to Advertise, Promote, and Market Your Business or Web Site — With Little or No Money*, is an excellent starting point for startups, new Internet entrants, or businesses looking to better their current efforts. He covers many of the dos and don'ts of Internet marketing and offers a solid starting point for any business looking to venture into Cyberspace.

— Jai Merchant
Senior Business Consultant
Internet Marketing Logic, Inc.
www.internetmarketinglogic.com

E-Commerce and Web Sites

E-commerce is a simple concept that you'll need to understand so that you can see exactly the steps you need to take to use the Internet for promoting your business. E-commerce is a broad term that we will discuss in great detail, all with the intent of providing you with low- or no-cost ways to improve your Web site marketing campaign.

> **E-commerce:** *Any sale or purchase that takes place using the Internet or through electronic means.*

Let's cover some of the basics of fundamental Web site terminology and theory. For a potential customer to visit your Web site, you must have a Web site and it must be hosted. There are thousands of companies that offer Web site design and hosting services, and some offer both services together. The first step is to obtain a domain name for your Web site. Most Web design firms offer inclusive hosting, Web site design, Web site maintenance, and domain name procurement. We highly recommend Gizmo Graphics Web Design (**www.gizwebs.com**) for their quality customer service, rapid site development, inclusive Web hosting, and domain name service as well as overall low cost. If you want to search for and buy your own domain name, we recommend GoDaddy (**www. godaddy.com**) as the premier service for domain name management. GoDaddy has proven time and again to be far superior than any other competitor in the domain name market. Once you have a domain name and a Web site established, you will need to ensure that the domain name server for your domain name is updated to point to your Web hosting company's DNS servers. GoDaddy simplifies this process by providing you with an intuitive Web-based management tool.

At this point we are assuming that you have a domain name, a completed and professionally designed Web site, and that your site is hosted, enabling access to anyone on the Internet. At this time you have what we would consider to be a "static" Web site. Your Web site may contain vast amounts of data and images about your products or services but offer no advanced or dynamic features such as shopping cart services or dynamically generated content.

There is nothing wrong with a static Web site, and, in fact, it is completely appropriate in most instances. The Silvermine Tavern (**www .silverminetavern.com**) in Norwalk, Connecticut, is a classic example of a superb static Web site. The Web site contains vast amounts of information about wine and dinner events, lodging, lunch and dinner menus, banquets, weddings, corporate events, and holiday gatherings. The site content is updated often to reflect new events, jazz artists, and unique culinary treats. Since the Silvermine Tavern Web site is designed to promote an establishment and not to sell products directly off the Internet, a static Web site is completely appropriate. Small and large businesses that wish to sell products online, such as Atlantic Publishing Company (**www.atlantic-pub.com**), have taken their sites much further by incorporating e-commerce into the Web site, enabling shoppers to buy and securely pay for products online. We will go into much more detail throughout this chapter.

The first thing that you need to understand is how e-commerce works: A consumer, or potential customer, accesses the Internet and navigates to your Web site. If you have a brick-and-mortar business, you'll want to have vital information on your Web site so that your customers can find you; as we discussed earlier, this would be a static Web site. This may include current products that are on special as well as other product listings that make consumers believe that your business is where they want to make their purchase and is both appealing and a good value to the consumer. Likewise, if you have an online business, you'll want to convince your potential customers or Web site browsers to make a purchase for the products you are selling from your Web site. Once consumers decide that they're ready to make a purchase, they'll need to be guided to an online transaction or secure Web server so that you can collect their personal and payment information using a secure encryption method. It is possible to create a Web site that can collect credit card and other sensitive data without offering encryption; however, most savvy shoppers will never enter credit card information into a non-secure Web site. Therefore, we highly discourage any attempt to create a simple shopping cart that does not include secure socket layer encryption of personal or sensitive data. Operating a Web site without encryption for personal or credit card data is a sure-fire formula for disaster and loss of potential customers.

To enable your Web site for e-commerce, you must install and configure your products in a shopping cart; we will offer you several low-cost and high-quality shopping carts. It is important to recognize the elements of a credit card transaction: your Web site contains the product pricing, description, and images, and the shopping cart is embedded into your Web site and stores the dynamic data regarding your product. When he or she is ready to "check out" from the Web site store, the customer typically clicks a "checkout" button and is taken to the encrypted version of the company Web site. The customer will typically continue with the checkout process by calculating shipping costs, entering personal information such as credit card data and a shipping address, and securely completing the transaction. All credit card companies charge a percentage of the sale as an overhead fee for using their credit processing services. The added service layer between your credit card processor and your Web site is known as a transaction service or gateway service. This layer recognizes an e-commerce transaction, performs immediate credit card authorization, and processes the transaction. While this service is not uncommon, it does add a layer of cost to operating your Web site, and we will discuss some lower-cost alternatives. There are two distinct possibilities that account for how your order may be processed: as discussed previously, after the order has been placed, all of the necessary information travels through a private gateway toward the "transaction/ gateway processing network." This processing network is where the transaction is approved or denied, depending on the credit history of the consumer and the funds available. Although this may seem like a long process, it takes only a few seconds to complete. For the business owner, offering an e-commerce service is an added service and an added fee. Another lower-cost option is to eliminate the transaction/gateway processing network. Many Web site owners prefer to manually "run" credit card payments through their desktop credit card processing/ authorization systems and merely use the shopping cart as an order processing and retrieval system, where the credit card is processed manually after the online session is completed. This low-cost alternative eliminates the cost of the middle-tier authorization and does not affect what the consumer sees after completing the checkout process. With both options, the consumer should be sent an order confirmation by e-mail. We will discuss the other shopping cart and authorization systems in detail throughout this chapter.

As mentioned, you will be able to use many different systems of payment to accommodate your online transactions, depending on how many transactions you average in one day. No matter what type of payment method you choose, you need to ensure that it is encrypted and secure so that the privacy and personal information of your customers is never jeopardized. As a reminder, never operate a Web site where you collect personal data or financial information without offering a secure and encrypted connection.

Digital Certificates

One of the first things that you're going to need to obtain when you're doing business on the Internet is a digital certificate. A digital certificate is also known as a "secure socket layer server certificate," or SSL certificate for short. A digital certificate is used to protect any communication that you have with your customers that contains private information. You'll need to have a digital certificate installed on your Web server so that you can take credit card orders in a safe and secure manner. You want to make sure that no one but you, your customer, and the bank receives your customer's financial and personal information. A digital certificate is going to ensure this privacy and security.

In most cases you'll be able to get a digital certificate through the Web hosting service where your Web site is hosted; however, it is not uncommon for them to mark up the cost of this service more than 100 percent over the cost of procuring the service directly from the providers listed below. If you wish to pursue buying your own SSL certificate, your Web hosting company will need to generate a key for your license from the Web server software (e.g., Microsoft Internet Information Server). You will need this piece of code (which will be sent to you in Notepad) to submit your SSL application with any service provider. After your SSL certificate is issued, you will be given a piece of code, or an encryption key, which you must provide to your Web hosting company. This ensures that encryption takes place and validates your corporate information to anyone wishing to view your certificate online. If you choose to buy an SSL certificate, you can expect to pay between $80 and $300 annually. The following are four reliable places to obtain your digital certificate:

1. **GoDaddySSL (www.godaddyssl.com)**
   Go Daddy will issue you a digital certificate using up to 256bit encryption for under $100 per year.

2. **Geotrust (www.geotrust.com)**
   Geotrust offers quick SSL certification for as low as $189 per year. Geotrust has always been a superior performer, and we highly recommend them.

3. **Thawte (www.thawte.com)**
   Thawte will issue you a digital certificate for $149.00. You can also receive a trial version for 21 days, and they typically offer other discounts.

4. **VeriSign (www.verisign.com)**
   VeriSign uses 128bit encryption for its digital certificates, ensuring your privacy and the privacy of your customers; however, it is also one of the most expensive services available.

Obtaining your digital certificate should be one of the first things that you implement if you're going to be doing business on the Internet. We do have some low-cost alternatives, which may be an option if you don't want to purchase an SSL certificate, are on a tight budget, or don't possess the ability to install your own SSL certificate on the Web hosting company's servers (some Web hosting companies will only allow you to utilize SSL certificates procured through them, and some don't offer SSL services at all).

- **Rich Media Technologies Just Add Commerce (www. justaddcommerce.com)** is a unique software/service which eliminates the need for a third-party SSL certificate and shopping cart since both are built into the JAC software. JAC is a plug-in to Microsoft FrontPage or Macromedia Dreamweaver software that allows you to quickly generate products and e-commerce enable your Web site in minutes. The HTML-based application is simple to use, cost effective, and includes SSL secure processing on the JAC Web servers, eliminating the need for both the SSL certificate purchase as well as the purchase of shopping cart software. You can even choose to incorporate a merchant credit card payment gateway or manually process credit card orders. When an order is placed by the customer, you are notified via e-mail of the order and then securely retrieve the order from the JAC Web site. The robust package includes e-mail order notification, customizable checkout templates, and good technical support. The service starts for around $329, with a reduced renewal for subsequent years. JAC is a very simple tool to use, and you don't have to be an advanced Web site designer to quickly implement e-commerce onto your Web site.

- **PayPal (www.paypal.com)** is a free alternative to buying an SSL certificate or a shopping cart. You will be required to open a business account with PayPal (which we highly recommend anyway). PayPal offers a very simple process to create an e-commerce-enabled Web site at no additional cost. Basic HTML (we suggest Microsoft FrontPage) is all that is required. One common myth is that for shoppers to utilize a PayPal shopping cart, they must also be PayPal users. This is not correct; there is no requirement for shoppers to join PayPal to allow them to securely shop and buy products from your Web site.

Web Hosting

Web hosting is an important aspect of e-commerce that you're going to have to establish before you can start doing business on the Internet, and typically before you complete your Web site design (which can be done without the Internet). Even if you are just planning to promote your traditional brick-and-mortar business online without e-commerce enabling your site, you must have a Web hosting account.

Shopping Carts

We have discussed, in general terms, the purpose of the shopping cart, which e-commerce enables your Web site, in conjunction with an SSL certificate and the Web server on which your site is hosted. A shopping cart is simply an application or program that keeps track of items a site visitor picks to buy from your site until he or she proceeds to the "checkout" phase of the buying process. As discussed earlier in this chapter, the shopping cart simply manages the process of keeping track of the products, financial data, and customer information, which is then passed to the credit card merchant gateway or is stored in a secure database, where the order is manually processed through a merchant credit card authorization process. The credit card merchant or payment gateway service, if implemented automatically, utilizes your Web site's secure connection through the appropriate financial networks and obtains an approval or denial for the credit card charge.

There are hundreds of shopping carts available—some are excellent, and some are not. They all have pros and cons, and we will recommend several for you. Before we make recommendations, it is important to understand the features available in a shopping cart so that you can determine which are desirable for your business.

There are many free shopping carts available, most of which are written in basic Perl language and may require extensive knowledge of scripting language as well as access to the Web server. Many Web hosting companies will not install third-party shopping carts, and most do not provide any technical support at all, so you need to be very cautious when selecting a shopping cart application. Full-feature shopping carts can cost upward of $800, so it is very important to review the features you truly need and select the most appropriate and cost-effective shopping cart solution.

As we already discussed, PayPal is one of the best free e-commerce shopping cart solutions. PayPal integrates basic shopping cart functions within your Web site, and it links via the PayPal network as the payment gateway. When the transaction is complete, the funds are automatically transferred and deposited into your PayPal account and can then be moved into your business checking account. The main resistance to implementing PayPal on a global scale by business owners was the reluctance of potential shoppers to join PayPal to complete a transaction; however, this was recently changed so that customers can complete a transaction without creating a PayPal account. Another advantage is that PayPal is universally accepted throughout the world, similar to major credit cards. With PayPal, there are no monthly fees, no purchase costs, and no setup costs. You are charged only a small percentage of each sale total. PayPal has an extensive program for fraud protection. Online merchants are offered a wide array of tools available from **www.paypal .com** to assist with the Web development and integration effort. The only "free" shopping cart we recommend is through PayPal.

Premium Shopping Cart Features

Shopping cart software has made tremendous strides toward easier integration, more robust features, and a wider array of configuration options. You need to be realistic in your expectations of a shopping cart. Amazon.com has the most powerful and robust storefront/shopping cart engines anywhere. You will not replicate all the features of Amazon.com for little or no cost, so you need to be realistic in expectations. Any shopping cart application will require a degree of technical knowledge. You must learn how to operate, manage, publish, support, and adapt the shopping cart to fit your Web site, and as with any new program, there will be a learning curve. A Web hosting company that supports your particular shopping cart may save you many hours of configuration nightmares. The following is a list of some of the features which may be available and will help you in determining which shopping cart is best suited to your needs.

AFFILIATES

Affiliate programs are one of the most successful and effective (and low-cost!) solutions for increasing your marketplace share, product visibility, and sales. The cost for incorporating an affiliate program is minimal, and the benefits can be tremendous. A robust affiliate module within a shopping cart application will take care of the new affiliate sponsorship/signup, process and track the transactions, provide detailed reports to the business and the affiliate, and process/feed payment information into a financial application, such as Quickbooks. Since the implementation of an affiliate program is so important to a sound Web strategy, we have created a separate chapter in this book dedicated just to affiliate programs.

CROSS SELLING

EBay and Amazon have mastered the art of cross-selling by making "suggestions" based on products similar to those which you have viewed or purchased previously, thus appealing to impulse buying by suggesting that you may be interested in these similar products. Some advanced shopping carts have the ability to implement limited cross-selling techniques. Just as in the physical world, impulse buying via the Internet is quite common, and some shopping carts have the ability to suggestively sell alternate and complementary products; for example, if customers select the "basic" version of a product, you can recommend that they consider the "advanced" version, or if customers choose a dinner entrée from an online menu, you can suggest that they also consider an appetizer to complement their meal.

QUANTITY DISCOUNTS

Most shopping carts allow you to incorporate a variety of discounts. You can offer discounts based on volume, quantity, and order total as well as shipping discounts. Most shopping carts also integrate coupons and gift certificates to offer additional discounts and incentives to new and returning customers.

Auto-Responders

Auto-responders are a feature of shopping carts that are often under-utilized or not adopted by business owners. This no-cost feature is perfect for providing follow-up correspondence to your customers with announcements, feature products, and discounts. We have dedicated separate chapters to auto-responders and Web site automation.

Other Features You May Wish to Consider

Online Credit Card and Check Authorization

These features offer built-in compatibility with multiple online payment service providers to allow real-time authorization of credit cards and checks. The following are some of the service providers available:

- VeriSign (Payflow Pro and Payflow Link, fully supporting VeriSign's Fraud Protection Services)

- CyberSource

- USA ePay

- TrustCommerce

- SkipJack

- PayPal

- LinkPoint

- EFT Secure

- Planet Payment

- PSIGate

- SurePay

- Moneris

- WorldPay

- MetaCharge

- AIM (used by providers such as AuthorizeNet)

Tiered Pricing Categories/Discounts

Tiered pricing categories offers the capability to adopt different price levels for various users, such as retail and wholesale customers. This feature may allow you to set percentage discounts for all items within your Web store, with the option of adjusting discounts for individual items. You may want to incorporate discount programs, where you can run sales and promotions just like traditional brick-and-mortar retail stores. Most shopping carts allow you to establish quantity discounts for each product, subtotal discounts based on the value of items in the user's basket, discounts based on users providing a discount code, or any combination of options.

Product Search Capability

You will definitely want to have the built-in ability for Web site customers to search your Web site and product database by a variety of methods, including product name, description, or keywords.

Adding Multiple Products or Options

When multiple products are displayed on a single page, some shopping carts allow customers to add quantities of multiple items to their basket with a single click.

XML Logging

Some business owners prefer the flexibility of XML (Extensible Markup Language) format data order logs, which can simplify the process of importing orders into any other third-party application that can read XML files.

Storefront/Product Builder

The hardest part in e-commerce enabling your Web site is the actual creation of the database and storefront. Built-in Store Builder dramatically improves this process by allowing for quick and maintenance-free integration that will not require changes to Web pages as products are added and removed from the store. This allows you to get your Web store operational by dynamically generating Web store pages based upon product category.

Quickbooks Integration

Many small businesses utilize Intuit's Quickbooks (**www.intuit .com**) for their financial ledgers. Most premier shopping carts feature Quickbooks integration, which allows you to export shopping cart data directly into Quickbooks.

Froogle/Yahoo! Data Feed

Many shopping carts allow you create a Froogle or Yahoo! Stores data feed from your product database. In turn, you simply submit this data file to Froogle, and your catalog will be available to anyone searching the Froogle or Yahoo! e-commerce site.

Web Development/HTML Automation Components

You may want a shopping cart that can be easily implemented and customized using any HTML editing software. Most offer components that make it easier to integrate with Macromedia Dreamweaver or with Microsoft FrontPage.

Sales Tax Computation

The ability to set up multiple tax rules to accommodate customers based on locality, including counties, city, ZIP code, state/province, and country.

Maximum and Minimums per Product

This allows you the flexibility to specify a minimum or maximum quantity allowed for purchase of an item on a per-item basis. If you have a promotional special, this feature is ideal to limit the purchase of that item to a certain quantity.

Compatibility with UPS and USPS Online Tools

Many shopping carts have the ability to work online with major shippers, including UPS Online Tracking and UPS Online Rates & Service Selection Tools. They also provide the ability for your customers to track their shipments directly from your Web site or from the UPS Web site.

Many also have the built-in ability to utilize the U.S. Postal Service's Web Tools, which provide rate quotes for USPS shipping services.

Softgoods/Digital Downloads

This is a highly desirable feature if you sell downloadable electronic files such as documentation, software, or music. Most premier shopping carts incorporate this ability, and you can specify how many times the customer may download the product.

Multi-Platform Compatibility

Not all Web servers are created equal or can be operated on several different platforms, such as Microsoft Windows NT/2000/2003 or Unix servers. Some shopping carts are platform-dependent, so you will need to verify what platform your Web hosting company is utilizing and validate that your prospective shopping cart software is compatible. Most of the supportable platforms or Web servers include:

- Microsoft NT/2000/2003

- Solaris (Sun or Intel)

- Apple's OS X

- Linux (RedHat, Mandrake, Slackware)

- FreeBSD

- BSDi

- Digital Unix/Tru64

- IRIX

- Cobalt (mips)

Frequent Shopper Points

Similar to how airlines reward repeat customers with "frequent flyer miles," many shopping carts can track points assigned to products and provide a summary of an order's total frequent-shopper points. This allows customers to accumulate points toward some future reward or incentive.

HTML-Based E-Mail Integration

Most shopping carts generate e-mail confirmation; however, more advanced carts provide HTML-based e-mails, which allow you to customize templates to suit your needs.

Choosing the Right Shopping Cart

There will be many questions you'll want to ask yourself when compiling a shopping cart requirements wish list. We recommend that you go through these nine questions and then compare your answers to the features desired, as outlined previously.

1. **What kind of shopping cart does my hosting service support?** Shopping cart scripts are written in many different coding formats: Perl, PHP, and ASP, just to name a few. To ensure compatibility, be sure to check with your host before purchasing a program. You should also inquire about support, since many installations and customizations require Web server administration support actions.

2. **What is our budget?** Web hosting, SSL certification, Web site development, and the cost of procuring and implementing a shopping cart can add up quickly. Make sure you consider all the costs involved, and buy the shopping cart that fits your needs and budget. If you only need a basic cart for fewer than 100 products, PayPal is free, simple to set up, and definitely fits into any budget!

3. **What delivery methods will I be using?** All shopping carts are designed for products that need to be packaged and mailed by a carrier. However, if you want to offer electronic softgood downloads, you need to make sure that your cart has that capability. The better the shopping cart, the better results your company will have. If you are considering softgoods for a delivery method, you should only consider carts that limit downloads or provide a temporary download URL (to prevent fraud, abuse, and distributing your product for free). Another softgoods delivery method may be to send the customer an e-mail confirmation with a hyperlink to download the product. This should also limit the user to a specific number of downloads.

4. **Where will my business be in a year?** You need to ensure that the shopping cart has the features you may "eventually" implement

so that you don't quickly outgrow your cart as your business grows and expands to offer more comprehensive options. Make sure you check the fine print as many shopping carts are modular in design and many advanced features are not included in the basic package.

5. **Is the cart software compatible with my credit card/merchant payment gateway?** We listed most of the major payment gateways, which integrate with the most shopping cart applications. Know which payment gateway you will use and ensure that it is 100 percent compatible with your shopping cart before you select your shopping cart application.

6. **What kind of payments are allowed by the shopping cart?** All shopping carts allow you to accept credit card transactions. You may consider other options for payment, such as purchase order, COD, e-checks, etc. Another payment option that is increasingly popular is PayPal. Most quality shopping carts integrate with the PayPal system to allow customers to pay via their PayPal accounts.

7. **Can I easily back up and restore my data?** All quality shopping carts provide support for backing up files and allow for export into a variety of formats. Equally important is the ability to quickly restore data in the case of a catastrophic Web server failure.

8. **How is the product support?** Most shopping carts are difficult to install and configure. Many companies do include free installation and setup, and we highly recommend this option. Make sure that you are prepared to invest in technical support as most offer limited or per-fee support only.

Many shopping cart software companies also offer free user forums as part of their service. This is unequivocally the best free support system available as technical experts and other users post similar problems or challenges, with actionable solutions for others in similar situations.

You need to carefully analyze your company's needs and weigh the costs and features of shopping cart applications. Be cautious in your decision to purchase based on promotional features, exaggerated claims, and features you will never utilize. Most reputable shopping cart companies feature trial versions of their software. Don't hesitate to try out several to see which works best for your business.

We do highly recommend the PDG shopping cart or E-Commerce Suite, which meets or exceeds all of our standards and contains all of the features discussed in this chapter. You can find details, pricing, free installation, and a sample demo at **www.pdgsoft.com**.

Ten Steps to Profitable E-Commerce

The following steps can be used as a checklist to ensure that you have everything in place for doing business on the Internet. Once your Web site is up and running, you'll be able to implement low-cost marketing and advertising techniques for promoting and managing your business.

1. **List goals and ideas.** Determine what your goals are for using the Internet for the promotion of your business and/or selling products on the Web. Sit down with the people who are going to be helping you with your online Web site and the e-commerce part of your business so that you can go over your ideas for design, implementation, and promotion. It's important not to discard any of your goals and ideas, no matter how silly and far-fetched they seem. You want to be as creative as possible to start with, and then you can fine-tune your list by getting rid of those ideas that are not cost effective or not considered for adoption. This is a good time to do a preliminary projection of your budget, incorporating all the potential costs so that you can set realistic expectations for your Web site and online storefront. You will adjust your budget later, after you complete steps 1–4.

2. **Review the products and services you intend to sell.** Take some time to carefully review the products and services that you're offering on or through your Web site. Things that you should be asking yourself include the following: What are the advantages and disadvantages to your business of selling or advertising online? Are you willing to accept payment online, and if so, what payment methods? What logistics will you have to consider about shipping your product, including cost, method, etc.? Are

you willing to consistently update and maintain your Web site to reflect current products, market trends, and pricing?

3. **Compare online e-commerce Web sites.** Find Web sites that are related to your business and take some time checking them out. Look at how they promote and advertise similar products or services as well as how each Web site is laid out and navigated. If a similar Web site uses a shopping cart for online purchases, try it out, stopping, of course, at the point where you're ready to commit to a purchase. See how smoothly the process works and what can be done to improve the process. Don't just look at e-commerce sites that are within your own country, since consumers won't limit their shopping to those businesses where they live. Look at the way other countries handle e-commerce Web sites so that you have a broad spectrum of Web sites with which to compare yours. A wide range of experience and knowledge of how competitors operate their online businesses is valuable information that you can use to get the upper edge on competition.

4. **Determine your target market.** Determine what market of consumers you want to target with your Web site. If you're using your Web site to promote your brick-and-mortar business, decide if you're going to be selling your products and services only locally or if you're willing to sell outside of your immediate market area. Since the Internet is global, there are many reasons to promote your Web site to the national or global marketplace. If you're selling your products or services online, you'll need to decide if you're only selling within your own country or if you're going to be an international e-commerce company. It's important to know who your Internet audience is going to be so that you can target them effectively. If you're selling your products internationally, you're going to have to be prepared for some potential language barriers.

5. **Budget for your Web site.** It's important that you have a predetermined budget for your Web site so that you can stay within the guidelines of what you can afford. There are many aspects to your Web site that you're going to need to take into account, including the development of your Web site, marketing

of your Web site and business, customer service and maintenance, Web hosting, the cost of a merchant payment system, secure server certification, domain names, search engine submissions, and any new staff that you may need to hire to maintain your Web site or to handle the inflow of new business. You want to know where your business costs are going so that you can allocate them appropriately. In most cases it is not necessary to hire a full-time Web designer. After your initial Web site design is completed, all you will need is monthly maintenance and updates in most instances.

6. **Determine your unique selling points.** Determine what the unique selling points are going to be for your business. There are many Web sites on the Internet that are going to be selling the same products and services that you are, and you must separate yourself from the competition. This means that you need to have selling features that will make consumers want to buy from you instead of the next Web site that they hit. Make a listing of unique selling points that you have currently and those that you're willing to consider for future use. The computer hardware and software industry is very competitive, yet NewEgg (**www .newegg.com**) is traditionally the industry leader with superior products, superior customer service, and one of the finest reputations in the industry. What are the unique selling points that set them apart from their competition?

7. **Create a marketing plan.** You need to have a solid marketing plan in place so that you know exactly where you want your business to go and how you want to get there. This should be a written plan that you can sit down and read logistically. An online marketing plan should address search engines and techniques for improving a Web site's visibility on the Internet.

8. **Decide on a Web site structure.** Determine what you want the structure of your Web site to be like. You want to know ahead of time what you want your Web site to do and how you want to achieve that function. This is crucial to implementing your Web site design plan and integrating how you want your shopping cart to act and perform within your Web site. Careful planning should be given to designing and laying out the structure and

organization of your Web site.

9. **Implement online Web services.** Have all of the services that you're going to need for your Web site ready to go. This includes Web hosting, a digital certificate, and your completed Web design, including detailed product or services descriptions (including digital images and pricing, if appropriate). Once you launch your Web site, ensure that you have ample amounts of product in your inventory ready for sales.

10. **Launch your Web site.** This last step marks your entry into the world of e-commerce. Keep in mind that you need to keep a close eye on your Web site when you first go live so that you can catch any mistakes or areas that need additions or improvements. Listen to customer feedback for potential problem areas or areas for improvement. Also, encourage friends and relatives to give your site a thorough "shakedown."

By following the above steps, you'll be well on your way to a live Web site for promoting your traditional brick-and-mortar business or for selling your products and services to the global Internet community. Having all of the above e-commerce concepts in place will ensure that your business is ready to earn you new customers and greater profits, and doing your research and planning will ensure that your e-commerce solution is obtained at the lowest possible financial investment.

E-Commerce Terms and Definitions

There are some terms and definitions that you should know so you can adequately understand what e-commerce is all about and so you're prepared when you encounter any of the following terms.

Source for terms and definitions: **http://ecomm.webopedia.com**

• **Commerce server.** Web software that runs some of the main functions of an online storefront such as product display, online ordering, and inventory management. The software works in conjunction with online payment systems to process payments.

• **Cookie.** A message given to a Web browser by a Web server. The browser stores the message in a text file. The message is then sent back to the server each time the browser requests a page from the server.

- **CRM.** Short for customer relationship management. CRM entails all aspects of interaction a company has with its customer, whether it be sales or service related.

- **Digital cash.** A system that allows a person to pay for goods or services by transmitting a number from one computer to another. Like the serial numbers on real dollar bills, the digital cash numbers are unique.

- **Digital certificate.** An attachment to an electronic message used for security purposes. The most common use of a digital certificate is to verify that a user sending a message is who he or she claims to be, and to provide the receiver with the means to encode a reply.

- **Digital wallet.** Encryption software that works like a physical wallet during electronic commerce transactions. A wallet can hold a user's payment information, a digital certificate to identify the user, and shipping information to speed transactions.

- **Domain name.** Location of an entity on the Internet.

- **EBPP.** Short for electronic bill presentment and payment. The process by which companies bill customers and receive payments electronically over the Internet.

- **EDI.** Short for electronic data interchange. The transfer of data between different companies using networks, such as the Internet.

- **ERP.** Short for enterprise resource planning. A business management system that integrates all facets of the business, including planning, manufacturing, sales, and marketing.

- **Opt-in e-mail.** A term that refers to promotional e-mails that have been requested by the individual receiving them. Unlike spam, promotional e-mails that get sent out to large lists of recipients without regard to whether or not they want the information, opt-in e-mails are only sent to people who specifically request them.

- **Page impression.** The exact number of times a specific Web site has been accessed or viewed by a user. A page impression acts as a counter for Web pages, informing site owners how many times their sites were visited.

- **SET.** Short for secure electronic transaction, is a standard that will enable secure credit card transactions on the Internet.

- **Shopping cart.** A shopping cart is a piece of software that acts as an online store's catalog and ordering process.

- **SSL.** Short for Secure Sockets Layer, a protocol developed by Netscape for transmitting private documents via the Internet.

- **Smart card.** A small electronic device about the size of a credit card that contains electronic memory and possibly an embedded integrated circuit (IC). Smart cards containing an IC are sometimes called Integrated Circuit Cards (ICCs).

- **XAML.** Short for Transaction Authority Markup Language. XAML is a vendor-neutral standard developed jointly by Bowstreet, Hewlett-Packard, IBM, Oracle, and Sun that is used to coordinate and process online business transactions.

CHAPTER 2

Starting Your Business

There are some major differences and similarities when it comes to starting a brick-and-mortar business or an online business. It is quite possible to have an online-only business without the traditional brick-and-mortar, such as Amazon.com, which has no retail storefronts, and quite often, existing businesses seek the Internet as an alternative source of sales and profits. It is also very common for traditional retailers and businesses to expand their business onto the Internet to draw in a wider customer base, sell products, or promote and market their business's products or services. As with any new business venture, including the expansion of a traditional storefront onto the Internet, you must go through a series of well-thought-out steps to develop and implement the strategy that will work best for your specific type of business and desired results. Although the steps may be different when it comes to using the Internet for the promotion of an online business as compared to a brick-and-mortar business, the analytical process is very much the same.

This chapter outlines the steps that you should take for starting and expanding a brick-and-mortar business onto the Web and provides general guidelines for starting an online business; it can be easily adapted for companies wishing to expand services to offer an e-commerce component or Internet presence.

Starting an Online Business

Although starting an Internet business is much like starting any other business, there are going to be some significant differences with which you will have to concern yourself. You're going to have to work on building the confidence of your customers by using a variety of techniques, which don't include the face-to-face exchange of a traditional brick-and-mortar retail store. You will need to clearly convey through your Web site that your company is fair and honest in its advertising; has fair prices for your products or services; provides superior customer service and satisfaction; and is committed to developing long-term customers. While these aspects certainly apply to any brick-and-mortar business, the challenge is implementing them over the Internet in a successful but low-cost solution. Our goal is to identify the steps required to launch your online business, while ensuring that it is cost effective and that you are marketing your site for the lowest possible cost. First, let's look at the advantages of starting your business online or expanding your traditional business to the Internet.

- **Startup costs.** Starting an online business requires significantly less capital than a traditional brick-and-mortar business. In fact, with some careful planning you can start your Internet business with only a few hundred dollars. You need to keep in mind that there are no get-rich-quick schemes to having an online business; the key to profits is having products that people want to buy, and customers must be able to find your Web site to buy those products. Profits and success come from successful marketing and advertising, which we will help you achieve. Keep in mind that sales and profits can come from much more than selling products. For restaurants, putting graphical images of their establishments and menus online for prospective patrons to review is a great, low-cost use of the Internet that can directly increase sales without ever selling a product online. The majority of Web sites don't actually sell any products at all; they simply advertise and market the business, products, or services offered and provide a convenient means of obtaining information and providing contact information for prospective patrons or customers.

- **Limitless potential.** The Internet has unlimited potential since it can reach a multitude of consumers, including a wide international audience. Every computer in the world is a potential customer or patron. There is no other method to disseminate your business information to a global audience like the Internet. If a picture is worth a thousand words, a well-designed Web site with graphics, text, and other information about your business or product is worth infinitely more.

- **Polished and professional look.** You can make your online business look extremely professional and experienced by designing a Web site that ties together style and content. This can be achieved with the use of a professional Web design firm such as Gizmo Graphics Web Design (**www.gizwebs.com**) or one of many other Web design firms. It is possible to achieve good results by designing a Web site yourself; however, it is typically best to go with a professional design service. Gizmo Graphics Web Design has all-inclusive Web design packages for as low as $575, which include site design, one year of Web site hosting, and free domain name registration. If you choose to attempt your own Web site design, we recommend you use a professional Web design tool such as Microsoft FrontPage or Macromedia Dreamweaver. There are thousands of great small-business Web sites that are rich on content, search listings, product information, and user-friendliness. Atlantic Publishing Company (**www .atlantic-pub.com**) incorporates a clean design, simple navigation, advanced search features, and an integrated shopping cart.

Web Design Mistakes to Avoid

Be aware of these common pitfalls when designing your site:

- **The home page does not quickly tell you what the Web site is all about.** You should be able to visit the home page of any Web site and figure out what the site is about, what type of products it sells, or what it is advertising within five seconds.

- **The poor use of popup windows, splashy advertising, splash pages** (pages with neat animations and sound but which you have to watch for five to ten seconds before you are taken to the real Web site), and other Web design features that draw interest away from your Web site, products, and/or services.

- **Poor Web site navigation.** This includes broken hyperlinks, hidden navigation, poor wording of navigational links, links that take you to pages with no links, links that take you to the same Web page, and pages with no links back to the home page (always include a link back to the home page so that regardless of where site visitors are, they can find their way back home!).

- **Believing that because you have a Web site, you have a marketing campaign or overall marketing and advertising strategy.** We will discuss the marketing of a Web site in great detail later in this book; however, you need to understand that your Web site is not your marketing strategy. Your Web site is just a part of your overall marketing strategy, depending on your business goals; for example, if you have a successful restaurant but want to advertise and promote your business on the Web. Creating a Web site is great, but if it is not promoted and advertised, no one will ever find it. By passing out business cards with your Web site URL embossed on them, you are using a traditional marketing campaign to promote your Web site. If you offer a downloadable/printable coupon from your Web site, you are successfully using your Web site as part of your marketing strategy to meet your goal of increased restaurant sales.

- **Failure to attain Web site relevance and content updating.** There is nothing more dissatisfying to a Web customer than visiting a Web site that is grossly out of date. Incorrect pricing, products no longer available, dated content, and ancient advertising all signify to the Web site visitor that your devotion to your Web site is suffering greatly. During an interview with Gizmo Graphics

Web Design, they revealed that one client has not updated their Web site in more than three years, yet the site contains dated information (schedule of events, an outdated e-mail address, etc). Although the client is proud of their Web site and it looks great, it does not take a visitor long to realize that this site hasn't been updated since before the last presidential election, and, typically, interest fades fast. Conversely, cramming your pages with non-relevant material will detract the visitor from getting the point of your Web site (the five-second rule mentioned earlier).

- **Avoid too many text effects.** Forget flashing text, reversing text, gymnastics text, or other eye-popping and dizzying effects, which do nothing more than annoy your site visitor. Don't create a "loud" Web site that contain so many blinking, flashing, twirling, and spinning icons, text, or graphics that visitors are overwhelmed by the effects and under-whelmed by the site content.

- **Limit the number of graphics on your Web site** so that you don't overwhelm your site visitors with "graphics overload." Don't use animated GIF images on your Web site. These were cool ten years ago, but in today's professional environment, they are just another "loud," annoying distraction that site visitors don't want to see.

- **Don't use Microsoft's themes** (built-in design templates) when creating a Web site with Microsoft FrontPage. While FrontPage is bashed on a regular basis, we stand by the fact that it can be used to design great Web sites.

- **Don't incorporate frames into Web site design.** The use of frames within a Web site will drive customers away faster than anything!

- **DO incorporate the proper Web site design elements** to ensure that your Web site is ready to be found by search engines (we cover this topic in significant detail later in this book).

Developing a Plan for an Online Business

An online business requires planning and the determination to succeed. You will want to have a business plan in place that takes you from the beginning to the end of starting your business.

The following steps are a good guideline of what you need to do to start your online business and establish an actionable and sustainable business plan. After following these steps, along with proper Web design and incorporation of the low-cost marketing and advertising solutions in this book, your Internet business will be up and ready for customers to find you.

STEP ONE: START WITH AN IDEA

The first thing that you need to start your online business is an idea that you believe in. This means that you need to have a product or service, a concept of how to sell it, good content ideas for your Web site, and the belief that you can make it all work. If you don't have all these things in place, you may be wasting your time and money and setting yourself up for a disappointing failure.

You need to have a business plan in place that is going to successfully implement your idea with your product in such a way that you can take it from start to finish with very definite milestones along the way. Your business plan should include your budget, a time frame within which to work, your product or service inventory, and other financial matters. If you're unsure of how to write a business plan, you should consult with someone who has some experience writing such a plan. To facilitate this process, we have enclosed a sample business plan with this book.

STEP TWO: LEGAL MATTERS

Make sure that you have all the legal information that you need to start your business online. You don't want to find out at a later date that you've overlooked something important. Some of the legalities that you may need to consider include the following:

- **Incorporate or not?** Find out the legal benefits of incorporating your online business. There are benefits and disadvantages to incorporating your business that include taxes and matters of ownership. Contact a lawyer or tax accountant for more information about incorporating your business. Other options may include sole proprietorship and limited liability corporations.

- **Copyrights/Trademarks.** It may not seem like an important factor, but liability issues surrounding intellectual property are something that you'll want to consider when you're doing business on the Internet. You can visit the U.S. Copyright Office for more information: **www.copyright.gov**.

- **Contracts and licenses.** Make sure that before you sign any contract you know exactly what you're signing and that you understand it fully. If you don't pay attention to contracts and licenses, you could end up being liable for any number of things, such as Web hosting regulations. There are several contracts that you might need to sign when you start your own business online that include hiring a Web site designer, a programmer, and/or digital certification. You will need a business license, which is typically administered through the local, county, or state government prior to commencing business. Detailed information on how to start a small business may be found at the Small Business Administration Web site at **www.sba.gov** as well as from your local, county, and state governments.

- **Internet legalities.** Make sure that you understand all the legal issues of doing business on the Internet such as the legalities behind obtaining a domain name. This is a dynamic and often confusing subject. We found a fantastic reference site sponsored by attorney Ivan Hoffman that contains a vast amount of information related to trademarks, domain names, and e-commerce as well as articles for Web designers, Web site owners, and addresses of many other legal concerns surrounding the Internet. Mr. Hoffman's Web site is located at **www.ivanhoffman .com**.

Step Three: Your Domain Name

An important aspect of your Internet business is having your own domain name. This is a requirement to have your Web site hosted, and it should uniquely identify your business. The general rule of thumb is that the shorter the domain name, the better, and it should be relevant to your company name, service, or products. If you already have an established corporate name or identity, you should try to base your domain name on that corporate identity. This allows customers to identify your company name with your domain name (i.e., Atlantic Publishing Company = **www.atlantic-pub.com**). We highly recommend you secure any similar-sounding domain names, as in the example above, atlanticpub.com, atlanticpub.net, atlanticpublishing.com, etc. Your primary domain name should be the domain name that is "hosted," while others may be parked at no additional cost and pointed to the main domain name URL. This allows you to only pay for one hosted domain name but utilize many domain names on the Internet, all directing site visitors to your main hosted site. We recommend GoDaddy (**www.godaddy.com**) to purchase and manage all of your domain names. After years of experience with many other domain name companies, none beat the quality of service, price, or features that GoDaddy offers. You can check the availability of domain names and even get other suggested domain names based on similarity.

Step Four: Choosing Web Hosting

You'll need to find a company that offers Web hosting so that you'll have an online presence. You need to find a Web hosting company that is going to be able to provide you with the following things:

- Technical support that is available when you need it (24/7).

- A good "uptime" or "availability" history so that you know your Web site will be available to potential customers (Web site availability should be in excess of 99 percent); you will also need this to ensure that when you make changes to your Web site, the changes will go into effect as soon as possible.

- A fast and reliable Internet connection (forget about dial-up service—go with high-speed broadband cable, DSL, or satellite).

- Technicians and staff that understand all aspects of e-commerce, including shopping carts and SSL certification.

- Compatibility with other providers of e-commerce on the Internet.

- Compatibility with your selected shopping cart product. This is critical as many companies invest in expensive shopping cart software that is rendered useless by Web hosting companies that don't support essential features, such as Web scripting, executable files, or other dynamic content.

Take your time when you're looking for a Web hosting company. Keep in mind that you are going to be entrusting a large part of the success of your Web site to this company. You want to choose a Web hosting company that has been in business for a long time, since there are many startup Web hosting companies on the Internet that come and go. One of the most costly things that you'll be paying for when you do business on the Internet is your Web hosting service. You want to make sure that you choose a company that is reliable and reputable. The following are several Web hosting companies that have gained a good reputation on the Internet for being top in the field of hosting Web sites:

- **Readyhosting.** Ideal for the small- or medium-sized business, featuring one of the lowest costs around, with a feature-rich hosting package: **www.readyhosting.com**

- **Verio.** This company is great for medium- to large-sized companies that need a Web presence. They also have a great Web hosting plan for small businesses that are just starting up on the Internet: **www.verio.com**

- **Rackspace.** Rackspace offers great Web hosting for small- to medium-sized businesses that are looking for a secure environment: **www.rackspace.com**

When you're looking for a Web hosting company, there are several features you should also consider:

- **Guarantee.** Many good Web hosting companies will offer you a money-back guarantee that shows confidence in their ability to host your Web site at a high reliability percentage.

- **Web hosting space.** Choose a Web host that offers you a large amount of hard drive space for your Web site so that you have room to grow. Most Web sites use a minimum of up to 10MB of hard drive space; however, large e-commerce-enabled sites may grow to more than 100MB in size. Readyhosting (**www .readyhosting.com**) offers 500MB of storage with superior reliability and low cost.

- **Data transfer.** Most Web hosting companies will allow you a certain amount of traffic to your site before they start charging you for any extra traffic. This is because the more traffic that you have to your Web site, the more their servers will have to work. Look for Web hosting companies that have a low cost for high traffic to your Web site. Readyhosting (**www.readyhosting.com**) offers unlimited data transfer, so this is not a concern with them. Other companies, such as Interland (**www.interland.net**), restrict your data transfer to as low as 25MB per month.

- **Security.** If you need to have a secure (encrypted) server space, you will have to pay an additional cost for the secure server certificate. If you are going to process personal data or credit card information on your Web site, you will need a secure certificate. It is important to note that if you elect to use PayPal (**www. paypal.com**) or JustAddCommerce (**www.justaddcommerce. com**), you do not need to buy a secure server certificate as they are included in these services. A digital certificate is used to protect any communication that you have with your customers that contains private information. You'll need to have a digital certificate installed on your Web server so that you can take credit card orders in a safe and secure manner. You want to make sure that no one but you, your customer, and the bank receives your customers' financial and personal information. A digital certificate is going to ensure this privacy and security.

- **Web site upload.** Find out what method is used for you to upload your Web site pages to the company server. Many Web hosting companies use FTP (file transfer protocol) for this upload. You'll want to make sure that if the Web hosting company that you're using uses FTP, you have a good FTP program for your computers. Most Web hosting companies provide a free FTP application; however, we recommend you purchase IPSwitch's WS_FTP software (**www.ipswitch.com**).

- **Software.** Find out what software or built-in scripts the Web host offers when you sign up with them. Some companies won't offer you any software tools, while others will have several free tools that can help you to operate your Web site easily and efficiently. Some of the software that you might be offered includes auto-responders to send e-mail to your customers, search engines so that visitors can find your business Web site, forms (guestbook, order forms, and questionnaires), bulletin boards and chat room access, file backup and recovery, an e-commerce shopping cart, and Web site management software. Microsoft FrontPage-hosted sites offer many advantages with built-in e-mail forms handlers, allowing you to create forms on the fly that will e-mail data result sets to pre-specified recipients. You do need to make sure that your hosting company offers and supports Microsoft FrontPage extensions, which enable most of these features. Readyhosting. com offers a free Web site management control panel, FrontPage extensions, free FTP software, and a variety of other tools for your use.

- **Know what your Web host will support.** Several years ago, Gizmo Graphics Web Design utilized the PDG shopping cart, a reputable hosting company, on one of its main accounts. They had a successful e-commerce operation, and the SSL certificate and shopping cart were operating perfectly. One day, the shopping cart stopped operating, and after much frantic research, Gizmo determined that its Web host provider changed their policy (overnight) about supporting the executable files that are required on the server to operate the PDG shopping cart on a Windows-based Web server due to "security concerns" and, subsequently, put Gizmo out of business with no advanced notice or warning. Despite Gizmo's attempts to convince them that its configuration was perfectly safe, the Web host provider flatly refused to support

Gizmo's shopping cart, and they were forced to change hosting companies at a significant expense. Needless to say, we don't recommend that particular Web hosting company, and you need to be careful of what hosting companies do and don't support, and what their notification processes are to ensure a smooth operation of your Web site. Nothing hurts an online business more than starting an active marketing campaign, only to have your site rendered useless by your Web hosting company.

We recommend that you thoroughly research any potential Web hosting companies to ensure they will support all of your needs. We have recommended the services of Readyhosting.com through this book; however, they don't support the PDG software shopping cart, which we also recommend. Therefore, they would not be the choice if we wanted a powerful e-commerce-enabled Web site. There are a variety of resources to review and compare Web hosting companies, including:

- **www.findmyhosting.com**

- **www.findmyhost.com**

- **www.Web sitehostdirectory.com**

- **www.ratemyhost.com**

If you wish to combine Web hosting and Web design services with one reputable and highly respected company, we recommend Gizmo Graphics Web Design (**www.gizwebs.com**) of Land O' Lakes, Florida.

STEP FIVE: DESIGNING YOUR WEB SITE

You can design your Web site yourself, or you can hire a professional to do the job for you. We have already provided you with significant amounts of information related to Web design and the pros and cons of attempting the job yourself. There are numerous high-quality/low-price providers that perform Web design services. Ensure that you review our list of Web site design mistakes and put emphasis on proper Web site design fundamentals. We will cover elementals of Web site design, with an emphasis on ensuring that your Web site is geared toward search engine and user-friendliness in later chapters.

Step Six: Marketing

You'll need to develop marketing plans so you can ensure that potential Web site visitors can find and navigate to your Web site. Marketing will be discussed in great detail later in this book, but here are some general guidelines for what you'll need to consider about marketing your online business:

- **Search engines.** Make sure that you list your business and Web site with at least 15 to 20 search engines. We will provide you with all the free tips on how to properly design your Web site for maximum search engine effectiveness as well as procedures on how to list with free and paid search engine services such as Google, Yahoo!, MSN, and AOL.

- **Pay-per-click.** We will cover pay-per-click and pay-per-impression advertising in detail and compare them to free advertising options. There may be circumstances where you may need to implement a paid advertising campaign, and we will show you how to most effectively implement the plan at the lowest possible cost.

- **Keywords and meta tags.** Using keywords and properly formatted meta tags will generate more traffic to your Web site as search engines use meta tags to link to and index Web sites. The meta tag is used by search engines to allow them to more accurately list your site in their indexes; however, this is not always the case. You can design a Web site without any meta tags and register the domain name or URL with search engines, and their automated "spiders" or "robots" will index your Web site automatically based on the page content. Without going into much detail, each search engine functions differently, and we will provide you with all the information you need to design meta tags and tackle search engines later in this book. There are definitive formats and rules for properly designed meta tags, and we will ensure that you have a clear understanding of them in order to properly design and implement meta tags into your Web site. It is important to note that good Web designers should already design and incorporate meta tags into your Web site design package; however, they are simple to create and implement yourself with little or no HTML or programming experience.

Step Seven: Interactive Web sites and Updated Content

You need to constantly and consistently update your Web site so that visitors aren't reading the same information and seeing the same design that they did the last time they visited. Be as creative as you can, while still staying within the guidelines of professionalism. Site visitors want to look at the latest products, news, and information—so give it to them!

Step Eight: Your Customer Database

One of your main tasks when you have an online business is developing and building a customer database. You want to have as many people on your list as you can so that your marketing program reaches a wide range of consumers. We will provide you with detailed information on developing databases and e-mail marketing campaigns, which you can manage at little or no cost.

Step Nine: Repeat Customers

Once you've built a solid customer database, you'll want to put in place processes to harness repeat customers. Repeat sales and developing a loyal customer base are the foundation of a successful business and continued profits. One of the ways that you can achieve repeat or return customer sales is by having good customer service and establishing ongoing dialogue and communication with your customers. You can accomplish this good communication by using the following techniques, all of which are low-cost options that lead to more sales and profits:

- **Establish an affiliate program.** An affiliate program is an advertising program offering a monetary incentive for Webmasters to drive traffic to your Web site. This eliminates the necessity for the advertiser to find Web sites with related content to list their banners. It also increases the response rate by giving the "affiliate" Web sites a stake in the response rate.

Affiliate programs are a great plan for the Web sites offering them. We have dedicated a chapter in this book to discuss how to implement an effective and profitable affiliate program.

- **Coupons for repeat customers.** These may be through targeted e-mail campaigns designed exclusively for your repeat customer base or through traditional mailings, where you promote the use of your Web site through a discount coupon.

- **Contests in which your customers can participate.** Everyone loves a good contest (free dinner, free hotel stay, gift certificates, etc.). Online contests are a great way to keep people interested in your products and services and will drive them back to your Web site to track contest results. Atlantic Publishing Company created the "Top 50 Restaurant Web sites" about six years ago. The free contest was simply to promote great Web site designs for small, newly established restaurants across the world. Atlantic had a panel of judges who not only rated the sites on a variety of requirements but also reviewed the menu, history, imagery, and overall appeal of the site. The reviewers wrote a small summary of how the site and actual establishment appealed to them, and winners of the award were presented with a logo that they could display on their Web site. For Atlantic Publishing Company, the benefit was a popular contest that drew thousands of site visitors per day to their Web site and encompassed reviews of more than 2,500 restaurant Web sites.

- **Newsletters that provide useful information.** The use of newsletters is covered in detail in later chapters of this book; however, the use of a well-designed and targeted newsletter (printed or online) is an extremely effective marketing campaign. Obviously, the benefit of online newsletters is you can track open, click-through, and other response rates.

- **A program that features banners.** When done with class and style and in limited quantities, banner advertising is a great way to promote your Web site by placing banners on other Web sites that link back to your Web site. Typically, this is done in conjunction with an affiliate program; however, that is not always the case.

- **A program for discussion groups and forums.** Depending on your Web site, a discussion group or forum is a great addition to your Web site (and is also free through **www.phpbb.com** or **www.ezboard.com**). The Stagecoach Property Owners Association (**www.stagecoachfl.org**) uses a discussion forum to discuss community issues, concerns, and events. Companies use discussion forums to discuss anything from current events to new products. Many restaurants are establishing discussion forums as a marketing tool to attract new clients, offer recipes, offer cooking techniques, or for patrons to discuss their dining experiences.

- **A chat room option for customers.** This may be a controversial addition to a Web site if you expect associates to interact with the public or each other (some employers don't allow employees to engage in chat sessions, use chat software, or get paid to "chat"). There are many free chat applications, and a "live" session between customers and the business is often productive as customers can get immediate support and answers to their questions or concerns about products or orders. You can find free chat rooms at **www.chat-avenue.com** and **www.parachat.com**.

STEP TEN: MAINTAINING GOOD BUSINESS RECORDS

Although this seems like common sense, it is also the one area with which most business owners and managers fail to comply, as revealed by numerous state and federal audits. You need to have good records of all your business transactions to ensure that your financial accounts as well as your sales and incomes tax records are in order. If you need to seek any type of financing in the future, having accurate accounting books will give potential investors a good look into the way your business is operated and will help them determine profit potential.

The above steps are a good, simple plan if you're going to be starting an online business or expanding your current business onto the Internet. Make sure that you have all bases covered by taking your time and completing all the steps before your Web site goes live; this will ensure that both you and your customers will be satisfied with the online experience.

CHAPTER 3

The Importance of Internet Advertising

Marketing and advertising a traditional brick-and-mortar business is a costly venture. Postage and mailing costs are high, return rates on mailings are typically less than 1 percent of the total mailing, and most catalog and direct sales marketing techniques are considered successful if they just break even. This is not the case when advertising your Web site on the Internet. Expanding your business to the Internet exposes your products or services to a dramatically larger potential customer base; however, without proper advertising and marketing skills and techniques, few will ever find your Web site. Over 200 million Americans went online in 2005, and nearly 1 billion people worldwide used the Internet during this same time period. Internet access grew more than 107 percent in 2005 in the United States and more than 165 percent worldwide. You can advertise and market your Web site in this enormous marketplace at little or no cost using the techniques we provide in this book. Today, Internet marketing is more important than any other form of advertising, including newspaper, television, and radio.

The Internet has changed the lives of everyone. In North America alone, over 220 million people log on to the Internet each and every day. The Internet is here to stay, and businesses need to take steps not be left behind with archaic advertising and marketing techniques. Traditional advertising is fine, but it will not work within the global online community.

Every facet of business is being affected by the Internet. This means that no matter what type of business you have, online or offline, chances are you're going to want to use the Internet to promote your products and services. As we have discussed, the Internet is not just for selling products online. Most people visit a Web site to solve one or more of the following three problems:

1. They want or need information.

2. They want or need to make a purchase or donation.

3. They want or need to be entertained.

The Internet is very different from other mediums of advertising and marketing in several ways. Not only is the Internet a channel for communication, but it is also a channel for distribution and transactions. This is because consumers are able to get all the information that they need to make their purchases and payments online and actually process those transactions. There is no other advertising medium that is able to accomplish all these goals at once.

Another way that the Internet is different from other forms of advertising is that it is extremely interactive and relies primarily on the consumer for this interaction. Consumers are able to find an online shopping site that interests them. They then visit other Web sites for more information, comparison shopping, product review, and expert advice. The Internet is able to meet the needs of people looking for product information in a way that other advertising mediums are unable to do. With so much interactive information and with such a vast number of resources available at their fingertips, consumers are able to make informed choices of what they want to buy and how much they are willing to pay, and they have confidence that they are making an informed and educated decision.

The other way that the Internet is significantly different from other marketing and advertising mediums is that it is full of multimedia content. This means that the Internet is comprised of graphics, text, video, and audio. The Internet can be used for all types of interesting advertising techniques that leave the consumer with high-impact marketing images, including audio and visual. Some of the Internet marketing techniques that rely on multimedia include banner ads, interstitials, advertorials, 3-D visions, and advertainment.

If you're wondering how advertisers and Web promoters know how much traffic is on the Internet, all you have to do is look at the many surveys and tracking applications that monitor, record, and report Internet traffic and trends. These include the following:

- **Web-centric (meaning it was designed for the Web).** This method of Internet tracking uses what are called log files to determine the number of Internet users that have visited the Web site. These log files are contained on a Web server. When you sign up for a Web hosting account at a reputable hosting company, you should have full access to a wide array of usage and visitor tracking reports.

- **User-centric.** This method of tracking Internet usage requires that software that will automatically keep track of the number of times a certain Web site is visited be installed on the Web server and client workstation. The combination of this information with demographics and other user information creates what is called a "profile" of Web users.

Since the Internet is such a busy portal of information, it's important that any online or offline businesses take advantage of its availability to people all over the world as a way to reach potential consumers. Since our goal is to provide you with low- or no-cost techniques, you will want to ensure that your Web hosting company provides you with access to detailed Web-centric statistical reports that show you the average number of site visitors per day, their length of stay, the type of Web browser used,

Web pages visited, geographical location, and if they were referred to your Web site (and if so, by whom). All these feature reports should be included in your Web hosting package at no additional cost.

Advertorials

Wikipedia (**www.wikipedia.org**) defines an advertorial as an advertisement written in the form of an objective opinion editorial and presented in a printed publication—usually designed to look like a legitimate and independent news story. The term "advertorial" is a portmanteau of "ad" and "editorial." Advertorials differ from publicity advertisements because the marketer must pay a fee to the media company for the ad placement, whereas publicity is placed without payment to the media company and with no control over the copy. Most publications will not accept advertisements that look exactly like stories from the newspaper or magazine in which they are appearing. The differences may be subtle, and disclaimers—such as the word "advertisement"—may or may not appear. Sometimes, euphemisms describing the advertorial as a "special promotional feature" or the like are used.

Advertorials commonly advertise new products or techniques—such as a new design for golf equipment or a new form of laser surgery. The tone is usually closer to that of a press release than that of an objective news story; advertisers will not spend money to describe the flaws of their products.

Product placement is another form of non-obvious, paid advertising. The advertorial is becoming a very popular way for businesses to reach yet another target audience. An advertorial is simply an endorsement or advertisement that is placed into the context of any Web site as information. The advertorial may seem to be part of the editorial text of the Web content but is actually a type of advertising message.

Although many businesses still use banner ads and other forms of advertising, the advertorial is becoming more and more popular as people recognize its potential in successful marketing and for driving more traffic to a Web site. A sample advertorial may be viewed at **www. pdedit.com/images/Shoreline.pdf**, courtesy of PDEdit (Paul Desmond

Editorial Services). PDEdit produced this one-page advertorial on a Shoreline Communications IP voice customer for the July 8, 2002, issue of Network World.

One thing to keep in mind is that although advertorials may not necessarily generate as much Web traffic to a Web site as pay-per-click or search engine advertising, they do generate traffic that is better in terms of "quality" in regards to the number of potential customers becoming actual customers. This is because people that reach your Web site after reading an advertorial are arriving because they trust the resource that endorsed your product or service.

You need to understand that when it comes to advertorials, endorsement is extremely important. If you're going to use advertorials as part of your advertising and marketing campaign, make sure that you understand the importance of affiliates and endorsements and how they work hand in hand. An endorsement from a recognized industry professional is extremely valuable and typically conveys faith in the products advertised within the advertorial.

Advertainments

Advertainments are another form of new advertising on the Internet that is becoming more and more popular. Advertainment is a form of advertising that is consumed and enjoyed by the consumer as if it were for entertainment purposes. Advertainments are advertisements disguised as entertainment.

Advertainments are targeted to consumers with an interest in the products advertised. Advertainments are extremely viral, meaning that they are easily shared and distributed as "entertainment" among peer-to-peer and other networks, among thousands of consumers, at no cost. Advertainments are very economical. Each year, billions of dollars in advertising are spent advertising to consumers who will probably never buy the particular product being advertised. Since an advertainment is targeted, it reduces costs by targeting selected marketing groups and increasing the likelihood of sales. Advertainments allow you to concentrate your efforts on your target audience, and this can save you thousands of dollars in advertising each year.

The Budweiser beer commercials viewed during the Super Bowl are examples of advertainment because the commercial advertisement is entertaining, while at the same time promoting the Budweiser product.

No matter what form of advertising you use to promote your online business or your traditional brick-and-mortar business, you can be assured that advertising and marketing are going to be a big aspect of your business.

Customer Loyalty

Customer loyalty is going to be vital to the success of advertising online. When you gain the loyalty of your customers, you'll have them coming back to your Web site to do business with you over and over again.

> "'Loyalty can be easier to achieve in a small business because you can know your customers well and take care of the relationships you have,' says Janice Anderson, vice president of CRM Solutions for Lucent Technologies. You get more of their wallet and loyalty since you have taken the time to care about them. According to Julie Fitzpatrick, 'Loyalty is the result of building past positive experiences with an individual. Recognize the unique situation of a customer at any point in time,' she says. Consider the customers' value, their current business situation, proximity to purchase and history of goodwill to the organization."

Source: *Business Week*
www.businessweek.com/adsections/care/relationship/crm_loyalty.htm

THE LADDER OF LOYALTY

The Ladder of Loyalty concept is simple to understand and is something that you should be striving for since it ties in all aspects of successful online advertising.

The Ladder of Loyalty has four steps that represent all groups of people who may visit your Web site: prospects, suspects, customers, and advocates. Every potential customer or customer with whom you communicate in some way will be on one of these steps. Where they stand on the Ladder of Loyalty will depend on what visitors know about your business and the products or services that you sell, what customers have bought from you in the past, how frequently customers have bought from you, and how much trust customers have in your business and the products or services that you sell.

The following list of potential customers identifies the four steps of the Ladder of Loyalty:

> "**Suspects:** *You'll find the suspects on the ladder bottom. All people fall into this category. No matter how hard you try you can't reach everyone who is a suspect, therefore you shouldn't put too much time and money into trying. However, this will also depend on what type of product or service that you're selling.*
>
> **Prospects:** *Prospects are those people who have shown an interest in your product or service but still aren't convinced that they should buy from you. You'll want to focus your marketing program on those prospects that have an interest but that still haven't committed to a sale. To help you target prospects you need to learn to ask the right questions so that you can find out more about the customers want.*
>
> **Customers:** *Customers have already bought something from you. Now your goal is to get them to become repeat customers.*
>
> **Advocates:** *Advocates are those customers that keep coming back time and time again to make another purchase. But advocates are much more than just repeat customers. Advocates give you power by referring you to other potential customers. And it's this referral that holds a strong weight with prospects and suspects."*

Source: *Success Net*
www.bni.com/successnet/

CHAPTER 4

Generating More Traffic to Your Web Site

Wikipedia **(en.wikipedia.org)** states that "Web traffic is the amount of data sent and received by visitors to a Web site. This is determined by the number of visitors and the number of pages they visit. Web sites monitor the incoming and outgoing traffic to see which parts or pages of their site are popular and if there are any apparent trends, such as one specific page being viewed mostly by people in a particular country. Web traffic is measured to see the popularity of Web sites and individual pages or sections within a site."

As we mentioned previously, Web site traffic analysis and reports should be included in your Web hosting package. Web traffic can be analyzed by viewing the traffic statistics found in the Web server log file, an automatically generated list of all the pages served. A *hit* is generated when any file is served. The page itself is considered a file, but images are also files, thus a page with five images could generate six hits (the five images and the page itself). A *page view* is generated when a visitor requests any page within the Web site—a visitor will always generate at least one page view (the home or main page) but could generate many more as site visitors travel through your Web site.

How to generate more Web traffic to your Web site so you can increase the success of your online business is a question you should frequently ask yourself. You should never get too comfortable or confident in your current marketing and advertising program as your position within search engines will change daily based not only on your marketing techniques and campaigns, but also on those of your competitors as well. There are many ways that you can increase your Web site traffic—all leading to greater sales and profit potentials. We will discuss a variety of options that will lead to increased Web site traffic.

Media Exposure

Media exposure, of all kinds, is one way that you can boost your Web presence visibly and increase the amount of Web site traffic. Media exposure can also be defined as "promotion and publicity" for the online success of your company. If you have an online business, or a traditional brick-and-mortar business that you want to advertise and promote online, you need to make sure that you get as much as you can out of media coverage without spending too much of your advertising budget. You need to make the media work for you, not against you, so that customers can easily find you, learn to trust you and your product, and keep coming back to your Web site for repeat sales as you develop loyal customers. Your potential and existing customers are only going to buy products and services from a business that they feel is trustworthy. To earn that trust and reliance, you have to make the most of media exposure so that you can build your credibility and find a secure position for your business as an expert in your target market. What is going to work best is a combination of effective online and offline publicity and public relations that is geared toward affirming your corporate trustworthiness, reliability, and credibility. There are proven techniques, as outlined in this chapter, that show you how to get media exposure without having to use up your entire advertising budget on advertising and public relations. You should think of the Internet as your own personal publicity and media tool. You need to learn how to develop your own public relations and media campaigns so that you can build up the value, creditability, and trust that creates satisfied customers and repeat customers. When you gain that credibility and trust, you get more sales and increased confidence from your customers, and you gain the public profile that you want and need for your online or traditional business.

CREATING MEDIA EXPOSURE

Many businesses pay thousands upon thousands of dollars for media exposure, publicity, and advertising. You can get free publicity and PR for your business Web site by using tried and proven methods that will garner media exposure. Many businesses pay upward of $5,000 to $10,000 for advertising with a rate card. Your company can get that same advertising exposure with little to no money over the Internet. By engaging in Internet media campaigns or "non-traditional" media methods for gaining media exposure, you can accomplish two things: 1) you can save a significant amount of money and 2) you get to be in full control of your own media techniques.

So just how do you gain media exposure? What you can't do is wait around for the media or customers to find your company Web site, or you may be waiting for a long time with very low sales results. Publicity concepts are very simple: You need to get out there and create your own media opportunities instead of waiting for the press to find you. You make media exposure work for your business, and at the same time you save thousands of dollars along the way.

Your customers are going to form negative or positive opinions about your business based on what they see and hear on the radio, on the television, or in print. Mass media, such as radio, television, and print, are often difficult and certainly very costly methods to promote your business, so we will concentrate on less costly methods to grab the attention of customers in a big way. By using positive media relations, you'll be taking the first step toward your successful positioning in the Internet marketplace. This will allow you to convert more of the traffic to your Web site into satisfied, paying customers.

Online Success

What do you do when you have a new (or even successful) online business, and you want to attract more customers by positioning yourself as an expert in your marketplace? You'll want to merge the proven success of positive media coverage and a successful online presence to give yourself the winning edge over your competitors. It is the combination of both successful online and offline publicity and promotion that will guarantee your credibility, trustworthiness, and dependability, which all lead to greater sales and interest in your products or services. Your success will lead to more sales, increased client confidence, increased exposure at speaking appearances, and the positive public profile that you want for your online business. People who look on the Internet for merchants will only buy from someone that they feel they know and trust.

THE IMPORTANCE OF MEDIA EXPOSURE

Media exposure is key to your successful online marketing profile. Your customers will form their opinions (positive or negative) based on what they hear and see in print, on television, on the radio, or on the Web. These "media" channels are not to be confused with the common short-form referral to online "multimedia" as media too. Recognizing the importance of media exposure can boost the sales of your products or services. That positive media exposure is also a major step toward maintaining credibility in your online marketplace and ensuring that you compel visitors to channel more traffic to your Web site.

The first thing you need to keep in mind is that media exposure, as with online marketing campaigns, will take some time to become effective. It's not going to happen overnight, and you will have to take the time to think about the direction in which you want that exposure to take you. Make sure you know the differences between online and offline media exposure. There are several things that you can do to promote your offline media exposure, including the following:

- Approach your local chamber of commerce and request that they write a short article about you and your business; even if you are an online-only business, the local exposure is great.

You can then take that article and publish it on your Web site as another promotion tool or use it in an online e-zine campaign. You will want to make sure that the focus of the article is just as much about you as it is about the business you are promoting. Remember that you want to promote yourself as well as your business. The best local media exposure results if you're being viewed as a leader in your community.

- Offer to be a speaker at a seminar or to lead a workshop in your area of expertise. This is a great way to gain media exposure that is incredibly positive and community oriented, thus gaining you credibility and trust among potential clients. Circulate your URL at the seminar, and give away a digital report via an auto-responder e-mail. Put your Web site URL on everything you distribute (flyers, promotional items, business cards, letterhead).

- Follow up any correspondence or phone calls from the media with a letter or phone call. Make sure to leave your Web site URL on the voice mail. This strategy gains you media exposure by building a reputation as a conscientious, courteous entrepreneur.

- Share your knowledge by writing articles and professional opinions for online publications and uploading them to automated, e-zine syndication sites. These syndication sites are perfect for having immediate hotlinks back to your Web site and other specific landing pages. Remember to include your e-mail or your picture in the byline as well as brief biographical information about yourself and your business. The more exposure you generate, the more successful your business will become.

Develop tactics to make media exposure and coverage work for you. Make media friends wherever and whenever the opportunity presents itself, all in an effort to increase media awareness and promote public relations. You are going to have to earn media exposure, but the time and effort that you expend will be your investment by having a positive public profile, both online and offline.

Keep in mind that most columnists will give their e-mail addresses in their byline at the conclusion of their articles. Send them notes with your comments and views, while offering your expertise as a source for future quotes. Optimize your media exposure whenever possible; the returns for your business will be substantial.

Gaining the Trust of Your Clients

Gaining the trust of your customers is extremely critical in developing a continuing relationship that rewards your online business with repeat customer sales. The one-time sale may boost your immediate sales numbers, but it's returning customers who take your business from mediocre to fantastic profits. Your goal is to build quality customer relationships and then maintain them. Gaining media exposure, both online and offline, opens the doors to a potentially long-term relationship with customers by using implied third-party credibility, thus legitimizing you as the expert in your field. Once you attract the prospects, you still have to deliver your goods/services and ensure that customers are completely satisfied. There are several rules that you should remember when it comes to building a relationship with your customers and gaining their trust: be honest, be upfront, and always do what you say you are going to do. By following these three simple guiding principles, you will have satisfied customers.

Increasing Your Public Profile

The more positive your public profile, the more success you will have both online and offline. This, of course, ties back in with gaining credibility with the public and with your customers. Your public profile is your trademark for success and profits. Just as important, your online profile and business rating is critically important to how customers perceive you. Your local and state Better Business Bureaus are great organizations to join and obtain positive ratings. Other online business profile ratings services worth considering are **www.resellerratings.com**, **www.epinions.com**, and **www.consumerreports.org**.

INCREASING YOUR PUBLIC PROFILE BOTH ONLINE AND OFFLINE

Take some time to determine just what type of public profile you want to project. Most likely, you'll want a successful, upbeat profile that is

based on your confidence and credibility and supported by
your products, services, and superior customer service and satisfaction.
You can increase your public profile by taking advantage of opportunities
that allow you to use your services and knowledge in a variety of venues,
thereby gaining public awareness and online marketing exposure without
spending your own funds on relatively expensive advertising. Think
outside the box. Don't always stick to convention just because
the business market dictates certain protocol. Check out Raleigh
Pinskey's book *101 Ways to Promote Yourself*, which is available at
www.PromoteYourself.com.

"Without promotion something terrible happens . . . Nothing!"

—P.T. Barnum

Positioning yourself, and actually becoming an expert in your
market, takes time, patience, and personal confidence. Just knowing
the advantages of effective marketing is half the battle in getting there.
Remember, it's the combination of media and marketing that really
communicates the benefits and unique aspects of your business, which in
turn drive customers to your Web site.

One of the most important methods of being an expert in your field
has already been touched on previously in "The Importance of Media
Exposure": publishing and sharing your knowledge. Publishing your
knowledge has several advantages for your online marketing strategy.
Foremost, publishing your knowledge puts you in the position of being
an expert in your industry, which draws traffic to your Web site and
contributes to your brand recognition.

Your goal when it comes to sharing your expertise is to publish for
free, thereby allowing many other organizations, news services, and other
publications or magazines to distribute your article throughout their
distribution network in return for links back to your Web site and direct
product promotions to thousands of potential new customers. There are
ways that you can publish a full-page ad promoting yourself and your
business without spending a dime. Contact editors of publications and
offer them your press release to add content to their next publication.
Many editors are looking for useful and relevant content so that they
can meet deadlines. You need to take advantage of this opportunity and
create the perfect article for publication.

You should be targeting newspapers, magazines, newsletters, Web sites, and Web magazines as ideal opportunities for displaying your article. Keep in mind that magazines that have both an offline and an online image are excellent for increased exposure for driving customers to your Web site. Atlantic Publishing has produced e-zine newsletters for more than four years and has grown a significant subscriber database. They routinely publish articles at no cost to professionals within the industry, providing a variety of hyperlinks, company and product descriptions, and other promotional material all at no cost, driving thousands of potential customers to their Web site.

Using Press Releases to Generate Exposure

We've already discussed the importance of media exposure. But what about using an online press release to get that same exposure to your customers? An online press release is part of the online medium of communication, and online communication is all about timing. Your press release, whether printed and faxed or online, is one method of communicating with your customers and your industry. It's up to you to make the most of a press release so that it has as much impact as possible.

Most companies use press releases to alert the public about a new product or service they offer. These press releases, while informative, tend to be somewhat dry, and consumers typically skim over them, sometimes even missing the key points. In fact, the bottom line is "If it's not NEWS-worthy, then you won't be selected by the media for coverage." That said, a press release promoting specific events, specials, or newsworthy items can be very effective. The Silvermine Tavern (**www.silverminetavern. com**) has utilized effective press releases for years by publishing written press releases, which are printed in the newspaper. Additionally, they publish the press releases online and also disseminate highlights through their online newsletter promotional program, gaining maximum promotional potential at virtually no cost. As an alternative to a written press release, you could try a multimedia approach. If you are giving a live press release, you can incorporate the audio or video files onto your Web site, either to complement a written press release or replace it altogether. It is highly recommended that you have a media section on your Web site to serve reporters, columnists, producers, and editors with your latest press release information. Many people find listening to an audio clip or, better yet, watching a video clip preferential to reading a written press release. There is so much written word on the Internet that trying another medium to get your message across could be just the boost your company needs. You should also think of other Web site owners as another form of media channel since everyone is looking for fresh content and expert advice.

Consider using an online press release service, such as **www.PRweb.com**, to generate successful media exposure for your online business. This free service is another tool to distribute your press release information to thousands of potential new customers or clients. Keep in mind the value of using highly relevant keywords often within the content of your online press release in order to utilize the benefits of search engine optimization (SEO). Including live links within your online press release is another way for you to ensure increased media coverage. Linking to relevant Web sites increases the credibility and functionality of your online business. You may also do your own press release through your own e-zine or e-mail campaigns, which are covered in detail later in this book.

ONLINE PUBLIC RELATIONS ARE EASILY MARKETABLE FOR SEVERAL REASONS

1. **Accessibility.** Using SEO and search engines can give you the visibility to drive traffic to your Web site.

2. **Affordability.** By using free online press release services, you can work within the tightest budget. You can also select small, tightly targeted press releases within a niche or specific industry. Even though you are paying for the press release, you won't be blowing your budget by sending the release to non-qualified markets or media outlets.

3. **Internet speed.** The speed of the Internet lets you seize business opportunities immediately. Millions can be made by tying your media events and campaigns to current events such as the World Series and the Super Bowl. It's up to you to follow up on all

customer sales and communication.

4. **Internet leverage.** The Internet deals with facts and information without focusing on the size or prestige of your company. Potential customers are using the Internet for research and obtaining helpful knowledge. Make yourself easy to find on the Internet.

Your focus when doing your own publicity and PR shouldn't circulate around a press release. Although useful, the press release shouldn't be your only technique when it comes to media exposure; rather, it should be treated as another tool in a well-stocked arsenal.

YOUR WEB SITE IS YOUR OWN MEDIA TOOL

Free media coverage is a great way to get your name out to the public and build your credibility. It's "free" if you do it yourself without hiring a media agency, but it does require an investment of your time, focus, and effort. There are several tactics you can employ to generate free media coverage. Paid advertisement may be important, but to the struggling small business, it is all about cheap or free media coverage. That said, paid advertising should still be considered as a feasible and desirable component of your overall online marketing portfolio if you can afford it, if you choose to implement it, and if it typically has the potential to be highly effective. It is vital to use your advertising dollars wisely, though, as you want to ensure that you get the most bang for your buck and make sure that your target audience is receiving as much information about your company as possible.

The Internet gives every individual a place where they can present their own media online. The Internet is a media channel, and you have the power to own your own PBS—Personal Broadcasting System. There are many ways that you can increase the amount of traffic to your Web site and generate more business from your site. You want to drive as many potential customers to your Web site as possible, even if each visitor does not result in a "sale." Depending on the type of business you operate, your goal may only be to increase Web site traffic. For example, if you are operating a restaurant and your Web site is an online marketing and advertising tool for your restaurant, acquiring an increase in the number of site visitors or page hits is considered a success, as your goal is to drive visitors to your site, which will, hopefully, in turn inspire them to dine at your establishment. If you are selling products, you can expect many comparison shoppers who are shopping for features, product reviews, or other product descriptive information as they consider purchasing the product. You should advertise your "press releases," "product promotions," or other information venues in the form of an opt-in form on your Web site. This form should be on the home page, easily found, and should capture each visitor's name and e-mail. Likewise, if you are engaging in face-to-face communications, you should ask for the customer's name, e-mail, and contact information, while starting a conversation that eventually leads to trust and, finally, that first purchase. The more media exposure you use to direct targeted traffic to your Web site, the more you increase your chances for successfully connecting with prospects who are prepared to buy. Use media exposure to get prospects to your Web site, but then, present your own media via your "PBS" section of your Web site.

Your e-presence isn't just about how good your Web site looks. You want to give your customers a reason to come to your Web site and do business with you instead of giving that business to your competitors. You need to pull out all the stops and build your e-presence via the media and Internet marketplace by providing quality content, unique experiences, ease and simplicity, savings, superior customer satisfaction, and other advantages. Building your online business again comes back to earning the respect and trust of your customers with the combination of media, marketing, and relationship skills. There are many ways that you can improve your online marketing success.

Five Ways to Improve Your Online Marketing

1. SITE DESIGN

Make sure that your Web site is professional and has a great design. You want your Web site to have a clean, tight look so that customers are compelled to return. Professional site design means having a Web site that is easy to navigate, has appropriate logos, has up-to-date information, answers customer questions, and doesn't look like an amateur site. Use the techniques we have given you to ensure that you have a professional-looking, quality Web site. Make sure you incorporate the techniques in later chapters of this book to ensure that your Web site is optimized for search engines.

2. Honesty

Never hide anything from your customers. Give them all the data that they need to make an informative decision about your products or services. Follow through on what you say you offer at your Web site to maintain credibility and trust. You don't want to be identified and exposed in the media as a poor company, scam site, or rip-off artist. Bad news travels fast, and it travels even faster on the Internet. A great example of this is in a PowerPoint presentation titled "Yours Is a Very Bad Hotel," authored by two extremely dissatisfied businessmen after their bad experience with a hotel. The hotel's poor customer service and failure to hold a "guaranteed" room reservation was widely distributed on the Internet. As a result of the negative publicity, the nationwide hotel chain changed corporate policies and no doubt suffered from the unwanted attention. This is a superb example of very negative exposure that was spread virally and very quickly around the world — literally.

3. Customer Incentive

Make sure that you give your customers a reason to visit your site, to spend time browsing it, to interact with it, and most importantly, to return to it. Offer incentives by showcasing featured products or promotions, and use creative and new Internet tools, such as video and audio, to create an interactive experience. For affordable and easy tools, check out **www. MyInstantVideo.com** or **www.audiomarketingon-line.com**. You can also import video clips from promotional products or CDs/DVDs or create your own video clips and add them to your Web site with Microsoft FrontPage.

4. DOMAIN NAME

Try to get your own domain name for your Web site. As simple as this concept may be, it makes the difference between prospects remembering who you are and moving on to your competition. Use brief, benefit-related terms for multiple-site URLs. Don't rely on only one domain featuring your name or organization. We have given you a significant amount of information related to selecting a "good" domain name; you should carefully review this prior to purchasing your domain name.

5. TESTIMONIALS

Using customer testimonials is a great way to promote the quality and reliability of your Web site and, more importantly, promote your products or services. This is an amazingly effective tactic. The media you create and the coverage that you get is a subtle, third-party referral to you. However, the strongest and most effective sales assistance comes from direct customer testimonials. We recommend using audio and video testimonials as well as printed quotes on your Web sites. You should include your customer's name, e-mail address, and Web address with each unsolicited testimonial to increase believability. A script which will rotate testimonials on your Web site is available from **www.willmaster.com**.

Remember that no matter how flashy or impressive your Web site may look, it is customer service, satisfaction, and reliability that keeps them coming back. The success of your online strategy relies on combining all of the above tactics for maintaining successful online positioning and presence.

Techniques for Improving Web Site Traffic

The following techniques may be employed to increase your Web site traffic.

- **Create a What's New or New Products page.** Site visitors like to see what is new, trendy, or just released. Make it easy for them.

- **Establish a promotion program.** The sky is the limit for promotions. You can offer free products, trial samples, or discount coupons. Everyone loves a bargain, so give it to them!

- **Establish a contest.** We already discussed Atlantic Publishing Company's Top 50 Restaurant Web sites contest, which drew thousands of site visitors. Similar contents cost nothing to create, are simple to manage, and draw visitors back.

- **Add content-relevant professional articles**, news events, press releases, or other topics of interest on a daily basis to draw back visitors to your site.

- **Establish a viral marketing campaign** or embed viral marketing techniques into your current advertising programs or e-zines. Viral marketing is when you incorporate such things as a "forward to a friend" link within the advertisement. In theory, if many people forward to many more friends, it will spread like a virus (hence the name viral) and eventually go to many potential customers.

- **Use signature files with all e-mail accounts.** Signature files are basically business cards through e-mail, so why not send your business card to all your e-mail recipients? Signature files are sent with every e-mail you send out and can contain all contact information, including your business name and Web site URL. Signature files can be created in Microsoft Outlook or Outlook Express.

- **Start an affiliate program and market it!** Include your affiliate information in e-mails, newsletters, e-zines, and on Web sites to promote your program. A successful affiliate program will generate a significant increase in Web site traffic.

- **Include your Web site URL on everything** (business cards, letterhead, promotional items, e-mails, etc.).

- **Add a free search feature to your Web site.** This is a great tool, which site visitors will love! There are dozens of free search services you can incorporate into your Web site. Just do a search on "free Web site search," and you will have plenty from which to choose.

- **Register multiple domain names with search engines** and "point" them to your main Web site. Owning similar or content-related domain names is a good investment to protect yourself from competitors stealing similar-sounding domain names and will help you with search engine rankings.

- **Win some awards for your Web site.** There are quite a few award sites that are nothing more than link-exchange factories; however, there are some reputable award sites such as **www.100hot .com** and **www .webbyawards .com**.

Web Site Promotion

Promoting yourself online means that you need to be aware of all the techniques outlined in this book. The better that you understand all of the terms and definitions contained within these pages, the more armed you'll be to take your position at the top of your chosen market or search engine. The following terms and acronyms will better define some of the methods of promotion and other commonly used marketing and search engine "lingo" that will help you decipher the vast amount of information on the Internet that you may want to consider for your business.

Promotion Terms and Definitions

Source for terms and definitions: **http://searchcio.techtarget.com /sDefinition/0,,sid19_gci211535,00.html**

Ad: For Web advertising, an ad is almost always a banner, a graphic image or set of animated images (in a file called an animated GIF) of a designated pixel size and byte size limit. An ad or set of ads for a campaign is often referred to as "the creative." Banners and other special advertising that include an interactive or visual element beyond the usual are known as rich media.

Ad impression: An ad impression, or ad view, occurs when a user pulls up a Web page through a browser and sees an ad that is served on that page. Many Web sites sell advertising space by ad impressions.

Ad rotation: Ads are often rotated into ad spaces from a list. This is usually done automatically by software on the Web site or at a central site administered by an ad broker or server facility for a network of Web sites.

Ad space: An ad space is a space on a Web page that is reserved for ads. An ad space group is a group of spaces within a Web site that share the same characteristics so that an ad purchase can be made for the group of spaces.

Ad view: An ad view, synonymous with ad impression, is a single ad that appears on a Web page when the page arrives at the viewer's display. Ad views are what most Web sites sell or prefer to sell. A Web page may offer space for a number of ad views. In general, the term impression is more commonly used.

Affiliate marketing: Affiliate marketing is the use by a Web site that sells products of other Web sites, called affiliates, to help market the products. Amazon.com created the first large-scale affiliate program and hundreds of other companies have followed since.

Banner: A banner is an advertisement in the form of a graphic image that typically runs across a Web page or is positioned in a margin or other space reserved for ads. Banner ads are usually Graphics Interchange Format (GIF) images. In addition to adhering to size, many Web sites limit the size of the file to a certain number of bytes so that the file will display quickly. Most banner ads are animated GIFs since animation has been shown to attract a larger percentage of user clicks. The most common larger banner ad is 468 pixels wide by 60 pixels high. Smaller sizes include 125 by 125 and 120 by 90 pixels. These and other banner sizes have been established as standard sizes by the Internet Advertising Bureau.

Beyond the banner: This is the idea that, in addition to banner ads, there are other ways to use the Internet to communicate a marketing message. These include sponsoring a Web site or a particular feature on it, advertising in e-mail newsletters, co-branding with another company and its Web site, contest promotion, and, in general, finding new ways to engage and interact with the desired audience. "Beyond the banner" approaches can also include the interstitial and streaming video infomercial. The banner itself can be transformed into a small rich media event.

Booked space: This is the number of ad views for an ad space that are currently sold out.

Brand, brand name, and branding: A brand is a product, service, or concept that is publicly distinguished from other products, services, or concepts so that it can be easily communicated and usually marketed. A brand name is the name of the distinctive product, service, or concept. Branding is the process of creating and disseminating the brand name. Branding can be applied to the entire corporate identity as well as to individual product and service names. In Web and other media advertising, it is recognized that there is usually some kind of branding value whether or not an immediate, direct response can be measured from an ad or campaign. Companies like Proctor and Gamble have made a science out of creating and evaluating the success of their brand name products.

Caching: In Internet advertising, the caching of pages in a cache server or the user's computer means that some ad views won't be known by the ad counting programs and is a source of concern. There are several techniques for telling the browser not to cache particular pages. On the other hand, specifying no caching for all pages may mean that users will find your site to be slower than you would like.

Click: According to ad industry recommended guidelines from FAST, an ad industry group, a click is "when a visitor interacts with an advertisement." This does not apparently mean simply interacting with a rich media ad, but actually clicking on it so that the visitor is headed toward the advertiser's destination. It also does not mean that the visitor actually waits to fully arrive at the destination, but just that the visitor started going there.

Click rate: The click rate is the percentage of ad views that resulted in click-throughs. Although there is visibility and branding value in ad views that don't result in a click-through, this value is difficult to measure. A click-through has several values: it's an indication of the ad's effectiveness and it results in the viewer getting to the advertiser's Web site where other messages can be provided. A new approach is for a click to result not in a link to another site but to an immediate product order window. What a successful click rate is depends on a number of factors, such as the campaign objectives, how enticing the banner message is, how explicit the message is (a message that is complete within the banner may be less apt to be clicked), audience/message matching, how new the banner is, how often it is displayed to the same user, and so forth. In general, click rates for high-repeat, branding banners vary from 0.15 to 1 percent. Ads with provocative, mysterious, or other compelling content can induce click rates ranging from 1 to 5 percent and sometimes higher. The click rate for a given ad tends to diminish with repeated exposure.

Click stream: A click stream is a recorded path of the pages a user requested in going through one or more Web sites. Click stream information can help Web site owners understand how visitors are using their sites and which pages are getting the most use. It can help advertisers understand how users get to the clients' pages, what pages they look at, and how they go about ordering a product.

Click-through: A click-through is what is counted by the sponsoring site as a result of an ad click. In practice, click and click-through tend to be used interchangeably. A click-through, however, seems to imply that the user actually received the page. A few advertisers are willing to pay only for click-throughs rather than for ad impressions.

Click-through rate: The percentage of people clicking on a link compared with the total number seeing that same link.

Co-branding: Co-branding on the Web often means two Web sites or Web site sections or features displaying their logos (and thus their brands) together so that the viewer considers the site or feature to be a joint enterprise. Co-branding is often associated with cross-linking between the sites, although it isn't necessary.

Conversion rate: The percentage of site visitors who respond to the desired goal of an ad campaign compared with the total number of people who see the ad campaign. The goal may be, for example, convincing readers to become subscribers, encouraging customers to buy something, or enticing prospective customers from another site with an ad.

Cookie: A cookie is a file on a Web user's hard drive (it's kept in one of the subdirectories under the browser file directory) that is used by Web sites to record data about the user. Some ad rotation software uses cookies to see which ad the user has just seen so that a different ad will be rotated into the next page view.

Cost-per-action: Cost-per-action is what an advertiser pays for each visitor that takes some specifically defined action in response to an ad beyond simply clicking on it. For example, a visitor might visit an advertiser's site and request to be subscribed to their newsletter.

Cost-per-click (CPC): The amount of money an advertiser will pay to a site each time a user clicks on an ad or link.

Cost-per-lead: This is a more specific form of cost-per-action in which a visitor provides enough information at the advertiser's site (or in interaction with a rich media ad) to be used as a sales lead. Note that you can estimate cost-per-lead regardless of how you pay for the ad (in other words, buying on a pay-per-lead basis is not required to calculate the cost-per-lead).

Cost-per-sale: Sites that sell products directly from their Web site or can otherwise determine sales generated as the result of an advertising sales lead can calculate the cost-per-sale of Web advertising.

Cost per thousand impressions (CPM): The amount of money an advertiser will pay for 1,000 ad impressions or views (M refers to the Roman numeral for 1,000, it is an industry standard measure for selling ads on Web sites).

CPTM: CPTM is "cost per thousand targeted" ad impressions, apparently implying that the audience you're selling is targeted to particular demographics.

(The) Creative: Ad agencies and buyers often refer to ad banners and other forms of created advertising as ""the creative." Since the creative requires creative inspiration and skill that may come from a third party, it often doesn't arrive until late in the preparation for a new campaign launch.

Demographics: Demographics is data about the size and characteristics of a population or audience (for example, gender, age group, income group, purchasing history, personal preferences, and so forth).

Filtering: Filtering is the immediate analysis by a program of a user's Web page request in order to determine which ad or ads to return in the requested page. A Web page request can tell a Web site or its ad server whether it fits a certain characteristic such as coming from a particular company's address or that the user is using a particular level of browser. The Web ad server can respond accordingly.

Fold: "Above the fold," a term borrowed from print media, refers to an ad that is viewable as soon as the Web page arrives. You don't have to scroll down (or sideways) to see it. Since screen resolution can affect what is immediately viewable, it's good to know whether the Web site's audience tends to set their resolution at 640 by 480 pixels or at 800 by 600 (or higher).

Hit: A hit is the sending of a single file whether an HTML file, an image, an audio file, or other file type. Since a single Web page request can bring with it a number of individual files, the number of hits from a site is a not a good indication of its actual use (number of visitors). It does have meaning for the Web site space provider, however, as an indicator of traffic flow.

Impression: According to the "Basic Advertising Measures" from FAST, an impression is "The count of a delivered basic advertising unit from an ad distribution point." Impressions are how most Web advertising is sold and the cost is quoted in terms of the cost per thousand impressions (CPM).

Insertion order: An insertion order is a formal, printed order to run an ad campaign. Typically, the insertion order identifies the campaign name, the Web site receiving the order and the planner or buyer giving the order, the individual ads to be run (or who will provide them), the ad sizes, the campaign beginning and end dates, the CPM, the total cost, discounts to be applied, and reporting requirements and possible penalties or stipulations relative to the failure to deliver the impressions.

Inventory: Inventory is the total number of ad views or impressions that a Web site has to sell over a given period of time. Usually, inventory is figured by the month.

Keyword: A word or phrase that a user types into a search engine when looking for specific information.

Media broker: Since it's often not efficient for an advertiser to select every Web site it wants to put ads on, media brokers aggregate sites for advertisers and their media planners and buyers, based on demographics and other factors.

Media buyer: A media buyer, usually at an advertising agency, works with a media planner to allocate the money provided for an advertising campaign among specific print or online media (magazines, TV, Web sites, and so forth), and then calls and places the advertising orders. On the Web, placing the order often includes requesting proposals and negotiating the final cost.

Meta tags: Hidden HTML directions for Web browsers or search engines. They include important information such as the title of each page, relevant keywords describing site content, and the description of the site that shows up when a search engine returns a search.

Opt-in e-mail: Opt-in e-mail is e-mail containing information or advertising that users explicitly request (opt) to receive. Typically, a Web site invites its visitors to fill out forms identifying subject or product categories that interest them and about which they are willing to receive e-mail from anyone who might send it. The Web site sells the names (with explicit or implicit permission from their visitors) to a company that specializes in collecting mailing lists that represent different interests. Whenever the mailing list company sells its lists to advertisers, the Web site is paid a small amount for each name that it generated for the list. You can sometimes identify opt-in e-mail because it starts with a statement that tells you that you have previously agreed to receive such messages.

Page view: A common metric for measuring how many times a complete page is visited.

Pay-per-click: In pay-per-click advertising, the advertiser pays a certain amount for each click-through to the advertiser's Web site. The amount paid per click-through is arranged at the time of the insertion order and varies considerably. Higher pay-per-click rates recognize that there may be some "no-click" branding value as well as click-through value provided.

Pay-per-lead: In pay-per-lead advertising, the advertiser pays for each sales lead generated. For example, an advertiser might pay for every visitor that clicked on a site and then filled out a form.

Pay-per-sale: Pay-per-sale is not customarily used for ad buys. It is, however, the customary way to pay Web sites that participate in affiliate programs, such as those of Amazon.com and Beyond.com.

Pay-per-view: Since this is the prevalent type of ad buying arrangement at larger Web sites, this term tends to be used only when comparing this most prevalent method with pay-per-click and other methods.

Proof of performance: Some advertisers may want proof that the ads they've bought have actually run and that click-through figures are accurate. In print media, tear sheets taken from a publication prove that an ad was run. On the Web, there is no industry-wide practice for proof of performance. Some buyers rely on the integrity of the media broker and the Web site. The ad buyer usually checks the Web site to determine the ads are actually running. Most buyers require weekly figures during a campaign. A few want to look directly at the figures, viewing the ad server or Web site reporting tool.

Psychographic characteristics: This is a term for personal interest information that is gathered by Web sites by requesting it from users. For example, a Web site could ask users to list the Web sites that they visit most often. Advertisers could use this data to help create a demographic profile for that site.

Reporting template: Although the media have to report data to ad agencies, media planners, and buyers during and at the end of each campaign, no standard report is yet available. FAST, the ad industry coalition, is working on a proposed standard reporting template that would enable reporting to be consistent.

Rich media: Rich media is advertising that contains perceptual or interactive elements more elaborate than the usual banner ad. Today, the term is often used for banner ads with popup menus that let the visitor select a particular page to link to on the advertiser's site. Rich media ads are generally more challenging to create and to serve. Some early studies have shown that rich media ads tend to be more effective than ordinary animated banner ads.

ROI: ROI (return on investment) is "the bottom line" on how successful an ad or campaign was in terms of what the returns (generally sales revenue) were for the money expended (invested).

Run-of-network: A run-of-network ad is one that is placed to run on all sites within a given network of sites. Ad sales firms handle run-of-network insertion orders in such a way as to optimize results for the buyer consistent with higher priority ad commitments.

Run-of-site: A run-of-site ad is one that is placed to rotate on all non-featured ad spaces on a site. CPM rates for run-of-site ads are usually less than for rates for specially placed ads or sponsorships.

Search engine marketing (SEM): Promoting a Web site through a search engine. This most often refers to targeting prospective customers by buying relevant keywords or phrases.

Search engine optimization (SEO): Making a Web site more friendly to search engines, resulting in a higher page rank.

Splash page: A splash page (also known as an interstitial) is a preliminary page that precedes the regular home page of a Web site and usually promotes a particular site feature or provides advertising. A splash page is timed to move on to the home page after a short period of time.

Sponsor: Depending on the context, a sponsor simply means an advertiser who has sponsored an ad and, by doing so, has also helped sponsor or sustain the Web site itself. It can also mean an advertiser that has a special relationship with the Web site and supports a special feature of a Web site, such as a writer's column, a Flower-of-the-Day, or a collection of articles on a particular subject.

Sponsorship: Sponsorship is an association with a Web site in some way that gives an advertiser some particular visibility and advantage above that of run-of-site advertising. When associated with specific content, sponsorship can provide a more targeted audience than run-of-site ad buys. Sponsorship also implies a "synergy and resonance" between the Web site and the advertiser. Some sponsorships are available as value-added opportunities for advertisers who buy a certain minimum amount of advertising.

Targeting: Targeting is purchasing ad space on Web sites that match audience and campaign objective requirements. Techtarget.com, with over twenty Web sites targeted to special information technology audiences, is an example of an online publishing business built to enable advertising targeting.

Unique visitor: A unique visitor is someone with a unique address who is entering a Web site for the first time that day (or some other specified period). Thus, a visitor who returns within the same day is not counted twice. A unique visitors count tells you how many different people there are in your audience during the time period, but not how much they used the site during the period.

User session: A user session is someone with a unique address that enters or reenters a Web site each day (or some other specified period). A user session is sometimes determined by counting only those users who haven't reentered the site within the past 20 minutes or a similar period. User session figures are sometimes used, somewhat incorrectly, to indicate "visits" or "visitors" per day.

User sessions are a better indicator of total site activity than "unique visitors" since they indicate frequency of use.

View: A view is, depending on what's meant, either an ad view or a page view. Usually, an ad view is what's meant. There can be multiple ad views per page views. View counting should consider that a small percentage of users choose to turn the graphics off (not display the images) in their browser.

Visit: A visit is a Web user with a unique address entering a Web site at some page for the first time that day (or for the first time in a lesser time period). The number of visits is roughly equivalent to the number of different people that visit a site. This term is ambiguous unless the user defines it, since it could mean a user session or it could mean a unique visitor that day.

ABBREVIATIONS

AJ – Ask Jeeves

AOL – America Online

ASP – application service provider

AV – AltaVista

B2B – business-to-business

B2C – business-to-consumer

CPA – cost-per-action

CPC – cost-per-click

CPS – cost-per-sale

CTR – click-through rate

DH – direct hit

FFA – free-for-all link list

HB – HotBot

IM – instant messaging

INK – Inktomi

LS – LookSmart

MSN – Microsoft Network

NL – Northern Light

NSI – Network Solutions

PFI – pay for inclusion

PFP – pay for performance

PPC – pay-per-click

PPCSE – pay-per-click search engine

PPL – pay-per-lead

PPS – pay-per-sale

PV – page view

RON – run-of-network

ROS – run-of-site

SEO – search engine optimization

SEP – search engine positioning

UV – unique visitor

WWW – World Wide Web

Y! – Yahoo!

CHAPTER 5

Branding

What Is Branding?

Branding is something that is talked about frequently in the world of marketing and advertising, both on and off the Internet. But just what is this "branding" all about? In a nutshell, branding is when you give your business or product a unique identity by using one or more of a combination of a design, a name, a sign or symbol, or a specific term. It is this "brand" that is going to make you stand out among the competition, and that is going to make your customers remember just who you are. Branding can be defined as the process by which a commodity in the marketplace is known primarily for the image it projects rather than any actual quality. Branding is a promise, a pledge of quality. It is the essence of a product, including why it is great and how it is better than all competing products. It is an image. It is a combination of words and letters, symbols, and colors.

Ever heard of eBay? In 1996, Jared M. Spool wrote an article about branding, which was when eBay was in its infant stages and not everyone had multiple PCs in their homes. While the article is an interesting snapshot ten years into the past, it certainly drives the point home on how eBay has effectively utilized branding.

Spool wrote: *"You may not have heard of eBay (ebay.com). We never had. Not until we went to a regional antiques fair and interviewed more than 90 antique collectors and dealers. The eBay site provides an online auction. At first glance, it's not very sophisticated. In fact, it's effectively a modified message board, where each thread is an item for sale and each reply is a bid. Other than the site logo, it uses few decorative graphics and consists mostly of user-supplied text, often all in uppercase. What graphics are on the site are images of the items the users have provided – mostly amateur-taken snapshots.*

When we showed eBay to collectors and dealers who had never seen it, they got excited when they saw all the great stuff they'd been looking for. This initial positive experience created the eBay brand for these people. In fact, users new to computing told us that eBay will be their first Internet destination when they get their own computers – showing us that eBay has developed the emotional ties that make branding successful."

There are many companies (online and offline) that successfully use branding so that you can easily identify them over their competitors. Some of these companies that successfully use branding are Wal-Mart, IBM, The Gap, Travelocity, eBay, Amazon, and Microsoft. These names have become trusted among consumers throughout the world. With the huge increase in business activity conducted on the Internet, more companies use branding to help customers find them and to remember who they are and what they stand for. When it comes to your own business, you may wish to use branding in such a way that your service or product stands out among the many Internet Web sites that are all vying for attention and customers.

Branding is a mixture of creativity and the type of relationship that you strive to establish with your customers. The creative part of branding is all about the logo (or other branding that you choose to use) and the way that you advertise on and off the Internet, using this logo. The relationship part of branding is all about the way you make your customers feel when they come to your Web site. You want your customers to feel that they can trust you and your products or services so that they generate sales for your business. In summary, branding (online and offline) is all about:

- How your product or service looks when it's on the Web site or on a shelf in your traditional store.

- How your customers feel when they access your Web site.

- How you handle customer orders.

- The credibility and trust that you earn with your customers using a combination of branding and successful Internet marketing.

Developing your own branding for your business is an important step when it comes to the success of your company. This means that you need to spend quality time coming up with the right branding for your products and services.

Developing a Company Image

When you're developing a company image, it means that you'll be creating a "personality" for your company with which customers can identify and want to do business. The personality of your company will be a combination of many things such as the facts, goals, and history of your business and the style of advertising that you choose to use. All these elements will tie together to leave a lasting impression on your customers that can make the difference between the success of your business or its failure. You want to leave a positive and lasting impression on the public and your potential customers.

Many large and successful companies have worked hard to develop their company image. Part of this image is having a logo, or brand, with which customers can identify. McDonald's has had a successful logo for years with which people all over the world identify: Ronald McDonald and the Golden Arches. Some of the most effective logos are by the following companies: Coca-Cola, Sony, Google, Dell, Yahoo!, and America Online. These companies maintain a corporate image that appeals to customers and helps to generate huge sales figures each year.

Developing your company image means that you need to identify many aspects of your business, including:

- Knowing just who your target markets are and how to reach them.

- Developing a company image that is constant and revolves around your target market.

How to Determine Your Target Market

It's important that you find out just who your target market is. You need to know just who you're trying to reach as customers and why you're trying to reach them. From the very first day that you launch your business, you need to know who your customers are and who you want them to be. Many businesses make the mistake of not focusing on a very specific market segment. This means that they waste a lot of time and money with advertising campaigns trying to attract customers who will probably never buy from them.

When you're developing your company image, you need to focus your time, energy, and money on the portion of the market that you know will be the most likely to buy your product or service. There are certain things that you need to identify about your customers so that you can attract the right kind of sales to your business. Some of the things that you need to know about your potential customers include:

- The buying habits of your customers.

- The type of lifestyle that your customers have, including their age, sex, and marital status.

- Where your customers live and what types of jobs they have.

- What type of budget your customers have.

- What customers like and don't like about your product or service.

- What customers like and don't like about your competitors' products or services.

Any information that you find out about your potential customers and your target market will be a huge factor in the success of your online or brick-and-mortar business.

The Importance of the Name of Your Business

You might think that a name is just a name and that it will have little impact on the success of your business; however, you would be mistaken. This is the mistake that many businesses make as they come up with names for their companies. What you call your company can be very important in providing you with a business identity that is strong and will leave a lasting impact. You want to choose a business name that is going to be a reflection of what your product or service is all about. If you choose a name for your business that is too unique and creative, you may find that customers have a harder time finding you on the Internet or associating your name with your products or services.

Another thing that you need to keep in mind when you're choosing a name for your business is that this name will be your first contact with your customers. The first impression that you present to your customers can often be a lasting one. If you have a business that is selling scrapbook products, you'll want to have a business name that lets customers know that your business is about scrapbooks. For example, "Creative Scrapbooks" lets customers find you easily on the Internet and describes the product that you're selling. A name such as "Creative Crafts" won't be as definitive when it comes to the core of what your business is all about. Some people choose to name a business after themselves, and although this may work for companies that already have an established presence, it won't work well if you're just starting your company, unless you include mention of the product that you're selling as well.

An example of a business that includes your name would be "Carter's Creative Scrapbooks." This not only uses your personal name, it also lets your customers know what your business is selling. There are some benefits that come from using your name in your business title, such as the following:

- Customers will be able to associate your personal name, corporate name, and your product together.

- You'll become better known in the business community, both online and offline.

- Your credit rating may be higher and stronger when your personal name is associated with your business. Keep in mind that if your business isn't successful, your credit rating may also pay the price. This is why many people, when they are first establishing a new business, choose to keep their personal finances separate from their business finances, which is typically recommended.

Choosing a name for your company is a task that you should research carefully before finalizing and selecting an identity. You need to make sure that you're not infringing on another company's name, or you may find yourself faced with a future lawsuit.

How to Choose Your Company Logo

The logo that you choose for your company will be how you are visually identified in the business world. There are many companies that have logos that are instantly recognized around the world, such as McDonald's and Tommy Hilfiger. These logos help promote the corporate image and increase product recognition and profitability, both on and off the Internet.

You may want to choose a logo that not only identifies your business but that also ties your product to a symbol or image. If your product is scrapbooks, you may want to include an image of a scrapbook in your logo. This symbolic identification can be a big advantage when it comes to establishing yourself in your target market as an emerging corporate entity. You may wish to draft a mission or purpose statement to help you design your corporate logo.

Creating a logo sounds easy, doesn't it? It can be. Just remember to keep your customers and the nature of your business in mind when you put it all together. In time, you'll have succeeded in building equity in your trademark, and it will become a positive and recognizable symbol of your product or service. When it comes to creating your company logo, there are some things that you should keep in mind:

- Your logo should be functional and multipurpose, and it should work well in color, in black and white, printed, on letterhead, or on vehicles.

- Make sure that your business logo is tasteful and not offensive in any way.

- Try to make your logo as original and creative as possible without copying some of the other logos that fall into your target market.

- Many times, simplicity is the best rule to follow. You want to leave a clear and precise image with your customers and potential customers that allows you to stand out from the rest of the competition. Studies show that customers are more able to remember companies that have simple logos that they can identify.

- Make sure that the logo you choose for your business has a marketable value. This means that you need to have a logo that you can use for the sale of your product or service, for advertising purposes, and for any future public relations.

- Use vector graphics, which can be resized easily without distortion.

- Protect your logo. You can find details at the U.S. Patent and Trademark Office (**www.uspto.gov**).

Your company logo should be able to adequately and correctly encompass all aspects of your business. Another thing that you should consider when choosing a company logo is how you want the public, and the business world, to view your business. Some images that you can create include an energetic and lively company, a conservative company, a company that is full of luxury, or a hip company. All of these company images can be created with the use of the logo that you choose.

When you're ready to create your company logo, remember that simplicity and tastefulness go a long way, including the colors that you use, the shape and dimensions of the logo, and the typeface on the logo. You will want a logo that performs and looks good on the Internet. The color of your logo will often convey a certain message to the public, and you want to choose colors that send a clear message to your customers. As a general rule to follow, dark colors are usually associated with conservative companies that are selling serious and functional products, while companies that are selling unique and fun products tend to choose logo colors that are bright. If you're selling scrapbooks, you'll want to use bright and fun colors to get your message of creativity across to your customers.

Although the shape of your company logo may seem to be a small thing, just look at the many logos out there and the shape to which they conform. Straight-edge logos are often used by more conservative companies, while circular logos are seen more often for businesses that sell unique and creative products. Typeface follows the same rules of convention as the colors that you use for your company logo. You can use typeface that is conservative, modern, or classical. You may want to come up with your own typeface that is unique to your company and logo. If you consider this route for typeface, you'll want to make sure that you trademark it for your exclusive use. No matter what method you choose to use for finding the right typeface for your logo, make sure that the letter characters match the logo that you've chosen. Your company logo is a cornerstone of corporate branding, and the investment spent carefully designing a logo will reap dividends with branding, corporate identification, and product familiarity.

Branding is an important step to developing a successful business, both on and off the Internet. You'll want to make sure that the impression that your company presents to the public is as precise as possible and one that they'll remember when they're looking for the product or service that you're selling. You want to communicate with those in your target market in such a way that they know who you are, that they trust you, and that they keep coming back time and time again.

Branding Summarized

Successful branding really is all about one thing: recognition from your customers, when your customers are able to identify just what your company, product, or service is all about and are able to separate you from your competition. At that point you've already taken one of the most important steps toward grabbing their attention. Branding uses several methods to ensure that your company name is at the top of the list and that your potential customers can find you among all the competition that exists on the Internet. Branding has one aim: to earn the trust of your customers so that they buy from you, buy repeatedly from you, and refer you to family and friends.

You will want to develop branding for your business Web site that lets your customers quickly recognize who you are, what your products or services are, and a logo that is easily identified with the image that represents quality, service, and value. Brand recognition should be a direct reflection of the products and services that you're selling as well as the personal style of your business. There are different methods that you can infuse into your branding marketing strategy so that you can gain that all important recognition for your business:

- **Packaging that is creative.** You want to create packaging for your products that can be easily identified by your customers and that they'll remember when they see your product online or offline in your brick-and-mortar store.

- **Communication that is visual.** You want to create a logo for your business that can be displayed on the packaging of your products or that symbolizes the services that you're selling. This type of visual communication with your customers will help them to recognize your business in an instant. Not only should your logo be displayed on your packaging, it should also display prominently on your business cards, catalogs, letterhead, brochures, and any other type of media that you use for the marketing of your business.

- **Advertising campaigns that boost your business.** Take every opportunity to expose your business to all kinds of media. You want to encourage and improve your company profile whenever you can so that customers trust and rely on you and your products. In later chapters we will discuss the use of e-zines and newsletters to promote your business. Inclusion of a recognizable logo is extremely important in a healthy and profitable e-zine campaign.

Make sure that you have strategies in place that implement successful and positive branding for your business. Some strategies that you should keep in mind include having clear and precise goals and knowing what your company stands for, having a mission statement that is strong and definite so that you know exactly where your business is going and how you want to arrive at that destination, being determined and constant in the way you deal with your customers so that they know what they can expect each time that they do business with you, and remembering that branding is all about reaching your customers and staying in touch with them. The bottom line is that branding allows you to sell your products or services to customers in a way that makes you stand out from the crowd of competitors, each of whom is looking for his or her share of Internet business.

Case Study in Branding

The following case study in branding can give you an idea of the success that this Internet advertising technique can bring to your business.

Online Branding? Yes Sir!

By George Anagnos

Those who registered for YesSirNoSir, a new concierge-type of service for rich (err... I mean well-off) busy people, sadly lost five minutes of their time for nothing. Their laundry won't be picked up and their kids won't be driven to school by the non-existent chauffer.

The YesSirNoSir service does not exist, never did and never will. It was just a brand created on the Internet with the sole purpose of measuring the resonance of an online brand. And it left a lot of campaign managers wondering what they need to change.

Behind the Scenes of an eBranding Scam

The folks at Dynamic Logic, who created the brand, have every reason to be happy. By creating an online-only brand they managed to quantify the unquantifiable -- the isolated branding effect on the Internet. Their idea came from a spoof billboard campaign in the 80's, when the demand for billboard advertising began to fall. An advertising firm back then created the fictitious brand to show the power of billboard advertising.

Simon Andrews, MD of e-brands (who co-operated with Dynamic Logic) said that "it's very easy to find something wacky to put in a fake campaign, but we wanted something that sounded reasonable ... The product had to be interesting but not trendy."

Given the current status quo with Internet advertising, even the biggest adspenders won't invest too heavily in Web ads. According to Morgan Stanley Dean Witter, only three out of the top 50 adspenders in the US spend more than 1% of their advertising budget on the Internet: Microsoft spends (or invests) 19%, while K-Mart and Disney each spend 2%.

The YesSirNoSir experiment proved that the old ways of measuring the effectiveness of online advertising, like Click-Through Rates (CTR), do not represent the effect that a banner has on users.

Therefore, the fact that the average CTR has dropped 25 times from 1994 to 2001 (10% to 0.4%, respectively) does not mean that the effectiveness of online advertising has decreased with the same rate.

How it Worked—and What it Proved

For the experiment, the Websites of FTMarketWatch and iVillage (both in Britain) gave away advertising space of around $80,000 USD. The Websites saw this act as an investment because, should the results prove to be positive, the market would grow considerably. And the results were positive:

The number of people who claimed to have seen the brand although they really hadn't was 1 in 25 (4%), which we shall call the control level. In layman's terms, this percentage is normal and expected in market research because interviewees think that some answers are right, are in a rush, or simply tick the box nearest to their mouse. That's why we regard this number to be our baseline.

The percentage of those who recognised the brand and had in fact seen it was 11%, which shows a 275% increase from the baseline. So, a net 7% of people actually saw the advert, even if wasn't a brand they immediately recognised. In measuring the effectiveness of the ad toward the brand's pre-selected target audience (men between 18-49 years of age, with an annual income of $120,000 USD or more), it was found that 19% of all users remembered the advert. That's an increase of approximately 475% (well, actually a bit less due to rounding of the figures).

After last year's advertising success of X10.com with their peeping-tom videocams, some were lead to believe that the only way to have significant results is to drown all available channels with their adverts, and then measure the effectiveness of this approach. But this is also a sure-fire way to burn your brand, because the users who are repeatedly exposed to your messages will associate you with annoying adverts. After they've seen the X10 advert 5 times and maybe visited your site once, they're not going to think twice about closing the ad down the next time it appears, are they?

Source for case study: **www.sitepoint.com/article/online-branding-yes-sir**

Automation of Your Web Site

Methods of Automation

One of the important aspects of running an online business, or advertising online for a brick-and-mortar business, is being able to automate as much of the work that you have to do as possible. The more parts of your business that you can automate, the more time you can spend taking care of other parts of your company business such as developing new products, developing new and better Web sites, and focusing on the goals of your company. There are many work tasks that you can automate, including:

- The way that you take payment for orders.

- The way that you process those orders.

- Your e-mail list and database.

- The way you deliver your products or services.

- Your invoicing.

- The "help" section of your Web site.

- E-zines.

- Web forms.

There are many areas of your Web site that you can automate to make your job as easy as possible and so that you don't let any important tasks fall between the cracks. Some of these important tasks, which need to taken care of each day, can make the difference between the success or failure of your business.

USING AUTO-RESPONDERS

An e-mail auto-responder is a software program that sends a pre-written reply to anyone sending a message to the auto-responder's e-mail address, typically an e-mail address that is accessible from your Web site. If someone sends an e-mail to an auto-responder's e-mail address, it automatically and immediately e-mails this person the reply; for example, "Thank you for contacting the Atlantic Publishing Group . . ." The auto-responder is one of the most popular ways to automate your Web site and allows you to take care of many of the messages that you need to communicate effectively with your customers. You'll have the ability to set up the response messages to your customers that will most benefit your company. You'll also be able to send out reminders to those customers who haven't visited your Web site in a certain amount of time, perhaps offering an incentive to return to your Web site and purchase items. We have dedicated an entire chapter of this book to discussing how to properly establish and set up auto-responders; however, we wanted to mention it here as the proper use of auto-responders can simplify and streamline your operations in regards to customer response.

METHODS OF PAYMENT

When you have an automated system that lets you accept credit card payments, you'll not only be simplifying your business, but you'll also be making sure that you have all bases covered when it comes to your payment plan. We spent a great deal of time in the e-commerce chapter discussing Web site development, shopping cart integration, and merchant payment gateway systems. We also discussed the pros versus cons of implementing an automated payment processing application. In most cases, there are fees for using online credit card authorization services; however, you reap the benefit of instant credit card approval or denial. One no-cost option for businesses with a limited number of products (typically fewer than 100) is to utilize the free PayPal system to accept credit card transactions. Even if you don't use PayPal as your payment processing system, you should ensure that your shopping cart is capable of accepting PayPal payments as the use of PayPal as a payment method has increased dramatically in recent years.

MANAGING YOUR E-MAIL DATABASE

We have discussed the importance of growing an e-mail customer database and mailing list. When your business is first starting out, you'll have time to manage your mailing list, which will most likely be very small as you begin your online venture. However, as your business grows, so will your mailing list, and you'll find that management of the database and e-mail list is time consuming and is a process ripe for automated management. You should incorporate an automated method to collect your e-mail addresses. The use of Web forms soliciting customers to "join our mailing list" on the Web site is the best place to start. Instead of having customers e-mail you with their contact information, why not connect the form to a Microsoft Access database on the Web server and allow the database to automatically capture that data for you? Then, when you need the data, you can simply export it out of the database. Microsoft FrontPage simplifies this tedious task for you by actually creating the database, the database fields, and the connection between your newly created Web form and the database.

MANAGING AND USING E-ZINES

The use of an online e-zine is one of the best promotional tools available to market and distribute product news, corporate information, discount promotions, new product announcements, and any other information that you feel may be of benefit to your customers and potential customers. This process can be almost entirely automated at little or no cost to you. There are several options that may be available to you, depending on the type of Web hosting service you use for your Web site, including:

- You can install scripts on your server to process bulk e-mails (Note: most Web hosting companies do not allow bulk e-mail service).

- You can buy third-party software to develop and process the mailing.

- You can outsource to a mailer service that does all the work for you.

- You can utilize an online service which processes your e-mail e-zines and provides you with all the tools and help needed to develop your own quality e-zines.

We highly recommend you choose te last option, which affords you the lowest possible price, highest degree of control and management, and superior results. We will discuss the process of e-zine development later in this chapter.

USE A SYSTEM FOR AD TRACKING

Whether you're selling your product and services online or advertising for a traditional brick-and-mortar business, you'll want to have processes in place that allow you to track the results of your advertising. An ad tracking system will not only let you track the number of hits that you get to your Web site, but you'll also be able to keep track of where those hits came from. All reputable Web site hosting companies should provide you with a feature-rich package for Web site statistics. Our preferred provider for e-zine management and distribution is

www.topica.com. One of the best features of using Topica is that they provide detailed reports for each e-zine sent, including number of times the e-mail is opened and number of clicks (per link). We will discuss these in great detail later in this chapter.

- **Software.** There are many different types of software that you can use to automate your Web site. Microsoft FrontPage and Macromedia Dreamweaver, for example, have a wealth of built-in tools designed to automate your Web site processes and forms. Just do a search on any search engine, and you'll find a multitude of results that you can choose from. When you use software to automate your Web site, you're the one who will be in charge of maintaining and updating your system, rather than giving the control to an outsourced company. Most Web site automation applications are script based, and therefore you must ensure that they are compatible and allowed on your Web hosting server. Web automation software/scripts may include calendars, news publishers, shopping carts, search engines, classifieds, statistics, content managers, site search engines, brochure providers, document managers, photo albums, refer-a-friend, and mailing list management.

How to Automate Your Web Site

If you're operating an e-commerce Web site to complement your existing brick-and-mortar business, then you most likely recognize the importance of Internet marketing and the integration of shopping cart solutions as part of the overall approach to Web site management. If you're going to sell online, you need a combination of powerful marketing systems and credit card processing systems to be efficient and profitable.

One of your goals should be to have as close to a hands-free sales and marketing system as possible, which runs on automatic while you are free to concentrate on other areas of your business. Automation of your Web site processes enables you to focus on other areas to grow your business, travel, do charitable work, spend more time with your family, or enjoy a favorite recreational pastime or hobby, all while your business continues to market and sell your products and services. You simply check in to ensure that your Web site is operating properly, credit card orders are processed, and other automated processes are working as designed.

BENEFITS OF AUTOMATION

The benefits of automation are so numerous that you can't afford to ignore them. If you automate your online processes correctly, then you'll reap the rewards from this type of "hands-free" marketing that lets you sell to customers 24 hours a day, 7 days a week. The importance of implementing a reliable automated order processing, marketing, and advertising system is of crucial importance to sustained Web site expansion.

- **Cost reduction:** Automation reduces your costs across the board, including everything from long-distance phone bills to direct mail postage in your sales and marketing department to reducing the need for additional hiring of staff for customer service and support.

- **Easy to run:** The number one complaint of most business owners is their inability to get away from the business. With automation, your online business becomes much easier to run, requiring less time-consuming attention and maintenance. With a properly implemented automated e-commerce solution, you can check your sales and customer orders from anywhere with a Web browser.

- **More time:** You can free up more time than you had ever expected so you can focus on priorities for the strategic growth of your company, addressing all those small problems that pile up and eat away your day.

- **Satisfied customers:** Automation lets you serve your customers faster and more efficiently. Staff can focus on other higher-value functions that require human intervention, or you can reduce the high cost of customer service representatives.

- **Targeted marketing:** While building your e-mail lists, your prospects can be segmented according to the offers and promotions to which they respond based on demographics. When they join your e-mail list, or as they e-mail you for a specific offer or question, they can be put on a demographics list that identifies them, the products they want, and their personal preferences. This lets you market to your prospects more effectively, efficiently, and personally.

Automation could be just what your business needs to give you the edge over your competition. By using automation properly, you will see your online sales profits excel beyond what you ever thought possible. The following steps will help you build a successful and automated business Web site.

Ways to Automate Your Web Site

ONLINE SHOPPERS

If you're trying to build your online business, it's going to be vital that you have a marketing plan in place. Letting your customers place orders on your Web site is a big part of your marketing plan that you can't overlook. A big function of e-commerce on the Web today is the ability to market to your target customer group and accept orders on the Internet. A shopping cart is, without question, one of the most innovative Web software applications to e-commerce enable the Internet. What better way to assist consumers in shopping your Web site than with a shopping cart that functions in exactly the same way it would in a grocery store? Anyone can understand what a shopping cart is for, and therefore anyone will be able to shop your Web site. What could be easier?

How exactly does a shopping cart work? The best way to think of using an online shopping cart is to compare it to a trip to the grocery store. Picture this: You're wandering down the aisles while pushing your shopping cart along, and you grab an item off the shelf. You can inspect it, read about it, and even look at the item. If you are convinced to purchase the item, you can then place the item in your cart and continue to browse and shop, adding more items to your cart. Once you finish shopping, you simply "check out" by following the checkout and payment process. The shopping cart application walks you through the process, providing you with an online receipt and, typically, an e-mail confirmation of your transaction. No long lines, no rude service, no traffic, no tax in many cases, and, typically, better pricing than in the retail establishments. You can even download your product instantly if it is software, music, or digital content. This is important because when it comes to the Internet, timing is everything! If you don't take advantage of an e-commerce tool such as a shopping cart, you're going to be missing out on a major part of the online market.

One of the questions you may ask about online shopping carts is this: Are they safe? A few years ago, most people were concerned about using their credit cards online. But with all the security features that Internet browsers have these days, using your credit card online is actually a lot safer than using it at your local store. Make sure you are using an encrypted Web site before giving out your credit card information, and if you are implementing a shopping cart on your Web site, ensure that you have a properly installed SSL certificate, which enables you to run your site in a secure, encrypted mode.

TAKING ORDERS ONLINE

When you're taking online orders for your business, there are a few things that you can do to push sales to even higher levels:

- **Set up a merchant account and gateway**, which will approve your credit card orders automatically through the bank.

- **Create custom, branded order forms** unique to your business to provide a highly professional image.

- **Consider limited use of audio/video** to sell your products and services; do not use background music on your Web site, or you will quickly lose customers.

- **Incorporate cross selling** to promote additional products to customers at checkout.

- **Offer incentives to close the transaction** (such as free promotional items). The final stage of checkout is where most customers are going to change their minds about buying your product and, thus, abandon your Web site. Shopping cart abandonment can be as high as 60 to 80 percent. You need to make sure your online ordering process is as efficient and streamlined as possible so that the remaining 25 percent of customers make repeat purchases.

SALES ADMINISTRATION

You need to keep track of all your sales and customer data information. Using automated marketing and sales processing applications is going to let you take care of all your sales administration in the easiest way possible. You can check on your sales statistics anywhere the Internet is available, without being at your own computer through your Web site hosting provider's statistics server. All information is real-time data so that you have all the latest, up-to-the-minute figures, including page hits, site visitors, and demographic information.

Sales reports give you the statistics that you need to track how your business is doing. Automated marketing lets you look at multiple sales reports for any number of those statistics such as reports by product, day, and the credit card used by your customers.

You can see who your best marketing partners and performers are by using automated marketing to administer your affiliate programs. When you know which campaigns or affiliates are the most profitable, you can concentrate your efforts there. Topica's e-mail marketing and sales solutions provide detailed reports for each e-mail transmission so you can know exactly how each of your e-mail blasts has done, and they even provide trend data so you can compare performance among several e-mail blast campaigns.

AFFILIATE PROGRAMS

An affiliate program is a Web-based pay-for-performance program designed to compensate affiliate partner Web sites for driving qualified leads or sales to your Web site. Typically, you will pay a percentage of any sales resulting from any click-through (via banner or text link) to your Web site from an affiliate partner's Web site. We have dedicated an entire chapter to affiliate programs; however, you should understand that once established, the majority of the processes are automated and require minimal manual intervention. The incorporation of an affiliate program into a Web site's marketing and sales portfolio allows you to market and sell your products through thousands of content-related Web sites throughout the world.

AD TRACKING

Ad tracking is a great way for you to know how many times a person clicks on a certain link on the Internet. This is extremely valuable data because it not only lets you determine how many times a banner was clicked, it also lets you know how much revenue was generated. This simply means that you can tell how many times a visitor was directed to your Web site from a link and made a purchase. Most affiliate programs provide tracking and click-through data, as do some search engines. We will discuss the use of pay-per-click and other advanced advertising campaigns in later chapters.

THE INTERNET IS A COMPETITIVE PLAYING FIELD

You need the right tools to give you an edge over your competitors. The technology and services that automated marketing offer are invaluable to your online business. Once you develop your tactics and strategies to build up your marketing plan, you'll start to see an increase in both sales and profits. By automating your online system, you'll increase your profits faster and more efficiently! When you invest in an automating service or software, you're using the best technology available that will make you money day and night, whether you're there or not.

Using Software for Automation

There are many different types of software from which you can choose that will help you to automate your Web site efficiently and effectively. There is automation software available that is easy to use, whether you have a home business, a small business online, or a traditional brick-and-mortar business. When you use software that is specifically designed for Web site automation, you're getting the functions and applications that are necessary to deal with all aspects of your business. Some of these tedious tasks that need to be completed each day include keeping track of your passwords, making submissions for your Web sites to search engines, monitoring traffic to your Web site, and testing the new features of your Web site. When you use automation software, you'll be able to have these tasks automated by a running script or function-specific software applications.

Different types of automation software will provide you with different functions, depending on the software bundle that you purchase, and many are included in the major Web site design packages, such as Microsoft FrontPage 2003. Some of the standard features for which you should be looking when you're choosing automation software include

- The automatic completion of forms.

- The automatic creation of Web databases to capture and process information submitted on Web forms.

- E-mail login and other e-mail features, such as standard customer responses.

- Organization, publication, and distribution of your e-mail lists.

- Password encryption for all your passwords and the passwords of your customers.

- Automation of the submissions that you make to search engines.

- Pay-per-click features and listings with search engines.

- Monitoring on the Internet so that you can keep an eye on your Web site and any problems that may occur, which you may not notice immediately. Free Web site monitoring and tracking is offered by **www.Internetseer.com**, and it will report to you when your Web site is down or not available. It also provides weekly reports of total uptime and availability — all at no cost to you!

The one thing that you need to keep in mind if you're going to be purchasing and using automation software is whether you have enough experience to successfully use the software. Although most software bundles are easy to use, they still require that you have some experience with the computer and how data is stored and used.

There are many different companies on the Internet from which you can choose when it comes to making your final decision for the automation of your Web site. Make sure that you do your research before you make your final choice so that you're completely happy with the features that you're purchasing. You can expect to pay anywhere from $100 to $1,000 for the right software bundle; however, we have found that most automations can be found for free or for a minimal charge at the following Web sites:

- **www.scripts.com**

- **http://javascript.Internet.com**

- **www.free-scripts.net**

- **www.dynamicdrive.com**

Outsourcing Your Web Site Automation

Outsourcing your Web site automation means that you'll be freeing yourself of the time-consuming job of many of the mundane maintenance tasks that need to be completed if you're going to have a successful Web site. There are many different types of automation from which you can choose, so you may have to decide which features are the most important; however, keep in mind that these services will cost you money. We recommend you consider the free options we have included in this book. Some of the common automation tasks that most hosting companies offer include the following:

- **Auto-responders.** Many companies will provide you with a different auto-responder for each e-mail address that your business has. This means that you can have a different type of customer response depending on what message you want to send and the impact that you want to make. (Note: Most reputable Web site hosting companies include free auto-responders with your e-mail accounts.)

- **Customer tracking.** You'll be able to find out where customers are coming from when they arrive at your Web site, how they found you, what keywords they used if they used a search engine to find you, and what they viewed when they were at your Web site.

- **A messaging system.** Although not a top priority, having some method of allowing your customers to leave you, and other customers, a message is a nice feature to have. This can be achieved using a chat feature or bulletin board. This way, visitors to your Web site can ask questions about your products or services and return for an answer during another Web site visit. Keep in mind that not all online or brick-and-mortar businesses will benefit from this type of communication with customers. There are also the free "chat" options we have provided you that may be adopted into your Web site.

- **Polling features.** Adding a different poll to your Web site every couple of weeks allows you to find out what your customers want and what they are thinking. For example, you could use the polling feature to find out what holiday most customers like to document in their scrapbooks. Once the poll is closed, you'll have a better understanding of what scrapbook items are most popular, allowing you to focus some portion of your marketing campaign on these products. Although there are many paid services that offer polling, you can do this yourself at no cost by visiting **www .freepolls.com**.

- **The expertise of professionals** who will make sure your Web site meets all of the legalities and standards to make it a success. In our chapter on search engine optimization, we will provide you with a vast arsenal of Web site tools, which can be used at no cost to you!

- **Shopping cart functions.** Many Web hosting companies will offer some type of shopping cart feature for your customers to be able to pay for your products or services. As we have stated numerous times, this is an area on which you need to put extra emphasis to ensure that your shopping cart provides you with the security, functionality, ease of use, and growth capability your emerging business needs. Most script-based shopping carts that come "free" with Web hosting packages are limited in functionality, have a steep learning curve, and come with no technical support. There are some things that you'll want to look for when deciding from which company to purchase your shopping cart application, such as how long the company has been in business, how readily available their support staff is when you have problems or questions, how easy they are to understand, how long the "free" technical support period lasts, and the cost of the software and additional technical support, if required. Make sure that you ask lots of questions before making your final choice.

E-mail is a very versatile medium. Formats range from simple text to HTML and rich media. Content can be one-size-fits-all or highly customized. Frequency can consist of fixed, frequent intervals, or sporadic intervals, with transmissions occurring only when something newsworthy comes along. Sophistication (and cost) can be very low or very high.

> *"Along with the power of e-mail comes the abuse of e-mail, commonly known as spam. Is spam e-mail considered marketing? Technically, the answer is probably yes, but it is certainly not responsible e-mail marketing. While some users fail to distinguish between permission marketing and e-mail spam, spam is actually a major threat to legitimate e-mail marketers, as a glut of messages could make the entire e-mail medium less effective."*

Source: **www.marketingterms.com**

Database Marketing

Database marketing is a form of direct marketing using databases of existing or potential customers to generate personalized communications in order to promote a product or service for marketing purposes. By incorporating demographic collections into your e-mail-collection program and e-zine or newsletter publication campaigns, you can target specific demographic areas and market segments and personalize your campaigns. Database marketing has very specific characteristics that define it precisely. Most companies fail to meet all of these characteristics, but your goal should be to incorporate as many as you can into your database marketing program. These characteristics include the following:

- Your marketing database should include repeat customers, one-time customers, potential customers, and new leads.

- Record information about all your customers, including identifying information, how to contact the customer, information about any previous transactions, and any and all previous communication with the customer.

- Every time a transaction takes place with the customer or a lead, all the information in the database should be available; this way, you and your company can decide how to successfully fulfill the needs of the customer.

- If you have a large company and have hired one or more marketing specialists, they'll use all of the information in the database to implement market divisions, making sure that your service or product is suitable for that division.

- Effective database marketing works incrementally. This means that it incorporates any improvements that need to be made to ensure that the customer is satisfied. This includes improvements in the rate of response, referrals, retention rates, any cross-sales, and the occurrence of sales.

- Successful communication with the customer is at the core of database marketing. When you have constant and beneficial communication with your customers, you ensure that they are happy. This increases your sales, builds trust and confidence, and encourages customers to refer your company or Web site to others.

The goals of your company are reflected in the way that you respond to your customers. This means that you have a clear and well-understood mission that is carried out in the way that you conduct your marketing program.

Concentrate your efforts on incorporating all of the above database marketing characteristics into your own marketing program. It may seem overwhelming to accomplish this at first; however, when broken down into milestones, you can achieve most of the characteristics for a successful database marketing program. Database marketing ties directly into your e-zine or newsletter publication service, and Topica. com includes all the tools necessary to simplify your journey toward successful database marketing.

BENEFITS OF DATABASE MARKETING

Database marketing allows you to understand the data that you accumulate so that you can effectively reach your customers and generate the sales and profits that you need to be successful. When you use database marketing the way it was meant to be used, you'll reap the following benefits:

- The ability to reach new customers and encourage them to try your products or services.

- The ability to reach current customers by sending out timely communications to them.

- Increased profits through more personal methods of communicating with your customers.

- Increased satisfaction among your customers that instills a large level of trust and encourages future sales.

- Increased potential of referrals from satisfied customers.

- Reduced overhead and expenses because you can use an automated method of managing your communication with customers.

You can begin the practice of database marketing immediately using tools you already have and data you have already collected. The time will come when you will wish to consider streamlining and modifying your data collection, data storage, and data processing practices, but in the beginning, all you will need is your existing customer data set and the desire to maximize the efficiency of your marketing operations.

First, you will want to start the process of organizing the data you have. What kind of data have you been collecting? From whom have you been collecting this data? How is this data stored? You will need to answers these questions by inspecting your current data-collection practices and analyzing your data storage systems and techniques.

Commonly stored information may include:

- Contact information

- Lead information

- Sales information

- "Service after the sale" information

- Forecasting information

DEVELOPING YOUR DATABASE MARKETING PLAN

When approaching the onset of the task of developing your database marketing plan, the following should be on your list of items to consider:

- **Analyze your current customer database.** What are the products you are offering that your customers have purchased? From the content of your data, in what are your customers generally interested? Which key points or segments of your database would be the most relevant or suitable for your offers? What are you doing with this data? Some companies simply use data they have for customers to send targeted e-mails and direct mail based on their purchasing habits, but have you thought about how you can take this a step further? For example, Amazon.com uses customer data to offer "rewards" for customers as well as a database-driven dynamic pricing scheme to learn more about price points and markup potential.

- **What assumptions can you make about your customers?** To which market you are selling? You can make assumptions based on your target demographic (you weren't planning to sell men's magazine subscriptions to elderly women, were you?). How have certain demographics behaved when shopping with you according to your data? Things to consider are customer age, location, sex, and marital status.

- **Plan your offers according to your answers to the questions**

above. Take a long, hard look at the information you have gleaned, and use this information to plan your strategy for special offers and other customer interaction.

4. **Build your database using what you have learned.** You will want to modify your data-collection techniques accordingly if you find glaring holes in the data you have been collecting. You should begin to think about how you can apply what you have learned in the above steps to refine the data you are collecting in your database. You should strive to collect detailed demographic information when possible from customers or site visitors who sign up for your mailing lists; however, you should not require them to complete this information to become members of your mailing list. There are many individuals who will never give away any demographic data but would still like to join mailing lists—we don't want to alienate those potential customers.

The Importance of Customer Segments

After you've collected the required data, it's important that you sort it into segments that you know will work for your marketing program. You'll need to use these segments so that you can target certain areas of the market for each specific marketing campaign that you launch. Database segmentation is defined as the grouping of your customers by their interests based on how and where they live.

Once you have your customers grouped into segments, you'll be able to target these segments with specific e-mail and newsletter campaigns. There are four basic perceptions of successful customer segmentation:

1. **Definite characteristics.** Each segment must be clearly identifiable by a certain set of conditions. An example of this would be a segment for seniors who make purchases to improve their health. People clearly will fall into this segment or not.

2. **Tactics.** Your entire database marketing program needs to take into account the importance of customer segments and must utilize the information. This means that the e-mail and newsletters that you send out to a specific segment must clearly target their needs and past buying trends.

3. **Communication.** Once you've established segments and prepared

a marketing program to target each segment, you need to be sure that the communication that you send out is precise and accurate, aimed clearly at the segment.

4. **Plan of attack.** You and your company must have a clear plan of attack that includes a definite budget, deadlines, and goals. Use Web site automation to simplify the process of segmentation marketing. Topica.com allows you to create segmented marketing campaigns based on selected demographic data.

Once you understand the importance of the four perceptions of customer segments, you'll need to make sure that you justify their use and potential. There are certain characteristics that exist for customer segments. These characteristics are important to ensure that segmentation works and that you spend the right amount of time and money concentrating on what will give you a payoff at the end.

CHARACTERISTICS OF EFFECTIVE SEGMENTATION

- A clear definition of what the segment is.

- The segment is large enough to justify spending time and money on further data collection.

- Use all of the customer information that you've collected in a profitable manner.

- Have a definite line between loss and profit so that you can focus your marketing program in the right direction.

- The segment is clearly justifiable for a marketing program on its own merit.

Along with these characteristics, you will need to understand how to read these segments. This means that you'll have to have the foresight to launch a database marketing program that looks at the potential of each segment. You will also need to be able to analyze the data that you collect and the data that you receive from the marketing program. This analysis also takes a look at how much the customer or company is spending on your product or service, the potential spending range of the customer, what products the customer purchases, and if the spending action of the customer can be changed in your favor.

You may consider adopting status levels for your customer segments such as Platinum, Gold, and Silver. Many large companies are using these types of segments to distinguish their customers; however, this is typically only for larger corporations or for those with very large marketing budgets. Another way to read customer segments is to take a close look at your successful marketing programs and those that have failed. Analyze where you went wrong, what you did correctly, and what you can do to improve the next group of marketing campaigns.

How to Get Customer Data

As mentioned previously, you'll already have a lot of customer data that you can utilize. This includes information that you've collected from invoices, customer communications, and existing customer lists. You'll also want to collect the information listed in this chapter. But just how do you go about capturing that information? There are several different methods that you can use to get the data that you need to build successful customer databases and segments.

The key thing to remember is to always be honest when you're acquiring any customer information. If you use deceptive means to get the information that you need, you'll be losing the trust of your customers. If being honest and aboveboard means that you lose some of those opportunities to capture customer information, then realize that the payoff will be the trust and respect that you instill in those customers, and potential customers, when they realize that you're doing exactly what you say you're doing: asking them to voluntarily provide you with certain information about themselves.

The following methods of capturing customer information are ways that you probably already use to keep track of sales and profit. This is information that can be found from the following sources:

- Customer order forms

- Warranty card information

- Servicing information (if you have a product for which you provide servicing)

- Records of returned products

- Questionnaires filled out at time of purchase

- Newsletter and e-zine registration forms on your Web site

This type of information is very helpful, but you'll need more to build a successful database that includes extensive customer data. This is where some of the newer methods of data capturing enter the picture. The Internet has provided you with some great opportunities to use technology to your benefit. Again, keep in mind that technology is a tool that you can use and not a means to an end. All this technology means that you can use some very interesting and successful methods for having your customers leave you the information that you need.

You may also consider the following methods for data collection and information gathering:

- **Opt-in with permission.** Ask visitors to your Web site for permission to put them on your e-mail list. Offer them information in the form of a newsletter in return for this information. Your responsibility is to provide useful information in the newsletter and not just a sales pitch. When customers say yes to giving you their e-mail address, you're that much closer to a sale.

- **Offer online contests** to create a large number of leads. This is a great way to capture customer information. Make sure that the prize for the contest is something of value.

- **Audio and video responses.** Prepare an audio or video presentation telling the visitors to your Web site all about your product or service. Offer to send them more information if they provide you with their e-mail address. Audio and video are a great way to get the instant attention of anyone visiting your Web site.

- **Protected pages.** Have pages of information on your Web site that can only be viewed if visitors provide you with certain information or access levels. You can have them fill out a questionnaire that asks them some questions about themselves.

This way you can gather useful information to add to your database.

How to Communicate with Your Customers

Once you've established that first contact with the visitors to your Web site, you'll need to communicate with them in an effective manner. This is where automation comes in, since automating your Web site and your database will allow you frequent and effective communication with your customers. Database marketing is all about collating the information that you've collected and using it to communicate using a marketing program that targets those specific customer segments that you've established.

Communication methods for database marketing include the following:

- Weekly newsletters

- Automated e-mail, targeting one-time customers, referrals, and repeat customers

- Free product offers to customers

- Mailed postcards

- Follow-up phone calls

Communicating with your customers is much easier after you've profiled them and know what they want to hear. Database marketing means that you learn as much as you can about your existing and potential customers before sending them any type of communication. Studies show that random communication that is sent to all of your customers almost always fails since you'll be spending a great deal of time and money to reach only a small percentage of those customers that feel you have something to say to them directly.

Determining Customer Lifetime Value

If you want to know the value of your company and the value of your database marketing program, you'll need to calculate your customer lifetime value. This will tell you the value that you should place on your customers and how much time and effort you should spend building relationships with some of these existing and potential customers. Before you calculate the customer lifetime value, you should understand the benefits of knowing this calculation:

- It helps you to calculate your long-term survival potential when the going gets rough.

- It will determine how much you have to spend to gain a new customer.

- It will determine how much time and effort you need to expend to gain a new customer.

- It will help to keep you focused on the products and services that you're selling that are of relevant interest to your customers.

MAXIMIZING CUSTOMER LIFETIME VALUE

Once you know your customer lifetime value, you can concentrate your efforts on certain areas of database marketing to reach those customers who are going to bring you the most value in the long run. The lifetime value calculation will help you maximize your profits in several ways:

- You'll know how much effort, time, and money you can spend to gain new customers.

- You can determine if the benefits of focusing on certain customers is worth the investment.

- You can change the focus of your database marketing program at any time to meet the needs of the calculated lifetime value.

- You can concentrate on your existing customers instead of spending too much time on suspects and prospects.

- You can alter your marketing offers and bonuses to reflect the lifetime value of certain customer segments.

- You'll know your bottom line when it comes to your budget.

DEVELOPING POSITIVE RELATIONSHIPS WITH CUSTOMERS

Developing positive relationships with your customers is crucial to your long-term success and profitability.

- **Auto-responders.** It's important to communicate automatically and frequently. Once you have a customer's e-mail address, you need to communicate with him or her frequently. You want to be able to follow your leads and convert more of the visitors to your site into customers. When you use auto-responders, you can personalize the messages that you send to customers. This can be accomplished in both the subject line and in the content of the e-mail that you're sending.

- **Newsletters.** Newsletters are a great way to communicate with your customers since there are an endless number of pieces of information that you can put into the newsletter. Remember to provide information that is relevant and factual. Studies show that when companies send out newsletters that contain nothing more than sales pitches for the products or services that they are selling, customers tune out these sales pitches and discard the newsletter. When this scenario occurs, you have no chance of developing a positive relationship with your customer.

- **Postcards.** If you have a budget that allows it, consider sending out postcards to reach your customers to communicate with them on a personal level. Don't target all the suspects, prospects, customers, and advocates in your database since that type of a marketing program would take too much money, time, and effort, yielding little results. Instead, choose one type of customer segment on which you want to focus, such as parents of small children, and focus your marketing there. Postcards are a cost-effective way to send useful information to a select group of customers. Consider joint mailings with other postcards to minimize costs.

- **Fulfill all your promises.** It's important that you do what you say you're going to do. This means honoring all special offers and bonuses that you promise. When you or your products fail to deliver on their promises, you lose credibility, which is crucial to establishing a trusting relationship with your customers.

- **Return all e-mail and phone calls.** When a customer makes an effort to contact you, make sure that you return the communication as soon as you can. This is the perfect opportunity for you to open up lines of communication. Follow the three basic rules when drafting e-mails to customers: (1.) professionalism (by using proper e-mail language, your company will convey a professional image), (2.) efficiency (e-mails that get to the point are much more effective than poorly worded e-mails), and (3.) protection from liability (employee awareness of e-mail risks will protect your company from costly lawsuits). Draft a corporate e-mail policy, that addresses e-mail etiquette. You should follow the rules of e-mail etiquette, which are as follows:

  - Be concise and to the point.

  - Do not make an e-mail longer than it needs to be.

  - Answer all questions.

  - Use proper spelling, grammar, and punctuation.

  - Make it personal.

  - Respond in a timely manner.

  - Do not attach large, unnecessary files.

  - Use proper structure and layout.

  - Do not overuse the high priority option.

  - Do not write in capitals.

  - Do not leave out the message title.

  - Read the e-mail before you send it.

  - Do not overuse "reply to all."

  - Do not forward chain letters.

  - Do not request delivery and read receipts.

- Do not ask to recall a message.

- Do not use e-mail to discuss confidential information.

- Use a meaningful subject.

- Avoid long sentences.

- Do not send or forward e-mails containing libelous, defamatory, offensive, racist, or obscene remarks.

- Do not forward virus hoaxes and chain letters.

- Do not reply to spam.

"By requiring employees to use appropriate, businesslike language in all electronic communications, employers can limit their liability risks and improve the overall effectiveness of the organization's e-mail and Internet copy in the process."

Excerpt from *Writing Effective E-mail*,
by Nancy Flynn and Tom Flynn.

If the customer is contacting you with a complaint, take the time to address the concerns and then attempt to rectify the situation. Once again, this is the perfect way for you gain the trust and confidence of your customers by being responsive to their needs and always using proper e-mail etiquette with less-than-satisfied customers.

- **Thank-you letters.** Make sure that you send out thank you letters for each sale that you generate. It's important to let your customers know that you appreciate their business.

- **Birthday cards.** Since you most likely have collected birth date information from your customers, a nice gesture is to send out birthday cards. This is just a small reminder to them that you are still out there.

- **Buying reminders.** Send out subtle reminders to your customers, and let them know that they may want to think about reordering or placing a new order.

- **Business anniversary cards.** For those of your customers who are making purchases for their business, find out when the opening date of the business was and send out an anniversary card.

- **Information about new products.** Whenever you have a new product or service, make sure that you let your customers know.

The more communication that you have with your customers, the stronger your relationship will be. You want to ensure that your customers trust you, listen to what you have to say, and return to buy more of your products and services.

CHAPTER 7

E-Zines and Newsletters

E-mail is the fastest form of communication to a wide audience, with nearly instantaneous results and at practically no cost. Harnessing the power of e-mail through targeted e-zines and newsletters is one of the most effective and cost-effective methods to advertise and market your e-commerce site, products, and services. With e-mail marketing you get direct and immediate communication with thousands of current and potential customers.

Building Your Customer Base

The value of a business comes down to the size and quality of the customer base. If there's no market demand and no customers are buying, then the business has little value or life expectancy. As an online business owner, you need to capture the names and e-mails of prospects when they visit your Web site. The fact that they clicked to your site shows that they have a level of interest in your company, and you need to capture the contact information where possible to expand the level of interest in your products and grow new customers. Rarely do customers buy on their first visit to a site.

PERMISSION-BASED, OPT-IN, AND SPAM E-MAIL

Opting in is the process by which a subscriber requests (by submitting electronically his or her e-mail address and any other required information) to receive information and advertising via e-mail from your company or organization. An opt-in e-mail list is also called a permission-based e-mail list. You should always seek permission from your visitors to put them on your e-mail list so you can send them additional information, e-zine marketing, or preferred access. Opt-in can be accomplished by a variety of methods, but we recommend you utilize the opt-in forms and automated processes that are built into Topica.com's E-mail Publisher application. At this point it is necessary to discuss and provide you with clear definitions of bulk e-mail, spam, opt-in, and opt-out e-mails. Solicited bulk e-mail is an important mechanism for allowing consenting customers to be informed of products or news. When bulk e-mail is solicited, it is valuable to the recipient and the sender. When this e-mail is unsolicited, it is what is known as spam. Spam is the unwanted receipt of e-mail by a recipient. Spam forces the recipient to deal with the unwanted advert, and it is also a theft of the unwilling recipient's time and resources. Typically, spam is associated with viruses or spyware attempting to infiltrate your servers or computers.

- **Opt-Out Unsolicited Bulk E-Mail:** Includes all bulk e-mail sent to recipients who have not expressly registered permission for their addresses to be placed on the specific mailing list and which requires recipients to opt-out to stop further unsolicited bulk mailings. The sending of unsolicited bulk e-mail is against all ISP terms of service worldwide and is illegal in many countries.

- **Unconfirmed Opt-In E-Mail:** If an opt-in request is unconfirmed, then it cannot be verified and is considered spam. In most cases, the bulk e-mail sender has simply purchased the address from another spammer. Unconfirmed opt-in is an excuse for spammers to harvest lists and simply claim "opt-in."

- **Confirmed Opt-In:** The recipient has verifiably confirmed permission for the address to be included on the specific mailing list by responding to the list subscription request verification. This is the standard practice for all Internet mailing lists, and it ensures that users are properly subscribed from a working address and with the address owner's consent. When an e-mail address is confirmed opt-in, it is legal to use this e-mail address for marketing and sales purposes.

The difference between senders of legitimate bulk e-mail and spammers couldn't be clearer: The legitimate bulk e-mail sender has verifiable permission from the recipients before sending, while the spammer does not.

Once visitors to your Web site have opted in to your list, they've "raised their hands" and identified themselves as prospects in your target market. Now you should feed them value-based, timely, rich-content e-zines or other marketing campaigns that encourage them to buy from your Web site and that convert them to customer status.

> ***Opt-in e-mail:*** *"Email that is explicitly requested by the recipient. The definition of opt-in email has been a matter of intense debate."*

> ***Single opt-in vs. double opt-in:*** *"The term single opt-in simply means that actions were taken to sign up for the e-mail in question. The term double opt-in means that the subscriber has actively confirmed their subscription, typically by responding to an automatically generated message sent to the e-mail address. Proponents of double opt-in may not actually use that term, as they feel any e-mail labeled 'opt-in' must be verified."*

> Source for terms and definitions: **www.marketingterms.com**

Capturing E-Mail Addresses

One of the important roles of your Web site is capturing the e-mail addresses of possible customers. Your mailing list is one of your most important marketing tools. You may want to offer promotions and other benefits over time to build your relationship in order to sell more, and more frequently, to your customers. You can offer special reports, insider information, mini-educational courses, advice, or free trials to entice visitors to share their names and e-mail addresses. When entered, they are automatically placed in your database and added to the appropriate list. Make sure you follow the guidance on opt-in to ensure you have a "clean" mailing list. Topica's E-mail Publisher ensures that your list will stay clean since it has a built-in opt-in manager.

BUYING E-MAIL ADDRESSES

There are literally hundreds of Web sites selling or renting e-mail addresses. They are typically expensive, and often, they are "harvested" e-mail addresses, which are not considered to be "opt-in" and are not in compliance with the "canned spam" act. We don't recommend or endorse buying, trading, or leasing e-mail addresses as this is very expensive, the quality of the e-mail addresses is suspect, and you cannot typically validate that they are, in fact, opt-in e-mail addresses.

Newsletter and E-Zine Creation

Customized newsletters and e-zines are a wonderful way to get people to promote and expand your business. Inclusion of a "forward to a friend" option, which is available in Topica's E-mail Publisher, enables recipients the ability to expand your customer base for you and even provides you with detailed reports to track how many "forward to a friend" links were initiated. An e-mail newsletter is a great way to stay in touch with your prospects. CustomerCatcherRadio.com is a good example of giving your possible customers something of value for free. CustomerCatcherRadio.com, which provides marketing and sales techniques, is free to use as long as people sign in first with their name and e-mail address. Topica E-mail Publisher services can be as low as $49.95 per month, which allows you to send up to two monthly e-zines for up to 5,000 names. Prices increase based on frequency and size of your mailing list; however, you can see the potential of promoting items directly to 10,000 e-mail addresses a month for only $49.95 per month. Topica does offer significant quantity discounts, and you can also obtain up to a 25 percent discount by paying in advance for the year. Topica's Online Marketing and Sales Solution enables businesses and organizations to find prospective customers and sell more online. By using Topica, marketers better leverage their current online marketing initiatives such as paid search, affiliate programs, and display advertising to convert more Web site traffic into first-time buyers and loyal, long-term customers.

Firmly committed to permission-based e-mailing, all Topica solutions are 100 percent compliant with state and federal privacy, permission, and anti-spam legislation.

Using a Successful
Auto-Responder

An e-mail auto-responder is a software program that sends
a pre-written reply to anyone sending a message to the auto-responder's
e-mail address; typically, an e-mail address that is accessible from your
Web site. If someone sends an e-mail to an auto-responder's e-mail
address, it automatically and immediately e-mails this person the reply
(for example: "Thank you for contacting the Atlantic Publishing Group …").
The auto-responder is one of the most popular ways to automate your
Web site and allows you to take care of many of the messages that help
you to communicate effectively with your customers. You'll have the
ability to set up the response messages to your customers that will most
benefit your company. You'll also be able to send out reminders to those
customers who haven't visited your Web site in a certain amount of time,

perhaps offering an incentive to return to your Web site and purchase items.

The auto-responder can be a very important tool when it comes to the management and automation of your Web site. This is because you may need to have a system in place that is going to allow you to respond to your existing and potential customers in a timely manner and with e-mail methods that pack the most punch per e-mail. You want to be able to send a simple e-mail such as sending a thank-you message that is personalized to each customer. Most of us have encountered auto-responders, which are often used by technical support departments of online businesses. When you submit your support request, you almost immediately receive a reply with a "canned" e-mail response. This e-mail response typically acknowledges your submission, provides you with a case number, and notifies you of response times. Often, auto-responders can be used to suggest alternative sources for you to answer your question, solve your problem, or provide you with more detailed product information.

You also want to be able to send e-mail to people on a regular schedule so that you can stay in touch with customers who haven't ordered in some time, remind customers to place another order, or contact those potential customers and remind them that you're still there. When you use an auto-responder, you're using a tool that has as much potential as you want to give it. You won't have to spend hours managing your e-mail list, and you won't have to hire someone to help you with this important part of running a successful business. An auto-responder lets you manage communication capabilities within each e-mail so that you can reach as many people as you want in a timely manner without missing crucial opportunities.

The larger your business grows, the bigger your e-mail mailing list will grow. You'll soon find that you won't have enough time to personally answer e-mail, and this means that you'll start to miss opportune moments to respond to a customer's e-mail question or comment. You'll want to think about implementing an auto-responder even in the early startup stages of your business so that you can take advantage of the tool and learn how to use it successfully. You'll also find that when you use an auto-responder, your customer mailing list will grow much faster, as people who visit your Web site "opt-in" to be on your mailing list.

The jury is out on auto-responders. We think the best approach is to use a personal e-mail reply whenever possible. If you can't do that, an auto-responder is a great solution to provide an immediate response, as long as you follow up with a personalized reply to questions, comments, or concerns.

Benefits of Automating Your Business

There are many benefits to you and your business when you start to use an auto-responder to manage your customer database and automated e-mail. You'll be able to save valuable time and be able to better implement and utilize your marketing strategy. Having an efficient marketing strategy is vital to the success of your online or brick-and-mortar business. When you start to use an auto-responder, you'll start to see your profits increase as your e-mail list increases.

As a quick summary, here are the main benefits that you and your business will experience when you use an auto-responder to save time and see more profits:

- The ability to e-mail and communicate with your customers and clients 24 hours a day.

- Send any number of followup e-mails to customers with no time or effort.

- Send personalized messages to as many existing and potential customers as you want.

- Choose the time of month/week/day that e-mail is sent to those people on your mailing list.

- Use auto-responder statistics to track followup e-mails with customers.

Marketing studies show that you need to be in touch with your potential customers up to seven times before they decide to make a sale or purchase. This may seem to be extremely time consuming, but when you have an auto-responder working for you, the correspondence becomes easy to manage. It's important that each followup e-mail is sent out at the appropriate time. You can program the auto-responder to send these followups on schedule so that you don't miss any crucial opportunity to communicate with what could become a repeat customer or client. The more efficiently that you send out your newsletters and other e-mail to people on your mailing list, the more organized you'll be with following up with those important potential leads. An auto-responder can implement this efficiency for you and your business.

Here is a list of some free auto-responders to help you get started:

- **www.getresponse.com**

- **www.sendthisfree.com**

- **www.sendfree.com**

- **www.freeautobot.com**

E-mail Unlimited 6.2, which is available at **www.officeautomation. com**, offers a feature-rich software application that sends HTML e-mails with pictures to customers, automatically follows up with leads and customers, lets you track exactly who views your e-mail and clicks on the links, and even has the capability to send bulk e-mail to up to 100,000 recipients in a matter of minutes.

If you are considering bulk e-mails, please review the requirements we discussed earlier on opt-in e-mails. Anti-spam laws vary state to state, and a good reference to review your specific spam laws is **www .spamlaws.com/state/index.shtml**. There are also federal laws that regulate spam, including the CAN-SPAM Act of 2003, along with numerous proposed pieces of legislation. The latest federal laws and proposed legislation can be found at **www.spamlaws.com/federal/index.shtml**.

The CAN-SPAM Act: Requirements for Commercial E-Mailers

The CAN-SPAM Act of 2003 (Controlling the Assault of Non-Solicited Pornography and Marketing Act) establishes requirements for those who send commercial e-mail, spells out penalties for spammers and companies whose products are advertised in spam if they violate the law, and gives consumers the right to ask e-mailers to stop spamming them.

The law, which became effective January 1, 2004, covers e-mail whose primary purpose is advertising or promoting a commercial product or service, including content on a Web site. A "transactional or relationship message" – e-mail that facilitates an agreed-upon transaction or updates a customer in an existing business relationship – may not contain false or misleading routing information but otherwise is exempt from most provisions of the CAN-SPAM Act.

The Federal Trade Commission (FTC), the nation's consumer protection agency, is authorized to enforce the CAN-SPAM Act. CAN-SPAM also gives the Department of Justice (DOJ) the authority to enforce its criminal sanctions. Other federal and state agencies can enforce the law against organizations under their jurisdiction, and companies that provide Internet access may sue violators as well.

THE LAW'S MAIN PROVISIONS

- It bans false or misleading header information. Your e-mail's "From," "To," and routing information – including the originating domain name and e-mail address – must be accurate and identify the person who initiated the e-mail.

- It prohibits deceptive subject lines. The subject line cannot mislead the recipient about the contents or subject matter of the message.

- It requires that your e-mail give recipients an opt-out method. You must provide a return e-mail address or another Internet-based response mechanism that allows a recipient to ask you not to send future e-mail messages to that e-mail address, and you must honor the requests. You may create a "menu" of choices to allow a recipient to opt out of certain types of messages, but you must include the option to end any commercial messages from the sender.

  Any opt-out mechanism you offer must be able to process opt-out requests for at least 30 days after you send your commercial e-mail. When you receive an opt-out request, the law gives you ten business days to stop sending e-mail to the requester's e-mail address. You cannot help another entity send e-mail to that address or have another entity send e-mail on your behalf to that address. Finally, it's illegal for you to sell or transfer the e-mail addresses of people who choose not to receive your e-mail, even in the form of a mailing list, unless you transfer the addresses so that another entity can comply with the law.

- It requires that commercial e-mail be identified as an advertisement and include the sender's valid physical postal address. Your message must contain clear and conspicuous notice that the message is an advertisement or solicitation and that the recipient can opt out of receiving more commercial e-mail from you.

PENALTIES

Each violation of the above provisions is subject to fines of up to $11,000. Deceptive commercial e-mail also is subject to laws banning false or misleading advertising.

Additional fines are provided for commercial e-mailers who not only violate the rules described above, but who also do the following:

- "Harvest" e-mail addresses from Web sites or Web services that have published a notice prohibiting the transfer of e-mail addresses for the purpose of sending e-mail.

- Generate e-mail addresses using a "dictionary attack" — combining names, letters, or numbers into multiple permutations.

- Use scripts or other automated ways to register for multiple e-mail or user accounts to send commercial e-mail.

- Relay e-mails through a computer or network without permission; for example, by taking advantage of open relays or open proxies without authorization.

The law allows the DOJ to seek criminal penalties, including imprisonment, for commercial e-mailers who do, or conspire to do, the following:

- Use another computer without authorization and send commercial e-mail from or through it.

- Use a computer to relay or retransmit multiple commercial e-mail messages to deceive or mislead recipients or an Internet access service about the origin of the message.

- Falsify header information in multiple e-mail messages and initiate the transmission of such messages.

- Register for multiple e-mail accounts or domain names using information that falsifies the identity of the actual registrant.

- Falsely represent themselves as owners of multiple Internet protocol addresses that are used to send commercial e-mail messages.

ADDITIONAL RULES

The FTC has issued additional rules under the CAN-SPAM Act involving the required labeling of sexually explicit commercial e-mail and the criteria for determining "the primary purpose" of a commercial e-mail. The Act also instructs the FTC to report to Congress on a National Do Not E-Mail Registry and issue reports on the labeling of all commercial e-mail, the creation of a "bounty system" to promote enforcement of the law, and the effectiveness and enforcement of the CAN-SPAM Act.

See the FTC Web site at **www.ftc.gov/spam** for updates on implementation of the CAN-SPAM Act.

Securing Your Server: Shut the Door on Spam

Your organization probably handles lots of Internet traffic every day — both to and from your clients and customers. The settings of your network servers may open your system to misuse.

If your mail server maintains an open door to the Internet, known as an "open relay," someone could access it and pass unsolicited commercial e-mail (spam) through it. And if your proxy server is "open," a spammer could use it to connect to your mail server and send bulk e-mail anonymously. Not only can these abuses overload your server, but they also could damage your organization's reputation. That's because it will appear that your system sent the spam.

How E-Mail Works

To send or receive e-mail, your computer must be connected to a mail server, a machine connected to the Internet that runs software allowing it to process e-mail. When you send an e-mail message from a secure server, software in one part of the mail server checks that you're listed as a user within your organization. If you are, it sends out your mail. When someone sends you an e-mail, software in another part of the server confirms that you're an authorized user and then accepts and delivers the e-mail to you.

But if the server is not secure, and some of its settings allow it to stay "open," it will forward e-mail to addressees who are not listed as users in your organization. Often called open relays, insecure relays, or third-party relays, these open mail servers are configured to accept and deliver e-mail on behalf of any user anywhere, including third parties with no relation to you or your organization. You don't benefit from allowing this e-mail to slip through your server; no one in your organization is receiving it or sending it.

Open relays are a vestige of the early days of the Internet, when many mail servers were kept open to allow e-mail to travel among different networks. Although they helped the Internet grow, they were abused by spammers, who have used them to disguise the origin of their messages.

THE CURRENT PROBLEM—OPEN PROXIES

Today, spammers are more likely to use an open proxy server to send their spam. A proxy is usually installed to be the only machine on your network that directly interacts with the Internet, providing more efficient Web browsing for your users. But if your proxy is not configured properly—that is, if your server is open—it also may allow unauthorized Internet users to connect through it to other hosts on the Internet. For example, a spammer can use your open proxy to connect anonymously to another mail server. Then, any mail that the spammer sends appears to have come from your system. In addition, an improperly configured proxy server can allow other types of unauthorized—and potentially damaging—network connections, including instant messaging, computer attacks, and file transfers.

Consequences for Your Business

When spam appears to come from your system, your server can be flooded with complaints from frustrated recipients. That could overwhelm your system and cause your server to crash. Repairing it could be time consuming and costly, both in financial terms and in the potential loss of goodwill from those who think you've sent the spam. The bottom line: An open proxy or open relay is an open door to the theft of your computer services and the impression that you're sending unwanted junk e-mail.

Securing Your Servers

To prevent these abuses, and the negative consequences for your business, check—and, if necessary, secure—your servers. It usually takes just a couple of commands. To find out whether you have an open relay on your system, evaluate the mail transfer agent software (MTA) your company uses to manage its e-mail.

To determine if your proxy server is vulnerable, consider these questions:

- Does your proxy allow connections from untrusted networks such as the Internet?

- Are you using the most current version of your proxy server software and hardware?

- Have you applied the latest patches or upgrades available?

- Are you using proper access controls for your server?

- Is someone regularly checking for unauthorized uses of your proxy server?

- Do you have and monitor an "abuse@[your domain name]" e-mail account where people can report abuses of your proxy server?

"Remove Me" Responses and Responsibilities: E-Mail Marketers Must Honor "Unsubscribe" Requests

Some marketers send e-mail as a quick and cheap way to promote their goods and services. Be aware that the claims that you make in any advertisement for your products or services, including those sent by e-mail, must be truthful. This means that you must honor any promises you make to remove consumers from e-mail mailing lists.

If your e-mail solicitations claim that consumers can opt-out of receiving future messages by following your removal instructions, such as "click here to unsubscribe" or "reply for removal," then the removal options must function as you claim. That means that any hyperlinks in the e-mail message must be active and that the unsubscribe process must work. Keep the following in mind:

- You should review the removal claims made in your e-mail solicitations to ensure that you are complying with any representations that you make.

- If you provide consumers a hyperlink for removal, then that hyperlink should be accessible by consumers.

- If you provide an e-mail address for removal, then that address should be functioning and capable of receiving removal requests; it may be deceptive to claim that consumers can "unsubscribe" by responding to a "dead" e-mail address.

- Any system in place to handle unsubscribe requests should process those requests in an effective manner.

The Federal Trade Commission Act prohibits unfair or deceptive advertising in any medium, including e-mail. That is, advertising must tell the truth and not mislead consumers. A claim can be misleading if it implies something that's not true or if it omits information necessary to keep the claims from being misleading.

Other points to consider if you market through commercial e-mail:

- Disclaimers and disclosures must be clear and conspicuous. That is, consumers must be able to notice, read or hear, and understand the information. Still, a disclaimer or disclosure alone usually is not enough to remedy a false or deceptive claim.

- If you promised refunds to dissatisfied customers, you must make them.

E-Mail Marketing Definitions and Terms

Source for terms and definitions: **www.marketingterms.com/ dictionary/4/**

E-mail: The transmission of computer-based messages over telecommunication technology.

E-mail marketing: The promotion of products or services via e-mail.

E-zine: An electronic magazine, whether delivered via a Web site or an e-mail newsletter.

E-zine directory: Directory of electronic magazines, typically of the e-mail variety.

HTML e-mail: E-mail that is formatted using Hypertext Markup Language, as opposed to plain text e-mail.

Opt-in e-mail: E-mail that is explicitly requested by the recipient.

Pass-along rate: The percentage of people who pass on a message or file.

Permission marketing: Marketing centered around obtaining customer consent to receive information from a company.

Sig file: A short block of text at the end of a message identifying the sender and providing additional information about him or her.

Viral marketing: Marketing phenomenon that facilitates and encourages people to pass along a marketing message.

CHAPTER 9

Search Engine Optimization

"Search engines are the entry point for most users when they want to look up something on the Web...Search engine visibility is the most important way of promoting Web sites..."

Jakob Nielsen, Ph.D. and author of
Homepage Usability: 50 Websites Deconstructed
October 2003

Advertising on the Internet is changing more and more each year as the competition becomes fiercer. A few years ago, all you needed to do to increase the amount of traffic to your Web site was submit your Web site information to one or more search engines. Soon, you were able to see more hits to your Web pages and an increase in the success of your business. These days, you have a more difficult task at hand as the number of Web pages on the Internet continues to increase. There are over two billion Web pages on the Internet. This means that there are many Web sites that are directly competing with yours for attention. You need to take drastic measures to ensure that your online business gets noticed and obtains the rankings within search engines that will deliver the results you desire.

This chapter will concentrate on proven, low-cost techniques designed to improve your:

- Search engine optimization.

- Proper meta tag formatting and inclusion.

- Proper use of ALT tags.

- Search engine registration.

- Search engine services.

- Privacy policy.

- About and Feedback pages to improve search engine visibility.

- Contentright pages.

- Web site marketing techniques.

Search engine optimization (SEO) is one of the proven methods that you can use to push up the ranking of your Web site within your target market on the Internet by using keywords that are relevant and appropriate to the product or services that you're selling. But just what does search engine optimization do, and how does it do it? When you use SEO, you use a process that allows you to make sure that your Web site is seen and read by the potential customers who need to see information about the product or service that you're selling. You need to have as many potential customers arrive at your Web site as you possibly can. SEO accomplishes this by taking the keywords that people would use to search for your product on the Internet using a search engine and placing these keywords in title pages, meta tags, and into the content of your Web site. When you properly use SEO and optimize your Web site based on sound Web site design principles, you know that your Web site is ready to be submitted to search engines and that you will greatly increase the visibility and ranking within the search engines, driving potential customers to your Web site and obtaining hits you need to increase your profits and the success of your business.

> *"The search market has become the Holy Grail of Internet advertising and continues to grow faster than our expectations. Our initial estimate of $7 billion by 2007 is most likely to be too conservative and we believe that we are still at the early stages of an expanding and large market."*

Deutsche Safa Rashtchy,
U.S. Bancorp Piper Jaffray's Senior Research Analyst
October 2003

Successful Search Engine Optimization

Understanding the concepts and actions necessary for successful search engine optimization can sometimes be confusing and hard to grasp when you're first starting out using SEO techniques. There are several steps that you need to make sure are followed so that you ensure you're getting the most out of your SEO. Some of these steps include:

- Making sure that your Web site is designed correctly and set up for optimal SEO.

- Choosing the right keywords that are going to bring you the most hits to your Web site.

- Using the right title tag to identify you within each search engine.

- The content writing that you use on your Web site.

- Using the right meta tags on your Web site.

- Choosing the right search engines to submit your meta information to and understanding the free and paid service options available.

Once you know which areas to focus on when it comes to successful SEO, you'll find that your ranking in search engines starts to increase, and you'll see many more hits to your Web site.

Meta Tag Definition and Implementation

Meta tags are just part of the overall search engine optimization program that you need to implement for your Web site. We can't stress enough that inclusion of properly formatted meta tags is not a magical solution to ensuring top search engine rankings. You need to be aware that you are competing against potentially thousands (or more) of other Web sites promoting the same products, using similar keywords, and employing other techniques to achieve a top search engine ranking. Meta tags have never guaranteed top rankings on crawler-based search engines. However, they do offer a degree of control and the ability for you, as the Web site or business owner, to impact how your Web pages are indexed within the search engines. When it comes to using keywords and key phrases in your meta keywords tag, you want to use only those keywords and phrases that you've actually included in the Web content of each of your Web pages. It's also important that you use the plural forms of keywords so that both the singular and plural forms will end up in any search that people do in search engines using specific keywords and key phrases. Other keywords that you should include in your meta keyword tags are any common misspellings of your keywords and phrases. Many people commonly misspell certain words, and you want to make sure that search engines can still find you despite these misspellings. Using misspellings in your meta keyword tags ensures that people will still find you at the top of the rankings for your business market. Don't repeat your most important keywords and key phrases more than four to five times in a meta keyword tag. Another thing to keep in mind is that if your product or service is specific to a certain location geographically, you should mention this location in your meta keyword tag. You want to make sure that those people who are searching for products and services specific to a certain area are sure to find you at the top of the search engine rankings.

Meta tags comprise formatted information that is inserted into the "head" section of each page on your Web site. To view the "head" of a Web page, you must view it in HTML mode, rather than in the browser view. In Internet Explorer, you can click in the toolbar on VIEW and then SOURCE to view the source of any Web page. If you are using a design tool such as FrontPage or Dreamweaver, you will need to use the HTML view to edit the source code of your Web pages. You can also use Notepad to edit your HTML source code.

This is a simple basic layout of a standard HTML Web page:

```
<!DOCTYPE HTML PUBLIC "-//W3C//DTD HTML 4.01//EN"

<HTML>

<HEAD>

<TITLE>This is the Title of My Web Page</TITLE>

</HEAD>

<BODY>

<P>This is my Web page!

</BODY>

</HTML>
```

Every Web page conforms to this basic page layout, and all contain the opening <HEAD> and closing </HEAD> tags. The meta tags will be inserted between the opening and closing head tags. Other than the page title tag, which is shown above, all other information in the head section of your Web pages is not viewed by individuals when they browse your Web pages. The title tag is displayed across the top of the browser window and is used to provide a description of the contents of the Web paged displayed. We will discuss each meta tag that may be contained within the "head" tags in depth.

THE TITLE TAG

Whatever text you place in the title tag (between the <TITLE> and </TITLE>) will appear in the reverse bar of an individual's browser when your Web page is viewed. In the example above, the title of the Web page to the page visitor would read as "This is the Title of My Web Page."

The title tag is also used as the words to describe your page when viewers add it to their "Favorites" list or "Bookmarks" list. The title tag is the single most important tag in regards to search engine rankings. The title tag should be limited to 40 to 60 characters of text between the opening and closing HTML tags. All major Web crawlers will use the text of your title tag as the text they use for the title of your page in your listings as displayed in search engine results. Remember, the title and description tags typically appear in the search results page after completing a search; therefore, it is critical that they be clearly and concisely written to attract the attention of site visitors. Not all search engines are alike: some will display the title and description tags in search results but use page content alone for ranking.

THE DESCRIPTION TAG

The description tag enables you to control the description of your individual Web pages when the search engine crawlers, which support the description tag, index and spider the Web site. The description tag should be no more than 250 characters.

Take a look at the "head" tag from the Web site **www.crystal riverhouse.com**, which is a Web site designed to promote the rental of a Gulf Coast vacation house on a secluded canal in Crystal River, Florida. The tag that says "name=description" is the description tag. The text you want to be shown as your description goes between the quotation marks after the "content=" portion of the tag (typically up to 250 characters is

allowed for search engine indexing; however, the full description tag may not be displayed in search results.

```
<head>
<meta http-equiv="Content-Type" content="text/html; charset=windows-
1252">
<title>Beautiful Crystal River Vacation Rental Home</title>
<meta name="keywords" content="Crystal River rental, Florida, Citrus
County, Grouper, Fishing, vacation home, Gulf Coast rental, florida vacation,
florida gulf coast">
<meta name="description" content="Casa Dos Crystal River vacation rental
resort. Located on beautiful canal off Crystal River.  Crystal River, Florida
is famous for its manatee watching, diving, grouper and other world class
fishing trips, world class golfing and many more activities.">
<meta name="language" content="en-us">
<meta name="robots" content="ALL">
<meta name="rating" content="SAFE FOR KIDS">
<meta name="distribution" content="GLOBAL">
<meta name="copyright" content="(c) 2005 APC Group, Inc.">
<meta name="revisit-after" content="30 Days">
<meta http-equiv="reply-to" content="info@crystalriverhouse.com">
<style>
<!--
.sitecredits {  color: #FFFFFF}
-->
</style>
</head>
```

It is important to understand that search engines are not all the same, and they index, spider, and display different search results for the same Web site. For example, Google ignores the description tag and generates its own description based on the content of the Web page. Although some major engines may disregard your description, it is highly recommended that you include the tag on each Web page since some search engines rely on the tag to index your site.

THE KEYWORDS TAG

A keyword is simply defined as a word that may be used by Internet users when searching for information on the Internet. Using the best keywords to describe your Web site helps get those searchers to visit your site. The keywords tag allows you to provide relevant text words or word combinations for crawler-based search engines to index. Again, although we maintain that the keyword tag is vitally important and should be included on every page, most crawler-based engines use your page content for indexing instead of the contents of the keywords tag. The truth is that the keywords tag is only supported by a few Web crawlers. Since most Web crawlers are content based (in other words, they index your site based on the actual page content, not the meta tags), you need to incorporate as many keywords as possible into your actual Web pages. For the engines that support the description tag, it is beneficial to repeat keywords within the description tag with keywords that appear on your actual Web pages. You need to use some caution with the keywords tag for the few search engines that support it, since repeating a particular keyword too many times within a keyword tag may hurt your Web site ranking.

If you look at the example earlier, you will notice that the keywords tag is the one that says <meta name="keywords" content=." The keywords you want to use should go between the quotation marks after the "content=" portion of the tag. It is generally suggested that you include up to 25 words or phrases, with each word or phrase separated by a comma.

To help you determine which keywords are the best to use on your site, visit **www.wordtracker.com**, which is a paid service that will walk you through this process. Wordtracker's suggestions are based on over 300 million keywords and phrases that people have used over the previous 130 days. A free alternative to determining which keywords are best is Google Rankings: **http://googlerankings.com/dbkindex.php**.

THE ROBOTS TAG

The robots tag lets you specify that a particular page within your site should or should not be indexed by a search engine. To keep search engine spiders out, add the following text between your tags:

```
<metaname="robots" content="NOINDEX">
```

You do not need to use variations of the robots tag to get your pages indexed since your pages will be spidered and indexed by default; however, some Web designers include the following robots tag on all Web pages:

```
<meta name="robots" content="ALL">
```

Other Tags

There are many other meta tags that exist; however, most provide amplifying information about a Web site and its owner and don't have any impact on search engine rankings. Some of these tags may be utilized by internal corporate or Web-based search engines on that particular Web site. In our example earlier, you can see some examples of other meta tags that can be incorporated (note that this is not a complete list of all possible meta tags):

```
<meta name="language" content="en-us">

<meta name="rating" content="SAFE FOR KIDS">

<meta name="distribution" content="GLOBAL">

<meta name="contentright" content="(c) 2005 APC Group, Inc">

<meta name="author" content="Gizmo Graphics Web Design">

<meta name="revisit-after" content="30 Days">

<meta http-equiv="reply-to" content="info@crystalriverhouse.com">

<meta name="createdate" content="4/8/2005">
```

You can also use the "comment" tag, which is primarily used by Web designers as a place to list a few keywords. A comment tag looks like this:

```
<!-begin body section for Crystal River Vacation House>
```

ALT Tags

The ALT tag is an HTML tag that provides alternative text when non-textual elements, typically images, cannot be displayed. The ALT tag is not part of the "head" of a Web page, but proper use of the ALT tag is so important that we wanted to emphasize it here. ALT tags are often left out of Web pages; however, they can be extremely useful for a variety of reasons, including providing detail or text description for an image or destination of a hyperlinked image; enabling and improving access for people with disabilities; providing information for individuals who have graphics turned off when they surf the Internet; and improving navigation when a graphics-laden site is being viewed over a slow connection, enabling visitors to make navigation choices before graphics are fully rendered. Text-based Web content isn't the only thing that increases your ranking in the search engines; images are just as important because these images can also include keywords and key phrases that relate to your business. If any visitors to your Web site should happen to have the image option off when hitting your site, they'll still be able to see the text that is associated with your images. Not all search engines can link to your images, but for those that do, images are an important part of search engine optimization techniques. These ALT tags are placed wherever there is an image on your Web site. It's key to remember not to use overly lengthy of descriptions when describing your images, but that you do include accurate keywords within the ALT tag to make sure that you're found by search engines. The keywords and key phrases that you use in the ALT tag should be the same keywords and phrases that you used in meta description tags, meta keyword tags, title tags, and in the Web content on your Web pages. A brief description of the image, along with one or two accurate keywords and key phrases, is all you need to optimize the images on your Web pages for search engines. Don't forget to include any misspellings and plural words in ALT tags so that you increase your chances in search engine rankings.

Most major Web design applications include tools to simplify the process of creating ALT tags. For example, in Microsoft FrontPage 2003, right click on the image, choose "properties" and the general tab, and you can enter ALT tag text information. To enter ALT tag information directly into a Web page, go to the HTML view and enter them after the IMG tags in the following format:

```
<img SRC="manatee.jpg" ALT="Manatee in Crystal River, Florida">
```

How to Use the Correct Keywords

When it comes to keywords, you need to guess at the words or word combinations for which your potential customers are searching when they look for products or services using a search engine on the Internet. If you start to optimize keywords that are incorrect, you may be wasting your time if your potential customers search using keywords that don't put you up there in the top rankings of search engines. You'll need to do some market research to find out what keywords are being used by people in search engines to find similar products or services to what you're selling. There are software tools on the market that you can use to find out just what these keywords are so that you can implement them into your Web content and into your meta tags. As we stated earlier, the importance of the keyword meta tag has faded over the years; however, using keywords within the content of your individual Web pages is critical and is the key to high Web site rankings.

Search engine optimization means that every page of your Web site will need to be optimized to the greatest extent possible. Keywords will vary based on the individual Web page content. By using the wrong keywords, you risk sending your potential customers in an entirely different direction than to your Web site. Always keep in mind that if you're not listed in the top rankings of search engines, your customers may have difficulty finding you, and your competition will have an edge over you.

You'll not only want to think about keywords for search engine optimization, you'll also want to think about the right types of phrases that people will use in search engines. General phrases often get lost in the shuffle of search engines, and phrases that are too broad in meaning will get no results as well. You need to find a fine balance between phrases that push you to the top of the rankings and phrases that leave you at the bottom of the pile. Unfortunately, there is no magic formula to developing search-engine-optimized and effective search phrases.

It's important that you determine just who your target customers are going to be and exactly what they'll be searching for when they use a search engine to look for similar products and services. Once you determine this, you'll be better able to optimize your Web pages. Make sure that you do a small market survey to find out what keywords people would use when searching for your product on the Internet. If you rely on your own list of keywords, you'll be limiting yourself from using keywords that other people are likely to use. Try to come up with a list of as many keywords and key phrases as you can so that you optimize your Web pages as much as you can.

As we mentioned, you will need to have a different list of keywords and key phrases for each Web page that you're optimizing for the Internet based on the content of the individual page. Keywords that work for some of your Web pages may not work for others. This is why you need to constantly assess how your search engine optimization campaign is progressing and be prepared to make changes along the way.

A good way to stay on top of top keywords is to keep an eye on your competition. Use a search engine yourself and use some of the keywords and key phrases that you know target your type of product or service. Take a look at the top-ranking Web sites and view the source HTML code as well as the keywords that they've used in their meta tags. The HTML code will show you the keywords that the site's creator used. You'll not only be able to come up with more keyword ideas, but you'll also be able to keep up with your competition so that you rank at the top of search engines as well.

> *"Shopping portals and search engines are attracting many consumers who rely on the Web to navigate through product offerings and efficiently research pricing and features."*

> Abha Bhaga
> Senior Analyst, Nielsen/NetRatings

The Optimization of Web Page Content

This is by far the single most important factor that will affect and determine your Web page rankings. It is extremely important that you have relevant content on your Web pages that is going to increase the ranking of your Web site in search engine rankings. The content on your Web site is what visitors to your Web site are going to read when they find your site and start to read and browse your Web pages, whether they browse to a page directly or via a search engine. You need to optimize your Web site with all the right keywords so that you can maximize your rankings within search engines. You can use software tools to find out what keywords people are using when they search for certain products and services on the Internet, and we will provide some of those to you throughout this book.

Not only are the visitors to your Web site reading the content on these pages, but search engine spiders and Web crawlers are reading this same content and using it to index your Web site among your competitors. This is why it's important that you have the right content so that search engines are able to find you and rank you near the top of the listings for similar products that people want to buy. Search engines are looking for keywords and key phrases to categorize and rank your site; therefore, it is important that you focus on just as many key phrases as you do keywords.

The placement of text content within a Web page can make a significant difference in your eventual search engine rankings. Some search engines will only analyze a limited number of text characters on each page and will not read the rest of the page, regardless of length; therefore, the keywords and phrases you have loaded into your page may not be read at all by the search engines. Some search engines do index the entire contents of Web pages; however, they typically give more value or "weight" to the content that appears closer to the top of the Web page.

If you want to get the best results from search engines, here are some tips that you should follow to optimize your Web site:

- Make sure that you have at least 200 words of content on each page. Although you may have some Web pages where it may be difficult to put even close to 200 words, you should try to come as close as you can since search engines will give better results to pages with more content.

- Make sure that the text content that you have on your Web pages contains those important keywords and key phrases that you've researched and know will get you competitive rankings and are the most common phrases potential customers might use to search for your products or services.

- No matter how much content you have after incorporating keywords and key phrases, make sure that the content that you have is still understandable and readable in plain language. A common mistake is to stack a Web site full of so many keywords and key phrases that the page is no longer understandable or readable to the Web site visitor—a sure bet to lose potential customers quickly.

- The keywords and key phrases that you use in the content of your Web site should also be included in the tags of your Web site, such as meta tags, ALT tags, head tags, and title tags.

- Add extra pages to your Web site, even if they may not at first seem directly relevant. The more Web pages that you have, the more pages search engines will have to be able to find you and link to. Extra pages can include tips, tutorials, product information, resource information, and any other information or data that is pertinent to the product or service that you're selling.

Optimizing your Web content and Web pages is one of the most important tips that you can use to ensure the success of your Web site. If you're unable to optimize your Web site yourself, you should hire an expert so that you get the most out of the Web content that you have on your Web site.

Web Site Optimization Tips, Hints, and Secrets

It is critically important that you explore and implement the wide range of tips, suggestions, and best practices to give your Web site the most competitive edge and obtain the highest possible rankings with search engines. The following pages contain various best practices, tips, and secrets.

- It is important to use your keywords heavily on your Web pages. Use key phrases numerous times, placing them close to the top of the page. Place key phrases between head tags in the first two paragraphs of your page. Place key phrases in bold type at least once on each page. Repeat keywords and key phrases often to increase density on your pages.

- Design pages so they are easily navigated by search engine spiders and Web crawlers. Search engines prefer text over graphics and also prefer HTML over other page formats. You must make your page easy to navigate by the search engines.

- Don't use frames. Search engines have difficulty following them, and so will your site visitors. The best advice we can give on frames is to never use them!

- Limit the use of Macromedia Flash and other high-end design applications as most search engines have trouble reading and following them, hurting you in search engine listings.

- Consider creating a site map of all pages within your Web site. While not necessarily the most useful tool to site visitors, it does greatly improve the search engine's capacity to property index all of your Web site pages.

- Many Web sites use a left-hand navigational bar. This is standard on many sites; however, the algorithm that many spiders and Web crawlers use will have this read before the main content of your Web site. Make sure you use keywords within the navigation, and if using images for your navigational buttons, ensure you use the ALT tags loaded with appropriate keywords.

- Ensure that all Web pages have links back to the home page.

- Use copyright and "about us" pages.

- Don't try to trick the search engines with hidden or invisible text or other techniques. If you do, the search engine will likely penalize you.

- Don't list keywords in order within the content of your Web page. It is perfectly fine to incorporate keywords into the content of your Web pages, but don't simply cut and past your keywords from your meta tag into the content of your Web pages. This will be viewed as spam by the search engine, and you will be penalized.

- Don't use text on your Web page as the page's background color (that is, white text on a white background). This is a technique known as keyword "stuffing," and all search engines will detect it and penalize you.

- Don't replicate meta tags. In other words, you should only have one meta tag for each type of tag. Using multiple tags (such as more than one title tag) will cause search engines to penalize you.

- Don't submit identical pages with identical content with a different Web page file name.

- Makes sure that every Web page is reachable from at least one static text link.

- Make sure that your title and ALT tags are descriptive and accurate.

- Check for broken links and correct HTML.

- Try using a text browser such as Lynx to examine your site. Features such as JavaScript, cookies, session IDs, frames, DHTML, and Flash keep search engine spiders from properly crawling your entire Web site.

- Implement the use of the robots.txt file on your Web server. This file tells crawlers which directories can or cannot be crawled. You can find out more information on the robots.txt file by visiting **www.robotstxt.org/wc/faq.html**.

- Have other relevant sites link to yours. We will cover the use of cross-linking your Web site with others later in this chapter; however, this is an often overlooked but extremely important way of increasing your search engine rankings.

- Design Web pages for site visitors, not search engines.

- Avoid tricks intended to improve search engine rankings. A good rule of thumb is whether you'd feel comfortable explaining what you've done to a Web site that competes with you. Another useful test is to ask, "Does this help my users? Would I do this if search engines didn't exist?"

- Don't participate in link schemes designed to increase your site's ranking. Do not link to Web spammers as your own ranking will be negatively affected by those links.

- Don't create multiple pages, subdomains, or domains with substantially duplicate content.

- Don't use "doorway" pages created for search engines.

- Consider implementing cascading style sheets into your Web site to control site layout and design. Search engines prefer CSS-based sites and typically score them higher in the search rankings.

More Web Design and Optimization Suggestions

Shelley Lowery, author of the acclaimed Web design course *Web Design Mastery* (**www.webdesignmastery.com**) and *Ebook Starter – Give Your Ebooks the Look and Feel of a REAL Book* (**www.ebookstarter.com**) offers valuable tips and suggestions for Web design and Web site optimization. You can visit **www.Web-Source.net** to sign up for a complimentary subscription to Etips and receive a copy of the acclaimed ebook *Killer Internet Marketing Strategies*.

ESTABLISH LINKS WITH REPUTABLE WEB SITES

You should try to find quality sites that are compatible and relevant to your Web site's topic and approach the Webmaster of that site for a link exchange. (Note: don't link to your competitors.) This will give you highly targeted traffic and will improve your score with the search engines. Your goal is to identify relevant pages that will link to your site, effectively yielding you quality, inbound links. You need to be wary of developing or creating a "link farm" or "spam link Web site," which offers massive quantities of link exchanges but with little or no relevant content for your site visitors or the search engines.

How to Establish a Reciprocal Link Program

Begin your link exchange program by developing a title or theme that you will use as part of your link request invitations. Your title or theme should be directly relevant to your site's content. Since most sites use your provided title or theme in the link to your Web site, be sure you include relevant keywords, which will improve your Web site optimization and search engine rankings. Keep track of your inbound and outbound link requests. Begin your search for link exchange partners by searching a popular engine such as Google and entering key phrases such as "link with us," "add site," "suggest a site," "add your link," etc. If these sites are relevant, they are ideal to being your reciprocal link program since they, too, are actively seeking link partners. Make sure that the Webmaster of other sites actually link back to your site as it is common that reciprocal links are not completed. If they do not link back to you in a reasonable time, remove the links to them as you are only helping them, with their search engine rankings.

You can use **www.linkpopularity.com** as a free Web source for evaluating the total number of Web sites that link to your site.

Free Link Popularity Report for http://www.atlantic-pub.com:

Google	click to view
MSN	826 links
Yahoo	519 links

ESTABLISH A WEB SITE PRIVACY POLICY

Internet users are becoming more and more concerned with their privacy. You should create a "privacy" Web page to let your visitors know exactly how you will be using the information you collect from them. This page should include the following:

- For what do you plan on using their information?

- Will their information be sold or shared with a third party?

- Why do you collect their e-mail addresses?

- Do you track their IP addresses?

- You should notify site visitors that you are not responsible for the privacy issues of any Web sites you may be linked to.

- Notify them that you have security measures in place to protect the misuse of their private or personal information.

- Provide site visitors with contact information in the event that they have any questions about your privacy statement.

ESTABLISH AN "ABOUT" PAGE

An "about" page is an essential part of a professional Web site for a variety of reasons. One reason is that your potential customers may want to know exactly who you are; and secondly, it is a great opportunity to create a text-laden page for search engine visibility. An "about" page should include the following:

- A personal or professional biography.

- A photograph of yourself or your business.

- A description of you or your company.

- Company objectives or mission statement.

- Contact information, including your e-mail address.

ESTABLISH A TESTIMONIALS PAGE

Another way to develop creditability and confidence among your potential customers is to include previous customer testimonials. You do need to make sure your testimonials are supportable, so include your customers' names and e-mail addresses for validation purposes.

ESTABLISH A MONEY-BACK GUARANTEE

Depending on the type of Web site you are operating, you may wish to consider implementing a money-back guarantee to completely eliminate any potential risk to customers in purchasing your products. By providing potential clients with a solid, no-risk guarantee, you build confidence in your company and your products.

ESTABLISH A FEEDBACK PAGE

There are many reason to incorporate a feedback page into your Web site. There are times when potential customers will have questions about your products and services or may encounter problems with your Web site, and the feedback page is an easy way for them to contact you. Additionally, it allows you to collect data from the site visitor such as his or her name, e-mail address, or phone number. A timely response to feedback is critical to ensuring customers that there is a "living" person on the other end of the Web site, and this personal service helps increase the likelihood that they will continue to do business with you.

ESTABLISH A COPYRIGHT PAGE

You should always display your copyright information at the bottom of each page. You should include both the word Copyright and the © symbol. Your copyright should look similar to this:

Copyright © 2006 Atlantic Publishing Company

How Do Search Engines Work?

There are several different types of search engines. They are crawler-based, human-powered, and mixed. We will discuss how each one works so you can optimize your Web site.

CRAWLER-BASED SEARCH ENGINES

Crawler-based search engines, such as Google, create their listings automatically. They "crawl" or "spider" the Web and index the data, which is then searchable through Google.com. Crawler-based search engines will eventually revisit your Web site, and therefore, as your content is changed (as well as that of your competitors), your search engine ranking may change. A Web site is added to the search engine database when the search engine spider or crawler visits a Web page, reads it, and then follows links to other pages within the site. The spider returns to the site on a regular basis, typically once every month, to search for changes. Often, it may take several months for a page that has been "spidered" to be "indexed." Until a Web site is indexed, the results of the spider are not available through the search engines. The search engine then sorts through the millions of indexed pages to find matches to a particular search and rank them in order based on a formula of how it believes the results to be most relevant.

HUMAN-POWERED SEARCH DIRECTORIES

Human-powered directories, like the Open Directory, depend on humans for its listings. You must submit a short description for your entire site to the directory. The search directory then looks at your site for matches from your page content to the descriptions you submitted.

How Long Until My Web Site Is Listed?

The chart below show the typical length of time it takes to get listed at each of the major search engines after you have submitted your Web page.

Search Engine	Typical Amount of Time to Get Listed
MSN	Up to 2 months
Google	Up to 4 weeks
AltaVista	Up to 1 week
Fast	Up to 4 weeks
Excite	Up to 6 weeks
Northern Light	Up to 4 weeks
AOL	Up to 2 months
HotBot	Up to 2 months
iWon	Up to 2 months

Using a Search Engine Optimization Company

If you are not up to the challenge of tackling your Web site search engine optimization needs, it may be to your benefit to hire a search engine optimization company so that the optimization techniques that you use are properly implemented and monitored. There are many search engine optimization companies on the Internet that can ensure that your rankings in search engines will increase when you hire them. One word of caution is to be wary of claims of anyone who can "guarantee" you a top-10 ranking in all major search engines; these claims are baseless. If you have the budget to hire a search engine optimization company, it may be extremely beneficial for you since you know the experts at SEO techniques are taking care of you and you can focus your energy on other important marketing aspects of your business.

CHOOSING THE RIGHT SEARCH ENGINE OPTIMIZATION COMPANY

- Look at the business reputation of the SEO companies that you're thinking about hiring. Ask the company for customer references that you can check out on your own. You can also contact the Better Business Bureau in their local cities or states or confirm their reputation at **www.bbb.org**.

- Do a search engine check on each company to see where they fall into the rankings of major search engines such as AOL, MSN, and Google. If the company that you're thinking about hiring to manage your own search engine optimization doesn't rank high in these search engines, how can you expect them to launch you and your business to the top of the ranks?

- You want to choose a search engine optimization company that actually has people working for them and not just computers. While computers are great for generating the algorithms that are needed to use search engine programs, they can't replace people when it comes to doing the market research that is needed to ensure that the company uses the right keywords and key phrases for your business.

- You need to make sure that the search engine optimization company uses ethical ranking procedures. There are some ranking procedures that are considered to be unethical, and some search engines will ban or penalize your business Web site from their engines if they find out that you, or the search engine optimization company that you've hired, are using these methods. Some of these unethical ranking procedures include doorway pages, cloaking, or hidden text, as we have discussed previously.

- The search engine optimization company that you decide to hire should be available to you at all times by phone or by e-mail. You want to be able to contact someone when you have a question or a problem to which you need a solution.

Once you've decided to hire a certain search engine optimization company, it's important that you work with the company instead of just handing over all the responsibility. How much control of your Web site you should allow your search engine optimization company is an area of debate.

How to Interact with Your Search Engine Optimization Company

- Listen carefully to the advice of the search engine optimization account managers. They should have the expertise for which you hired them and typically can provide factual and supportable recommendations. Search engine optimization companies are expected to know what to do to increase your ranking in the search engines; if they fail to deliver, you need to choose another company.

- If you're going to be making any changes to your Web site design, make sure that you let your search engine optimization account manager know. This is because any changes that you make can have an effect on the already-optimized Web pages. Your rankings in search engines may start to plummet unless you work with your search engine optimization account manager to optimize any changes to your Web site design that you feel are necessary to make.

- Keep in mind that search engine optimization companies can only work with the data and information that you have on your Web pages. This means that if your Web site has little information, it will be difficult for any search engine optimization company to pull your business up in the search engine rankings. Search engine optimization relies on keywords and key phrases that are contained on Web pages that are filled with as much Web content as possible. This may mean adding two or three pages of Web content that contain tips, resources, or other useful information that is relevant to your product or service.

- Never change any of your meta tags once they've been optimized without the knowledge or advice of your search engine optimization account manager. Your SEO company is the professional when it comes to making sure that your meta tags are optimized with the right keywords and key phrases needed to increase your search engine ranking. You won't want to change meta tags that have already proven successful.

- Be patient when it comes to seeing the results of search engine optimization. It can take anywhere from 30 to 60 days before you start to see yourself pushed into the upper ranks of search engines.

- Keep a close eye on your ranking in search engines, even after you've reached the top ranks. Information on the Internet changes at a moment's notice, and this includes where your position is in your target market in search engines.

Search engine: "A program that indexes documents, then attempts to match documents relevant to a user's search requests.

Information: The term search engine is most commonly used to refer to Web search engines, although other types of search engines exist. Web search engines attempt to index a large portion of pages on the World Wide Web. Other search engines are topic-specific, region-specific, and even site-specific.

*There is also some confusion about the difference between a search engine
and a search destination. A search engine powers the search process
and provides results for a search destination. A search destination can
use its own engine, a 3rd-party engine, or a combination. Knowing
the difference between an engine and a destination is important when
submitting URLs; a destination using its own engine can accept direct
submissions, while a destination using external engines may or may not
provide a submission option."*

Source for terms and definitions: **www.marketingterms.com**

SEARCH ENGINE REGISTRATION

It is possible to submit your Web site for free to search engines;
however, when you use paid search engine programs, you'll find that the
process of listing will be faster and will bring more Web traffic to your
Web site more quickly. Other than pay-per-click and other advertising
programs, such as Google Adwords, it is not necessary to pay for search
engine rankings if you follow the optimization and design tips contained
in this book and have patience while the search engine Web-crawling and
indexing process takes place. At the end of this chapter, we have provided
a wealth of tools and methods to submit your Web site to search engines
for free. If you do decide to hire a third-party company to register you
with search engines, we have provided some basic guidance to ensure
you get the most value for your investment.

SUBMITTING TO HUMAN-POWERED SEARCH DIRECTORIES

If you have a limited budget, you'll want to make sure that you
have at least enough to cover the price of submitting to the directory at
Yahoo! (called a "directory" search engine because it uses a compiled
directory), which is assembled by human hands, not a computer. For
a one-time yearly fee of approximately $300, you'll be able ensure that
search engines that are crawlers (a search engine that goes out onto the
Internet looking for new Web sites by following links) will be able to find
your Web site in the Yahoo! directory. It may seem like a waste of money
to be in a directory-based search engine, but the opposite is true. Crawlers
consistently use directory search engines to add to their search listings.

If you have a large budget put aside for search engine submissions, you might want to list with both directory search engines and crawler search engines, such as Google. When you first launch your Web site, you may want it to show up immediately in search engines and don't want to wait the allotted time for your listing to appear. If this is the case, you might want to consider using what is called a "paid placement" program.

SUBMITTING TO CRAWLER SEARCH ENGINES

Submitting to search engines that are crawlers — search engines that look throughout the Internet to seek out Web sites through links and meta tags — means that you'll likely have several Web pages listed within the search engine. The more optimized your Web site is, as discussed previously in this chapter, the higher you'll rank within the search engine listings.

One of the top Internet crawler search engines is Google. Google is extremely popular because it is not only a search engine, it also is the main source of power and information behind other search engines, such as AOL. The best thing that you can do when getting your Web site listed at Google is to make sure that you have links within your Web site. When you have accurate links on your Web site, you ensure that crawler search engines are able to find you. One thing to keep in mind is that if you have good links and you listed your Web site with a successful directory search engine, such as Yahoo!, you may find that crawlers are easily able to find you, thus eliminating your need to list with Google in the first place. However, don't let this stop you from building good links into your Web site and constantly updating them.

USING SEARCH ENGINE SUBMISSION SOFTWARE

There are dozens of software applications that can submit your Web site automatically to major and other search engines. We have reviewed most of these products extensively, and we recommend Dynamic Submission (**www.dynamicsubmission.com**). Dynamic Submission, currently in version 7.0, is a search engine submission software product that proclaims to be "multi-award winning, Web promotions software package, the best on the market today." Dynamic Submission search engine submission software was developed to offer Web site owners the ability to promote their Web sites to the ever-increasing number of search engines on the Internet without any hassles or complications. Dynamic Submission search engine submission software helps you submit your Web site to hundreds of major search engines with just a few button "clicks" and drive traffic to your Web site. To use Dynamic Submission, you simply enter your Web site details into the application as you follow a wizard-based system, which culminates in the automatic submission to over one thousand major search engines, including Google and Froogle.

As about 85 percent of Internet traffic is generated by search engines, submitting your Web site to all the major search engines and getting them to be seen on the search engine list is extremely important. Search engines are the most effective way of promoting your Web site on the Internet. In order to maintain a search engine placement near the top for your chosen keywords, it is essential to regularly submit your Web site details to these Web directories and engines. Some search engines de-list you over time, while others automatically re-spider your site. Dynamic Submission is available in four editions (including a trial edition, which we highly encourage you to try) to fit every need and budget. Here are the major features of Dynamic Submission 7.0:

- Automatic search engine submission.

- Supports pay-per-click (PPC) and pay-per-inclusion (PPI) engines.

- Support for manual submission.

- Keyword library and keyword builder.

- Link popularity check.

- Meta tag generator.

- Web site optimizer.

- Incorporated site statistics service.

Search Engine Optimization Checklist

There are many aspects to search engine optimization that you need to consider to make sure that it works. We have covered each of these in depth earlier in this chapter, but the following checklist can serve as a helpful reminder to ensure that you haven't forgotten any important details along the way.

- **Title tag.** Make sure that your title tag includes keywords and key phrases that are relevant to your product or service.

- **Meta tags.** Make sure that your tags are optimized to ensure a high ranking in search engine lists. This includes meta description tags and meta keyword tags. Your meta description tag should have an accurate description so that people browsing the Internet are interested enough to visit your Web site. Don't forget to use misspelled and plural words in your meta tags.

- **ALT tags.** Add ALT tags to all the images that you use on your Web pages.

- **Web content.** Use accurate and rich keywords and key phrases throughout the Web content of all your Web pages.

- **Density of keywords.** Use a high ratio of keywords and key phrases throughout your Web pages.

- **Links and affiliates.** Make sure that you have used links, and affiliates if you're using them, effectively for your Web site.

- **Web design.** Make sure that your Web site is fast to load and easy for visitors to navigate. You want to encourage people to stay and read your Web site by making sure that it's clean and looks good.

- **Avoid spamming.** Double-check to make sure that you're not using any spamming offenses on your Web site. Some spamming offences include cloaking, hidden text, doorway pages, obvious repeated keywords and key phrases, link farms, and mirror pages.

Always be prepared to update and change the look, feel, and design of your Web pages to make sure that you're using search engine optimization techniques wherever and whenever possible.

Free Web Site Search Engine Submission Sites

- **http://dmoz.org/** Open Directory Project

- **http://tools.addme.com/servlet/s0new**

- **www.submitexpress.com/submit.html**

- **www.ineedhits.com/free-tools/submit-free.aspx**

- **www.submitcorner.com/Tools/Submit/**

- **www.college-scholarships.com/free_search_engine_ submission.htm**

- **www.quickregister.net**

- **www.global.gr/mtools/linkstation/se/engnew.htm**

- **www.scrubtheweb.com**

- **www.submitawebsiteWeb site.com/free_submission_top_ engines.htm**

- **www.nexcomp.com/weblaunch/urlsubmission.html**

- **www.submitshop.com/freesubmit/freesubmit.html**

- **www.buildtraffic.com/submit_url.shtml**

- **www.mikes-marketing-tools.com/ranking-reports/**

- **http://selfpromotion.com/?CF=google.aws.add.piyw**

- **www.addpro.com/submit30.htm**

- **www.websiteWeb site-submission.com/select.htm**

Note: There are many other free services available on the Internet, and we make no guarantee as to the quality of any of these free services. We do recommend you create and use a new e-mail account just for search engine submissions (for example, **search@yourwebsite.com**).

Free Web Site Optimization Tools

- **www.websiteoptimization.com/services/analyze**
  Free Web site speed test to improve your Web site performance. This site will calculate page size, composition, and download time. The script calculates the size of individual elements and sums up each type of Web page component. On the basis of these page characteristics, the site then offers advice on how to improve page load time.

- **www.sitesolutions.com/analysis.asp?F=Form**
  Free Web site analysis to determine if you are effectively using meta tags.

- **www.mikes-marketing-tools.com/ranking-reports**
  Search Engine Rankings offers instant, online reports of Web site rankings in seven top search engines, including Google, Yahoo! Search, MSN, AOL, Teoma (Ask Jeeves), AltaVista, AllTheWeb, and the top three Web directories, Yahoo! Directory, Open Directory (Dmoz), and LookSmart, all for free.

- **www.searchengineworld.com/cgi-bin/kwda.cgi**
  Free, fast, and accurate keyword density analyzer.

- **www.hisoftware.com/accmonitorsitetest**
  A Web site to test your Web site against accessibility and usability: Section 508, Complete WCAG, CLF, XAG standards.

- **www.wordtracker.com**
  The Leading Keyword Research Tool. It is not free, although there is a limited free trial.

- **https://adwords.google.co.uk/select/KeywordSandbox**
  Gives ideas for new keywords associated with your target phrase but does not indicate relevance or give details of number or frequency of searches.

- **http://inventory.overture.com/d/searchinventory/suggestion**
  Returns details of how many searches have been carried out in the Overture engine over the period of a month and allows a drill

down into associated keywords containing your keyword phrase as well.

- **www.nichebot.com**
  Wordtracker- and Overture-based tools as well as a nice keyword analysis tool, which focuses on Google's results.

- **www.digitalpoint.com/tools/suggestion**
  Gives search numbers on keywords from Wordtracker and Overture sources.

Web Site Design and Optimization Tools (Free, Trial, or for Purchase)

- **www.webmastertoolscentral.com**
  A large variety of tools, guides, and other services for Web design and optimization.

- **www.htmlbasix.com/meta.shtml**
  Free site that automatically creates properly formatted HTML meta tags for insertion into your Web pages.

- **www.coffeecup.com – CoffeeCup HTML Editor**
  The CoffeeCup HTML Editor 2005 is two editors in one!

- **www.coffeecup.com – CoffeeCup Direct FTP**
  The only drag and drop FTP client that edits HTML, previews images, and more!

- **www.coffeecup.com – CoffeeCup VisualSite Designer**
  Now anyone can make a Web site . . . no experience needed!

- **www.coffeecup.com – CoffeeCup Flash Firestarter**
  The fastest and easiest way to make killer Flash effects for your Web site.

- **www.coffeecup.com – CoffeeCup Flash Form Builder**
  Create Flash e-mail forms without using HTML or scripts!

- **www.coffeecup.com – CoffeeCup Live Chat**
  Live chat with users on your Web site.

- **www.coffeecup.com CoffeeCup – Flash WebsiteWeb site Search**
  Add customized search to your Web site in a flash!

- **www.coffeecup.com CoffeeCup – Google SiteMapper**
  Create powerful Google site maps in seconds!

- **www.coffeecup.com – CoffeeCup RSS News Flash**
  Add headlines and news to your Web site fast!

- **www.coffeecup.com – CoffeeCup Flash Blogger**
  Easily create and modify your own online journal!

- **www.coffeecup.com – CoffeeCup Password Wizard**
  Password protect your site quickly and easily with Flash.

- **www.coffeecup.com – CoffeeCup PixConverter**
  Easily resize your digital pictures for Web sites, e-mail, CDs, and more.

- **www.coffeecup.com – CoffeeCup MP3 Ripper & Burner**
  Easily rip MP3s or burn music CDs now!

- **www.coffeecup.com – CoffeeCup Image Mapper**
  Often imitated, never duplicated – the original image mapper!

- **www.coffeecup.com – CoffeeCup StyleSheet Maker**
  Create advanced Web sites using cascading style sheets.

- **www.coffeecup.com – CoffeeCup Button Factory**
  The most popular button software on the Net now makes Flash!

- **www.coffeecup.com – CoffeeCup GIF Animator**
  The coolest animation software on the planet now does Flash!

- **www.coffeecup.com – CoffeeCup WebCam**
  Putting live WebCam images on your Web site has never been easier.

- **www.coffeecup.com – CoffeeCup PhotoObjects 10,000**
  Over 10,000 ready-to-use graphics that are perfect for Web design.

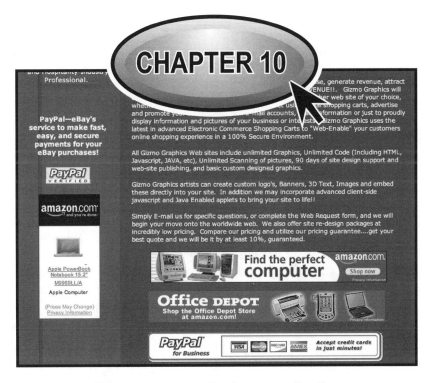

Banner Advertising

Everyone has heard about banner advertising, but very few really know what banner advertising is and how it works. A Web banner or banner ad is simply a form of advertising on the World Wide Web. Banner advertising involves embedding an advertisement into a Web page. Banner ads are designed to draw traffic to a Web site by linking them back to the Web site of the advertiser. The advertisement is typically comprised of an image (GIF or JPEG) but can come in Flash or other technologies. Banner ads are typically placed on pages with relevant content. The Web banner is displayed when a Web page that references the banner through its source code is loaded into the browser. When the banner is loaded into a site visitor's browser, this is what is known as an "impression." When the site visitor then clicks on the banner, the visitor is directed through a hyperlink embedded in the banner ad to the Web site advertised in the banner. This is what is commonly known as a "click-through." Banner ads are commonly "served" through a centralized ad server; however, they may also be embedded directly in the Web pages. Even if they are embedded, they can be rotated through a variety of scripting methods or from features within the Web design application, such as Microsoft FrontPage.

Many banner ads operate under a "pay-per-click" system. Software tracks the number of "clicks," and each click will generate revenue to the content provider of the banner ad (not the advertiser). Typically, this is less than $0.10 per click. The advertisers do not make any commission on the "click-throughs"; instead, they get the direct sales if a customer buys from them. Banner ads are very similar to traditional road-side banner or billboard advertisements. They notify potential consumers of the product or service and strive to create enough interest to get you to click the banner and travel to their Web site and buy their products or services. Banner ads also allow you to be much more dynamic when it comes to your advertising techniques because you can change the way the image looks at any time and you can add unique forms of animation to the banner ad. Banner ads are typically annoying, and many Internet users consider them as spam or a nuisance. Most recent versions of Web browsers have the ability to block most pop-up banner ads.

There are several reasons why online or brick-and-mortar businesses may choose to use banner ads to promote their products and services. Some of the reasons include:

- To increase the amount of Web traffic to your Web site.

- To increase the sales of your products and services.

- To let your customers know about any special deals that you're offering or any new products or services that you're selling.

- To get your name out onto the Internet so that potential customers know who you are.

How Do Banner Ads Work?

Each year, more and more people are using the Internet to make money. This means you may wish to participate in some of the many

Internet advertising techniques that typically obtain good results. Advertising is one of the biggest money makers on the Internet, and banner ads are still one of the most successful methods of prosperous advertising.

Banner ads are essentially an image with embedded HTML code that launches a hyperlink when launched. The HTML code tells the Web browser, or server, to pull up a certain Web page when someone clicks on that particular hypertext that is displayed in the banner as text or graphics or a combination of both. Typically, a third-tier server is utilized to track the impression and click-throughs. Obviously, banner ads are an integral part of an effective affiliate program, which we will discuss in detail later.

Overall, banner advertising success is on the downhill trend. Click-through rates have dropped steadily, and there has been much discussion about the untimely death of the banner ads. We can't argue the fact that banner ads are no longer the cash cow they used they be; however, they are still an effective, low-cost form of advertising, and many companies still use banner ads in their marketing and advertising portfolio.

Click-through rate (CTR). Defined as the measure of how effective an ad is. CTRs range from the industry average of about 0.35 percent to 10 percent. As a general rule, the more targeted the site, the higher the expected CTR. As we mentioned earlier, some banner ads will only be displayed when a particular keyword is entered.

Cost per sale. If the click-through rate does not equate to selling a product, then it is certainly not an effective banner ad or is not placed on relevant Web sites. The cost per sale is the cost, by Web site, for you to advertise your products with the banner ad campaign.

Branding. We have already discussed branding in depth earlier in this book; however, it is important to discuss branding as it relates to banner advertising. Banner ads certainly promote branding techniques, as potential customers become familiar with your "brand" and recognize it when displayed in banner advertisements. The idea is that potential customers will identify with your brand and thus choose your brand over a competitor's brand.

Different Types of Banner Ads

Using banner ads doesn't mean that you're limited to one kind of ad to advertise your product or service. In fact, there are many different types of banner ads from which you can choose, including altering the shape and size of the banner ad to suit your purposes. There are eight different unique sizes of banner ads from which you can choose, as indicated by the IAB (Internet Advertising Bureau). Each of these banner ad sizes is based on a pixel, which is the unit, or section, of color that creates the images that you see on your computer or on a television. The standard specific sizes for banners, as dictated by the Internet Advertising Bureau, are as follows:

- A full banner: 486 by 60 pixels

- A vertical navigation bar on a full banner: 392 by 72 pixels

- A half banner: 234 by 60 pixels

- A vertical banner: 120 by 240 pixels

- A square button banner: 125 by 125 pixels

- Button size, number 1: 120 by 90 pixels

- Button size, number 2: 120 by 60 pixels

- A small, or micro-size, button: 88 by 31 pixels

The most commonly used banner size is the full banner, at 486 by 60 pixels. However, you'll find all sizes of banner ads in all areas of the Internet, with many variations of the standard sizes. The above banner sizes aren't the only banner sizes that you need to stick to, but they are by far the most common, and you should stick to the standards whenever possible. Keep in mind that banner size is also dictated by the amount of memory size that can be given to the banner. The majority of Web sites limit memory to anywhere from 12K to 16K. Banner ads will add to the final size total of the Web page, and therefore many Web sites will limit the amount of memory that is allotted to banner ads and other forms of Internet advertising. The more memory size that a Web site is, the longer it will take to load on the Internet. You want your Web sites to load fast and clean, and once again, this requirement will put a limitation on the size of the banner ad.

When you look at the existing banner ads on the Internet, you'll notice that there are many different varieties of graphic and other animated creativity to be found among banner ads. Some of the most simplistic banner ads will have only one JPEG or GIF image on them that link the banner ad to the main Web site of the company doing the advertising. By far, the most popular of all the banner ads is an animated ad that uses a GIF animation tool. GIF animation allows the banner ad to change over a few minutes, showing various GIF images one after the other, and many times in a flowing sequence. These ads instantly grab the attention of visitors to the Internet and are sure to make people notice your banner ad. There are many programs available that help you create animated GIF images; our favorite is included with Corel's Paint Shop Pro (**www.corel.com**).

Another type of banner ad is known as a banner ad that uses media-rich tools, such as Shockwave programming, Java programming and audio and video techniques. Keep in mind that these types of banner ads will also add to the Web site memory size since they have larger files in which to store the rich media programming. These tend to make up the bulk of the annoying, nuisance-type banner ads, in addition to being more expensive to create. Animated GIF ads are simple to create on your own.

Reasons for Using Banner Ads

When you decide to use banner ads for the advertising of your Web site and business, you want to entice visitors to click the ad so that they go directly to your Web page. The visitor to your Web site wouldn't have arrived at your site if it weren't for the banner ad. This means that the person may not have been searching for the product or service that you're selling, so you need to keep that in mind when designing the ad as it may or may not generate a sale from the banner ad click. Statistics show that banner ads do amount to a certain percentage of Internet sales. If you are going to host ads on your Web site, there is no cost to doing so, and you will get paid for the click-throughs generated, regardless of whether they result in a sale or not. Including a small amount of tasteful, low-bandwidth banner ads on your site is a good idea. If you wish to use banner ads as an advertising campaign, there are many services that offer banner ad hosting, exchanges, and marketing. Banner ads are also very effective when used in conjunction with an affiliate program, which we will discuss in a later chapter

But how do you measure the success of your banner ad? There are several ways that you can measure how successful your banner ads are and if you need to do something to change them.

- **Number of page views.** Page views are also known as "page impressions." Page views are determined by how many times a particular Web site is requested to be seen from the server. You won't be able to measure the success of your branding techniques or how many sales you have achieved through the banner ad, but you will be able to determine how many people are reaching your Web site by clicking on your banner ads. Most space for banner ads is sold according to the cost of one thousand page views, or impressions, you receive. This is also known as CPM (cost per thousand).

- **Clicks.** Also known as "click-throughs." This is the number of times that Web surfers click on your banner ad. Many Web sites will sell banner ads according to the CPC (cost-per-click).

- **Click-through.** This information about your banner ad indicates the ratio between clicks to page views, or CTR (click-through rate). This ratio measures the number of people who have actually arrived at your Web site by clicking on a banner ad. Keep in mind that the number of people who find your Web site may be less than 1 percent, but this 1 percent is necessary to the success of your Web site.

- **Cost-per-sale.** The cost-per-sale will indicate the amount of money that you spend on advertising to make a sale of your product or service. You can use what are known as Internet cookies to keep track of the amount of traffic to your Web site from banner ads. All of this information is important in helping you determine how to effectively use your banner ads.

How to Make Banner Ads

Even if you have minimal knowledge about computers, you'll be able to make a simple banner ad for your Web site. Making a banner ad is simply a matter of coding and imaging with HTML hyperlink tags that are going to link back to your Web site. You'll be able to develop the graphics for your banner ad with the use of software such as Paint Shop Pro or most other graphics programs such as Microsoft Digital Image Suite. The following is the simple coding that is used for a banner ad:

```
<a href="http://www.YourWebSiteHere.com"> <img src="http://
static.YourWebSiteHere.com/gif/banner-ad-static.gif"> </a>
```

You can make simple banner ads on your own without too much computer knowledge, and keep in mind that GIF-animated banner ads aren't that much more difficult to make yourself than any other banner ads. If you want to use banner ads that are filled with media, such as Shockwave programming, Java programming or audio or video techniques, you might want to hire someone to do the banner coding for you; however, this is typically not cost effective for emerging online businesses. You want your banner ads to look as professional as possible so that you keep up with your competition.

If you really want your banner ads to stand out in the crowd, you may want to hire a professional designer for banner ads. You want to hire a professional who is able to create a banner ad that promotes your products or services and quickly grabs the attention of Web visitors so that they want to click on your banner ad. The price that you pay for your professionally designed banner ad can vary from as low as $75 to as much as $1,200, depending on what type of banner ad you want and how much you're willing to spend from your business budget for advertising with banners.

You can find some Web sites that will allow you to create your own banners free of cost to you. You'll be able to combine different banner sizes with font, color, and images to create the banner that you want for your advertising purposes. If you're wondering why these Web sites offer this type of service, the answer is easy: 1) they want to post their own banner on your Web site, 2) they make a certain amount of money from the advertising that is located on their own Web sites, or 3) banner creation is their own hobby, and they want to share and use the banners as a personal reference. Some free banner creation sites that you can use include:

- **http://members.tripod.com/atomicarts** – Atomic Arts

- **http://makeyourbanner.com** – Make Your Banner

- **www.abcbanners.com/mlinks/links.pl** – ABC Banners

The type of banner ad that you develop can be as simple as you like or as elaborate as possible. The choice is yours when it comes to how much time and money you're willing to allocate from your business budget for banner ads.

Successful Banner Ads

When it comes to creating and designing your banner ads, there are no strict guidelines that you need to follow. Different banner ads are successful for different reasons, and it's up to you to find out what works for you and your business and what you need to change. You may have to try a particular type of banner ad for a while and track how well it does before making changes and modifications. There are no rules to what works in Internet advertising and what doesn't work. There are, however, some things that you should know about banner ads so that you stand a fighting chance when it comes to designing your first ad.

One definite formula for success is to place your ads on Web pages that have some type of content that has a relationship to the product or service that you're selling. If you're selling chocolate, your banner ads might not be too successful if they appear on Web sites that are focused on diet-related information. Internet advertising studies show that the more relationship there is between banner ads and the Web sites on which they appear, the greater the number of clicks that take place. When you're creating your banner ads, you may want to make sure that the ad promotes your products or services and not your Web site, as the appeal is in the products, not necessarily your Web site. When Web visitors see a banner ad advertising a Web site, they are less likely to click and find out more than if the banner advertises a certain product that they're interested in. Banner ads should be a reflection of the things that you're selling and not about your Web site alone. Banner ads should take Web visitors directly to the portion of your Web site where that product or service is sold or promoted. You don't just want banner ads to link to your home page, since this means that visitors will have to read your site to find the product that they just clicked. Banner ads are designed to get you the sale, not to find potential customers who have time to browse your Web site.

If you have the choice and the option, put your banner ads at the top of a Web page. The farther down on a Web page your banner ad is displayed, the less likely it will be noticed. Web visitors are usually browsing through Web sites at a fast rate, and you need to have your banner ad in a location where it can be seen and clicked quickly.

The main point of your banner ad should be simple and easy to understand. Studies show that the more complicated your banner ad is, the less likely Web visitors are to read it long enough to want to click. You want the statement on your banner ad to be catchy, simple, and accurate. Internet advertising studies also show that animated banner ads do better than those ads that are stationary. Animated ads grab the attention of Web visitors long enough to make them read the message and for you to get the click-through. Another thing that you should pay attention to when it comes to the design of your banner ads is that the graphics that you display on your ads should reflect your product or service in a way that people can understand without having to guess. Web visitors are less likely to click on banner ads if they have no idea what the graphic is trying to tell them than if they have some idea of what you're advertising.

You want to make sure that the Web page on which your banner ad is displayed loads quickly, or Web visitors will give up and continue browsing to another Web site. The smaller your banner ad is, the faster the Web page it is on will load. Large banner ads are not only slow to load, they are also too big and intimidating and often deter Web visitors from clicking on them. The types of banner ads that do well on the Internet are ads that are attractive and interesting to look at. Banner ads also need to be placed on a Web page so that they make sense and are aligned in an order that is easy to understand. You'll have to experiment and try different things when it comes to the design and layout of your banner ads. As the Internet continues to grow, advertising techniques also continue to change to adapt to the needs of Web shoppers who are faced with more choices than ever as they search the Web for deals and unique products.

One of the key elements of using banner ads is to make sure that you target the right Web visitors. "Targeting" is a technique that focuses on the type of Internet browsing that a person does on the computer. Web visitors who are searching for a specific item that they type into a search engine are then presented with Web site results that match their keyword search. If your banner advertisements match these keywords, then your ad is more likely to be found by people, and you increase your page views and click-through totals.

Advertising and Banners

When you take the steps necessary to implement banner ads for advertising your product or service, there are options that can simplify the process for you. There are three basic options from which you can choose:

- You can pay certain Web sites to be hosts for your banner ads.

- You can do an exchange program, where you post the banner ads for other advertisers, and they post your banner ads on their Web sites.

- You can pay a fee to what is called a "banner network," where you can post your banner ads on a certain number of host sites according to the amount of money that you've paid. An example of a successful "banner network" is DoubleClick (**www .doubleclick.com/us/**).

You'll need to decide which of the above options are best for you and your business. You may want to choose the exchange program option with another advertiser if you don't have the budget to post your banner ads on other Web sites for a fee to eliminate any costs. If you decide to exchange banner ads, there are two methods that you can use. The first is to establish working relationships with advertisers on other Web sites so that you can both exchange your banner ads and host them on your sites. This way, you'll be able to put your banner ads on those Web sites that closely match your own or where you know potential customers might see your banner ads and be interested enough to link back to your Web pages. The only disadvantage to this method is that you need to spend a lot of time looking for banner exchange partners for you to have a significant number of banner ads on the Internet.

The second method of getting your banner ads online is to use what are called banner exchange programs. You'll become part of a huge network of Internet advertisers that each host a variety of banner ads on their Web sites, whether or not there is a similarity between the Web sites or even any relevant content on the site. Banner exchange programs are discussed further in the next section. No matter what method you choose to use, when it comes to getting your banner ads on the Internet, you'll be giving your Web site and business that cutting edge that you need to stay on top of your competitors.

Banner Exchange Programs

A banner exchange program is a great way for you to get your banner ads onto the Internet without spending any money. The exchange program works like this: When you host banner ads on your Web site, the exchange program will host the same number of your banner ads on other Web sites. In most cases you'll be hosting more banner ads than you're posting elsewhere, but this is the way that the banner exchange program makes its own profits. This means that the banner exchange program can sell the extra banner ads that they don't use on your site to their paying customers so that they can stay in business and realize a profit. When it comes to statistics and ratio figures, the usual ratio is something like 2:1, two of their banner ads to your one banner ad. This arrangement allows you to have your banner ads on many Web sites, while at the same time allowing the banner program to make a profit from those extra banner ads.

The main advantage to you of using a banner exchange program is that it doesn't cost you anything, which is great if you have a small (or nonexistent) budget for advertising. You get to post your banner ads on various Web sites so that you maximize the amount of exposure that your Web site gets on the Internet. There are disadvantages to using a banner exchange program: You lose most of the decision making about where your banner ads are placed and about which banner ads you display on your own Web site, plus these banner ads may overwhelm your site visitors. Most banner exchange programs control the decision making about where your banner ads are hosted, and there may be many times when you disapprove of where your banner ads appear. In most cases these banner programs will try to make some logical choice about banner ad placement, but there will be times when you wonder about the logic that placed your banner ad where it appears or the type of banner ad that you're required to host on your Web site.

Here are a couple of the more popular banner exchange programs:

- **www.LinkExchange.com**

- **www.FreeBanners.com**

You'll find that participating in a banner exchange program is simple and easy to set up. The listed exchange programs above will help you through the signup process and quickly have you on your way to effective banner ad placement for your business. Take your time when looking around for just the right banner exchange program since different programs will each have their own advantages and disadvantages. You'll find that some banner exchange programs focus more on accurate banner ad placement than others, while a different exchange program will concentrate more on providing Web sites for your banner ads that are related to the products and services that you're selling. In most cases, banner exchange programs won't cost you anything, but you may want to look for a program that gives you a better ratio exchange by having you pay a reasonable fee.

How to Buy Advertising

One way that you can increase the effectiveness of your banner ads is by buying advertising space on the Internet. There are several ways that you can buy advertising:

- Join an affiliate program.

- Join a banner exchange program.

- Contact Web sites on your own to buy advertising space.

- Hire an agency that specializes in Internet advertising.

You will find that there are benefits and disadvantages to using each of the above methods for buying advertising.

USE AN AFFILIATE PROGRAM

Using affiliate programs is a very effective way to place your banner ads on other Web sites as well as to save you time and money. You can join other affiliate programs, or you can start your own affiliate program that will enable you to pay those sites that are hosting your banner ads only when there are results to show for the click of your ad or when a customer actually makes a purchase that is a direct result of the banner ad. The nice thing about using affiliate programs is that you won't have to buy a large number of page views or click-throughs. Instead, you'll be paying only a certain amount of the profits that you generate from obtaining a new customer, which amounts to a minor percentage of your overall profits. We will discuss affiliate programs at great length in later chapters of this book.

JOIN A BANNER EXCHANGE PROGRAM

As discussed previously in this chapter, a banner exchange program is a great way to get your banner ads on many other Web sites. When you use an exchange program, you won't have to do the legwork and contact other Web sites about hosting your banner ads. Essentially, a banner exchange program is a system of brokers, where the program acts on your behalf to place your banner ads on appropriate Web sites on the Internet. A network of banner ad programs is much the same as a banner exchange program, but there is one drawback to using a banner ad network: You are giving up most of the final decision making power about where your banner ads are going to be placed as well as what banners ads you'll be hosting on your own Web site.

Make sure that you spend some time looking around before choosing a banner exchange program or network. Some of the larger banner networks will sell some great advertising space on some quality, highly traveled Web sites; however, you may find that the fee for advertising on these high-traffic sites is too high for your advertising budget. One thing that you should definitely be looking for when it comes to using a banner network are those programs that will sell what they call "an excess of banner locations." These are simply banner spaces that they haven't been able to sell at the regular price and now need to get rid of at a discounted price.

Another decision that you're going to have to make if you're choosing to use a banner exchange program is whether you want to use click-throughs or page views (impressions) when determining the success of your banner ads. You'll find that banner ad networks will deal with one or the other method of tracking the number of hits to your banner ads.

Some large banner networks that measure banner ads by page views (impressions) include:

- **www.burstmedia.com**

- **www.ContentZone.com**

- **www.doubleclick.com**

A couple of large banner networks that measure banner ads by the click-through method include:

- **www.eads.com**

- **www.BannerSpace.com**

CONTACT WEB SITES ON YOUR OWN

You can approach Web sites on your own to see if they'll place your banner ads on their Web pages. Although this can take up a lot of your valuable time, it has several benefits that you might be able to take advantage of. One of the biggest advantages is that you'll be in charge of the final decisions about on which types of Internet Web sites you place your banner ads. You'll be able to determine what Web sites will most benefit and relate to the products and services that you're selling. You'll have the ability to target Web sites that don't have a lot of other banner ads on them so that your own banner ads become more effective. Many times, being selective about where you place your banner ads can result in a big payoff when you target those sites that have a certain appeal to those same people who are interested in your products.

You'll have to do your research before you contact the Web sites where you want to place your banner ads to make sure that the site is what you're looking for. Many Web sites will have certain processes in place that you need to follow before you can place your banner ads on any Web page. You first need to see if the Web site has Web pages that have room for any type of advertising. If you're unsure about whether the Web site will accept banner ads, the only way to find out is to contact them using e-mail. You want to take your time choosing the right Web sites to target so that you don't waste your valuable time contacting sites that just don't fit into your banner ad campaign.

Many of the larger Web sites that will accept banner ads will have some type of a package available for Internet advertising. Along with this advertising package may come a high cost that will quickly eat up your advertising budget. Most of these large Web sites will use CPM (cost per thousand) of tracking page views, or page impressions, which means that you'll be paying anywhere from $10 to $125 for each thousand page views that you receive from your banner ads. Those Web sites that have a high traffic volume will charge more for CPM than less traveled Web sites, so you'll want to do your research before you make a final decision about on which Web sites you want to place your banner ads. Usually, you'll be buying bulk packages of page views (impressions) at one time. Some typical page view packages are anywhere from 50,000 page views to 200,000 page views.

A good thing to keep in mind is that many smaller Web sites that have less traffic won't have advertising packages available for you to place banner ads. This means that many times, you can make special deals with these smaller Web sites that will mutually benefit each of you.

HIRE AN AGENCY THAT SPECIALIZES IN INTERNET ADVERTISING

The last method of buying advertising is to hire an agency that has a great deal of expertise about advertising on the Internet. If you hire an advertising agency that offers all the available services, you'll have very little to do when it comes to your banner ads. These advertising agencies will help you to find the best Web sites to place your banner ads on and will find the best price for your advertising budget. You can also hire an agency that will help you create your banner ads as well as manage all of the advertising for your online or brick-and-mortar business. Many times, you'll find that large advertising agencies are able to get a more competitive price than if you were looking for Web sites yourself on which to place your banner ads. This is because agencies are able to buy page views (impressions) in large quantities.

Although there are many advantages when it comes to using advertising agencies, there are some disadvantages that you'll need to consider before making your final decision about whether to use an agency or not. One of the most significant advantages is that many advertising agencies won't deal with small Web sites that are looking for help with their banner advertising. Each advertising agency will have different services that they offer, and this may include what is called an "account minimum." If you have a small Web site as well as a small advertising budget, you may not find an advertising agency that is going to start an account with you and your Web site.

Make sure that you look around before making your final decision about which advertising agency you want to use to help you with your banner ads and other advertising needs. The questions to which you want to find answers before making your choice are as follows:

- How much experience does the agency have?

- What are the rate costs associated with the different services that the advertising agency offers?

- What services do they offer?

- Are customer referrals or client testimonials available?

If you have a large Internet-based or brick-and-mortar business, it may be worthwhile to hire an advertising agency since they'll be able to give you the knowledge that you need to stay in competition with your competitors and their banner ads. Even if you're a smaller company, with a smaller Web site to promote, you may want to consider hiring an agency so that you gain the Web presence that you need on the Internet to reach your customers and potential customers. Internet advertising can be tricky if you don't understand all the elements that go into successful advertising. You want to have as much of an advantage as you can when it comes to getting your company name out there so that you can increase your profits as well as your customer database.

How to Sell Advertising

When you have a Web site on the Internet, you not only can buy advertising, you can also sell it. When you sell space on your Web site, you'll be able to receive some revenue that you can turn around and put back into your own Web site or business. However, selling banner ad space on your own Web site can be a bit cumbersome.

BECOME PART OF THE BANNER AD NETWORK

The easiest way for you to sell advertising on your Web site is to become part of a banner ad network so that you don't have to be in charge of the advertising that you have on your site. The banner network will allow you to keep track of the amount of money that you earn from selling advertising space as well as take charge of the banner ads that are placed on your Web site. The only thing that you need to keep in mind if you're going to be using a banner ad program to sell Web space for advertising is that it will take a certain percentage of the profits that you see from selling this advertising.

There will always be more Web sites selling space for advertising than there will be Web sites that are interested in buying the space. It's for this reason alone that banner ad programs will be a bit particular about the advertisers that they list. You'll find that most of the banner ad networks have monthly Web site traffic minimums that they require to participate in banner ad programs. For instance, there are some banner ad networks that set the minimum of at least 250,000 Web site visitors before you can join the banner network. Some other banner ad networks have a set of tiers that determine how much you pay based on the amount of traffic that hits your Web site each month. A tier system works well for smaller Web sites so that you can choose a banner ad program that your advertising budget can handle.

If you have a Web site that gets a large amount of traffic each month, such as more than 90,000 page views (or impressions) each month, you'll have no problem joining a banner ad network that uses this CPM method of calculating Web site traffic. However, if your Web site generates less Web traffic each month, you'll most likely need to look at those banner ad programs that calculate Web traffic using the click-through method. Don't forget, though, that the click-through method of Web traffic calculation means that you won't be making much money on the banner ads that you host on your Web site. This is because you won't actually be paid until a Web visitor clicks on the banner ad and links to the Web site that is being advertised. The average click rate is less than 1 percent, so your revenue from the click-through method won't amount to much at the end of each month.

How Much Revenue Can You Make Selling Advertising Space?

Although you won't get rich each month selling banner advertising space on the Internet, you'll still be able to collect some revenue that you can then turn around and put back into your own business advertising budget.

Most of the banner ad networks on the Internet have what is called a "run of site" type of ad that they sell to businesses advertising on the Web. For each of these ads, they are getting approximately $4 to $5 per page view, or page impression (CPM). From this total, the banner ad program will deduct anywhere from 30 to 50 percent as its share of the earnings. This leaves you with about 0.2 to 0.3 cents on each page impression that occurs on your Web site. You need to have about 100,000 page views, or impressions, to earn $250 to $300 for that month.

Sell Your Own Space

When you join a banner ad network program, you usually will have little say about the type of banner ads that are placed on your Web site. This means that visitors to your business Web site will be seeing ads that may have nothing to do with the product or service that you're selling, and in some cases you may feel that these banner ads are having a negative effect on your Web site. If this is the case, you can sell your own advertising space and be a bit choosy about the type of banner ads that appear on your Web site.

If you're going to be selling your own Web advertising space, you need to be aware that there are many other Web sites selling advertising space as well. This means that you'll need to have a Web site that stands out from the rest and on which advertisers want to see their banner ads. Many advertisers are looking for Web sites that have a certain type of content and that also have a high volume of traffic each day. This is because quality Web sites receive more page views, and this means a higher chance of Web site visitors clicking on banner ads hosted on those sites.

When you're looking for advertisers to place their banner ads on your Web site, you need to be influential in having them decide that putting their ads on your Web page is going to be good for their own business. You'll need to provide potential advertisers with some statistics about your Web site such as providing them with information about the type of visitors your Web site receives and what your traffic volume is per day and per month. You will also need to show them that your own products and services have some relevance to the business that they are promoting.

The next thing that you'll need to make sure is in place if you're going to be selling advertising space on your own is that you have the technology available to host banner ads. You'll need to be able to host the banner ads as well as keep track of the number of visitors to your Web site as accurately as possible so that you're able to charge the advertisers on your Web site accordingly. Selling your own advertising space will be more time consuming than if you joined a banner ad network program and let them do all the work for you. However, if you want to have the Web site for your business grow in the direction that you want to take it, you might want to invest the time and effort that it takes to sell your own advertising so that you get the look and feel to your Web site that you're looking for.

The Future of Banner Ads and Advertising

As we discussed at the beginning of this chapter, there is some speculation that banner ads will soon be a thing of the past since more and more Web visitors are avoiding clicking on these ads. However, there will always be something to replace banner ads and continue the trend of successful Internet advertising. Another advertising trend that is very popular (and equally annoying) is the pop-up ad, which displays to the Web visitor in a small browser window of its own. Most people find the pop-up ad to be very annoying and close them as quickly as they can without paying attention to the advertising content, and most Web browsers provide automatic blocking of pop-up Web pages.

Another up-and-coming advertising technique is a "text link," where the advertising message is inserted into the content of the Web page. These non-intrusive advertisements are a subtle way for advertisers to get their messages across to Web visitors without being overwhelmed by large banner ads.

Yet another advertising technique is "interstitial ads." These ads are much like pop-up ads because they display to the Web visitor in a separate browser window. The advertising link is clicked, and then the interstitial ad appears, after which the Web visitor is taken to the corresponding Web page. These interstitial ads will close on their own, so unlike the pop-up ads that you have to close with a mouse click, the interstitial ad is there briefly and then gone, leaving an impression in the mind of the person viewing the ad on which they may or may not act. It's probably safe to say that the banner ad won't disappear completely but that it will undergo some significant changes over the coming months and years.

Advertising Specifications

In order for you to better understand the standards on the Internet for developing your ads, including banner ads, you need to have an understanding of the specifications that are required. The reason that these specifications are in place is so that there is a norm for all advertisers to follow.

Banner Ads Terms and Definitions

Source for the following terms and definitions:
www.marketingterms.com/dictionary/3/

Advertising specifications: A graphical Web advertising unit, typically measuring 468 pixels wide and 60 pixels tall (i.e., 468 x 60).

Beyond the banner: Online advertising not involving standard GIF and JPEG banner ads.

Button ad: A graphical advertising unit, smaller than a banner ad.

HTML banner: A banner ad using HTML elements, often including interactive forms, instead of (or in addition to) standard graphical elements.

Interstitial: An advertisement that loads between two content pages.

Pop-up ad: An ad that displays in a new browser window.

Pop-under ad: An ad that displays in a new browser window behind the current browser window.

Rectangle ad: Any one of the large, rectangular banner sizes suggested by the IAB.

Rich media: New media that offers an enhanced experience relative to older, mainstream formats.

Skyscraper ad: An online ad significantly taller than the 120 x 240 vertical banner.

Text ad: Advertisement using text-based hyperlinks.

Surround session: Advertising sequence in which a visitor receives ads from one advertiser throughout an entire site visit.

Vertical banner: A banner ad measuring 120 pixels wide and 240 pixels tall.

CHAPTER 11

Business Directories

When you're trying to promote your online or traditional brick-and-mortar business on the Internet, you will want to ensure that your business is listed in as many places as possible so that you have a better chance of reaching as many people as you can, and even more importantly, you want to provide all possible resource avenues for them to reach you. You need to connect with a lot of potential customers before they become actual customers and you generate sales revenue from them. As we discussed earlier in the book, as you gain customers, your goal is to retain repeat customers, developing a strong relationship and growing a loyalty in your customers toward your products and services. Word-of-mouth advertising is incredibly important and can only be gained through sustained loyalty and customer satisfaction among your existing and new customers.

Business directories can be found all over the Internet; in a sense they are typically nothing more than search engines combined with Web-based white and yellow page services. The primary purpose of business directories is simple. They exist to help you find:

- Products

- Services

- Companies

- Jobs

- People

There is really no reason not to have your business and Web sites listed with all of the business directories, and typically, the listing is free. Business directories, such as SuperPages.com and YellowPages.com on the Internet, can help send traffic to your Web pages, no matter what type of business you have. Directories place a listing of your business, product categories, Web site address, and other pertinent information into a consolidated listing that many people browse each day. Oftentimes, people are looking for exactly what you're selling or the services you are offering, and they can locate you through a business directory. You can find Web business directories that are specific to location, products or services, or by random selection. We highly recommend that you have your business listing in a variety of business directories so that you increase your chances of being noticed by Web visitors.

The following is a list of some of the more popular business directories that you can find on the Internet:

- **www.smartpages.com**

- **www.business.com**

- **www.europages.com**

- **www.business-directory-uk.co.uk**

- **www.hoovers.com/free**

There are many more online business directories from which you can choose. An Internet search using any search engine will yield you many results; however, the business directories can provide more detailed information about a particular company or organization.

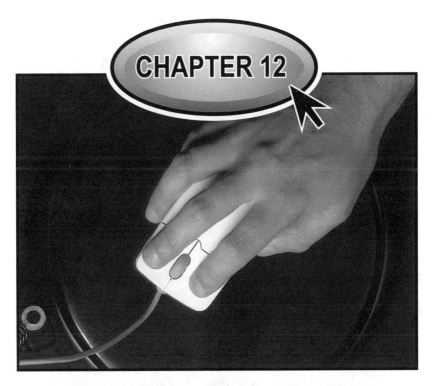

CHAPTER 12

B2B Web Communities and Portals

The Internet is a vast network where anyone can do business, exchange information, get an education, or search for any kind of data that they can imagine. With so much potential at your fingertips, it's important that you take advantage of being part of business-to-business (B2B) Web communities or, in some cases, business-to-consumer (B2C) Web communities. For the purposes of the success of your online advertising, this chapter will focus on the B2B Web communities, how you can become part of one, and what the community will do for you.

There are many different B2B Web communities on the Internet that you can take part in, and if you can't find the right community for you and your business, you can build your own community. So just what is a business-to-business Web community?

Business-to-Business Web Community Defined

B2B is often used to describe Web sites that sell goods or services to other businesses. Therefore, these businesses are serving other businesses as opposed to consumers. The difference between a B2B e-commerce Web site and a B2B Web community is in the type of information and degree of functionality that is offered. A B2B Web community is a full-service centralized clearing house of data, which presents content such as news, industry analysis, e-mail, purchasing, an industry-indexed search engine, trading exchanges, electronic storefronts, and career information, just to name a few.

Web communities are cropping up both in vertical and horizontal e-markets. Examples of vertical e-markets are chemicals and food and energy. Horizontal e-markets include organizations such as Perfect Commerce (**www.perfect.com**), which offers complete source-to-settle solutions coupled with deep supply chain expertise and The Open Supply Network. A horizontal e-market sells everything from toys to home furnishings to services for translating from one language to another.

A B2B Web community is a community that exists on the Internet much like a big virtual marketplace that centers around a specific topic, product, service, or other types of information. Other functions that the B2B Web community can provide for you and your business include:

- A search engine within your product or service category.

- A place to trade industry information.

- A place to join discussion groups about your specific business.

- A way for you to find out what the market value is of the products and services that you're selling.

All of these elements combined are ways that you can improve your knowledge of the business or industry in which you're involved, so that you can become more successful as a merchant.

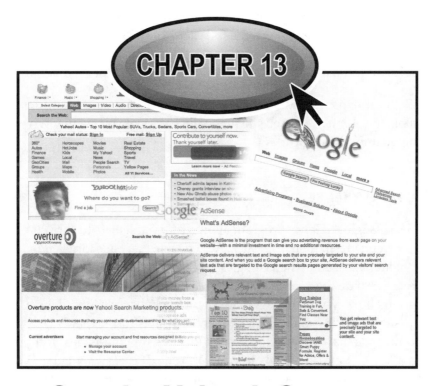

Google, Yahoo!, Overture, & Froogle Advertising

"Google saw a sizeable increase in advertising revenues for the quarter that ended March 31, 2006. Total advertising revenue was $2.2 billion, up 79% year-on-year and up 17% from the previous quarter. Total advertising revenue in 2005 were $6 billion, up from $3 billion the year before."

AdAge, April 2006

Google

Advertising on Google is one of the smartest decisions you will make for your online business. With Google you can actually generate revenue from your Web site or obtain immediate exposure on the world's most popular search engine on the Internet. You will immediately gain exposure to potential customers. Google offers two advertising programs: Google AdWords for advertisers and Google AdSense for Web publishers.

Before we discuss either of these programs, you should know it is possible to submit your Web site manually to Google by visiting **www .google.com/addurl.html**.

GOOGLE ADSENSE

The Google AdSense program allows Web publishers to earn more revenue from their Web sites. AdSense delivers ads targeted to content pages, and when Google WebSearch is added to the site, AdSense also delivers targeted ads to search results pages. The AdSense program allows your business to make money when visitors click on ads associated with your business. It enhances visitors' experiences by including ads that are relevant to what they see on your pages. You can even add a Google search box to your Web site. It is easy to manage your AdSense account and track earnings online with easy-to-use tools.

> *"At the beginning I was very concerned that I might lose traffic to competitors. I only used AdSense on a limited number of the site's pages, and I watched the stats very carefully. If the traffic, pages per visitor, or conversion rates dropped I knew I could easily pull the ads... Since implementing AdSense, our ad revenue has increased more than tenfold, and 100 percent of my available inventory is now sold through AdSense."*

—Vik Kachoria, Entrepreneur, Real Adventure.

> *"Instead of spending money to hire an additional sales rep to sell ad banners, Google ads have become a virtual sales tool for us. Now we're able to reap thousands of dollars in additional advertising revenue each month that we would very likely have missed without Google AdSense."*

— Robert Hoskins, Editor and Group Publisher, Broadband Wireless Exchange

"Google shows targeted ads reflecting the sorts of information and services SeatGuru visitors want. For a small business like mine, this is the best approach to advertising. You set it up easily, it automatically serves relevant ads, and it takes very little of my time."

—Matt Daimler, Founder,
SeatGuru.com

"We're seeing this impressive new revenue stream without incurring any cost. We're maximizing our previously unsold inventory, and our revenue per page figure continues to grow."

— Scott Zucker, Executive VP and COO,
Intelligent Content Corp, PetPlace.com

GOOGLE ADWORDS

The Google AdWords program reaches people actively looking for information related to the product or services offered by your business and sends targeted visitors directly to your Web site. AdWords uses cost-per-click pricing, which means you pay only when people click on your ad. There is a nominal, one-time activation fee for Google AdWords. After that you pay only for clicks on the AdWords ads, which you control by telling Google how much you are willing to pay per click and per day.

With AdWords, ads for your business appear alongside or above results on Google search results pages for Google Web search, Google Groups, and the Google Directory (see the example on the following page—your ads will appear in the right side of this page and will only appear when a relevant keyword is searched). Ads can also appear on the search and content sites and products in the Google Network, which is an extensive online advertising network. Google's global search network includes America Online, Netscape, CompuServe, AT&T Worldnet, AskJeeves, The New York Times, Earthlink, and Shopping.com. Google's content network of consumer and industry-specific Web sites includes USNews.com, ABC.com, TheStreet.com, WhatYouNeedtoKnowAbout.com, Economist.com, Thomson, Lowestfare.com, Lycos, InfoSpace, National Geographic, Viacom, Forbes, FoxSports, LinuxWorld.com, and Macworld.

Google Adwords is a great program in which to place the advertisements for your business because the program is used by people who are looking for specific information about the products and services that you are selling. If an individual clicks on your advertisement, he or she is taken directly to your business Web site. You will pay a fee for each time a person clicks on your advertisement, whether the visitor buys from your Web site or not. You will also find that keyword values are weighted, and the more valuable the keyword, the higher the cost of the click. As mentioned earlier, you do have to pay a one-time startup fee to join Google AdWords, after which time you'll only be paying for each of the clicks that hit your specific business advertisement in Google AdWords. You get to determine how much you're willing to pay per click, and you let Google know this price when you first sign up with them.

Google Adwords offers robust reports and performance history to track your ad performance. You can also adjust your keywords or advertisements to increase your visibility and widen your potential sales market. There is no reason to hire a professional to manage your Google campaigns as they are simple to set up and monitor. While we strive to provide low- or no-cost options for you to increase your sales, there is no money better spent than with Google advertising at present.

> *Both Google and Yahoo!, along with search-site rivals like Microsoft's MSN and Ask Jeeves (recently bought by Barry Diller's InterActiveCorp), are developing much broader ranges of marketing services. Google, for instance, already provides a service called AdSense. It works rather like an advertising agency, automatically placing sponsored links and other ads on third-party websites. Google then splits the revenue with the owners of those websites, who can range from multinationals to individuals publishing blogs, as online journals are known.*

Source: Economist.com

Froogle

Froogle is a price engine Web site launched by Google, Inc. Users can type product queries to return lists of vendors selling a particular product as well as pricing information. The name Froogle is a portmanteau of the word frugal, which means thrifty, and the name of the company, Google.

The best advice we can give is to start making plans now to submit your data to Froogle. Most major shopping carts can export your data into a Froogle data feed, including PDG Software's shopping cart (**www. pdgsoft.com**). You want to start positioning your products now to grab your share of the potential marketplace offered through Froogle. Froogle can already accept data feeds, even in beta or development mode, so you should take advantage of this sure-to-be-popular service.

In the image on the next page, you can see the results from a Froogle search, where multiple companies are displayed along with their product pricing and product descriptions. Froogle is poised to take over the marketplace for price-comparison shopping sites.

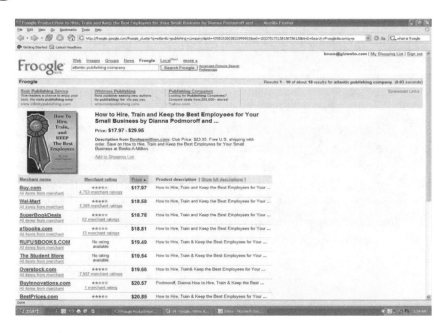

Yahoo! Search Marketing and Overture Advertising

Advertising on Yahoo! is another great portal that you may want to consider when deciding where to place your advertisements on the Internet. Yahoo! utilizes the services of "Overture," which was recently renamed to Yahoo! Search Marketing. Yahoo! Search Marketing has many great ways to get you the leads and the Web site traffic that you're looking for. This is because when you list your business with Yahoo! Search Marketing, you're also listing on their many partner sites, such as MSN, Metacrawler, WebCrawler, AlltheWeb, Yahoo!, Search.com, and Dogpile. Yahoo! Search Marketing is the direct competitor of Google, and between the two, they control most of the major search engines. With such market share between Google and Yahoo! Search Marketing, there is no reason, other than budget constraints, to limit advertising to one or the other. We recommend you establish pay-per-click accounts with both Google and Yahoo! Search Marketing.

When you list your business with Yahoo! Search Marketing, your Web site will be seen by customers around the world who are looking for your specific product or service online. The keywords that you choose to describe your business should closely link with the same keywords that Web visitors are likely to use when entering search information into search engines. Yahoo! Search Marketing uses the pay-per-click method, which means that you'll only be paying when Web visitors click to your site through the search engine.

Advertising using some of the large search engine portals such as Google and Yahoo! Search Marketing will give you the edge that you need to stay on top of your competition and to push your rankings in the search engine war. You want to be able to reach as many customers and potential customers as you can so that you can increase the size of your existing client database.

You can submit your Web site to Yahoo! for free by visiting **https://login.yahoo.com/config/login?.src=srch&.done=http://submit.search.yahoo.com/free/request**.

Yahoo! Search Marketing comprises the following marketing and search engine components. You may implement some or all of them.

YAHOO! DIRECTORY SUBMIT

Yahoo! Directory Submit is part of a suite of services created to help businesses get more out of Yahoo!, more efficiently. Yahoo! Directory Submit provides an expedited review of your Web site for possible inclusion in the Yahoo! Directory.

For Web sites that do not feature adult content or services, the Yahoo! Directory Submit service costs $299 (nonrefundable) for each directory listing that is submitted. Furthermore, for each listing accepted into the directory, there is a recurring annual fee of $299 to maintain the listing in the directory for the subsequent year.

YAHOO! PRODUCT SUBMIT

With Yahoo! Product Submit, your products will be featured prominently in Yahoo! Shopping (**http://shopping.yahoo.com**) and appear in highly relevant areas across Yahoo!, giving you access to millions of motivated buyers. Inclusion in Yahoo! Product Search and buyer's guide pages is based on a cost-per-click price that varies by product category. You pay only for leads directly to your site. Yahoo! features extensive Web-based account management and reporting tools.

YAHOO! SEARCH SUBMIT

Yahoo! offers several ways for you to submit Web pages and content so your business can appear in algorithmic (non-sponsored) search results. It is important to keep in mind that these are non-sponsored search results only. Yahoo! offers two versions of the Search Submit product, which enable you to submit your important URLs quickly and easily. Both Search Submit Express and Search Submit Pro feature daily reporting and refreshing every 48 hours. Search Submit Pro provides a dedicated account manager as well as other premium features. A comparison of options is portrayed in the chart below.

	Search Submit Express	Search Submit Pro
URL submission	X	X
Structured feed to simplify high-volume listing submission		X
Title, description, and meta data submission for better control over message and relevance		X
Daily Reporting: Clicks & search terms	X	X
Rank for each search term	X	X
Queries		X
Customization		X
Auto download		X
Dedicated Account Manager		X
48-Hour Refresh	X	X
Submission Format	Individual URLs	XML-like IDIF feed

	Search Submit Express	Search Submit Pro
Pricing	Annual fee + category-based cost-per-click	Category-based cost-per-click
Recommended number of URLs	No limit	1000+ URLs or $5,000+/month

YAHOO! SPONSORED SEARCH

The more search engines your listings appear on, the more customers you attract. And Yahoo! Sponsored Search lists your business in the search results on six of the top U.S. search properties: MSN, Yahoo!, AltaVista, InfoSpace, AlltheWeb, and NetZero.

Sponsored Search's top three listings appear in search results on the Web's leading sites. Yahoo! states that their advertisers receive over 170 million highly targeted sales leads each month. Like Google Adwords, Yahoo! Sponsored Search puts your Web site directly in front of customers searching for what you're selling. Pricing is similar to Google Adwords in that you pay per click, and keywords are weighted, so some are worth more per click than others.

> *"The prequalified traffic Sponsored Search delivers is the main reason it outperforms our CPM banner and portal sponsorship buys. And Yahoo!'s reach gives us the volume of registered leads needed to satisfy our sales force."*
>
> — Pat Lashinsky, Vice President, Marketing, zipRealty

This year the combined advertising revenues of Google and Yahoo! will rival the combined prime-time ad revenues of America's three big television networks, ABC, CBS and NBC, predicts Advertising Age. It will, says the trade magazine, represent a "watershed moment" in the evolution of the Internet as an advertising medium. A 30-second prime-time TV ad was once considered the most effective – and the most expensive – form of advertising. But that was before the Internet got going. And this week online advertising made another leap forward.

This latest innovation comes from Google, which has begun testing a new auction-based service for display advertising. Both Google and Yahoo! make most of their money from advertising. Auctioning keyword search-terms, which deliver sponsored links to advertisers' websites, has proved to be particularly lucrative. And advertisers like paid-search because, unlike TV, they only pay for results: they are charged when someone clicks on one of their links.

Source: Economist.com
www.economist.com/agenda/displayStory.cfm?story_id=3908700

CHAPTER 14

Affiliate Programs

Once you have established your Web site, completed search
engine optimization, and begun to manage your e-commerce site,
implementing an affiliate program may be the right option to extend your
online presence beyond your Web site. Nothing could be easier these days
than setting up a Web site for your online or brick-and-mortar business.

Definition of Affiliate Programs

Affiliate programs have been around for a long time due to the
success that they have achieved for thriving online businesses. Another
name for an affiliate program is an "associate program." An affiliate
program is when an individual or company promotes products and
services provided by a merchant in return for a commission. The concept
is fairly simple. You have your Web site with your products for sale on it.

You allow businesses to become "affiliates" of yours, and they can then promote your products on their Web sites. When a site visitor attempts to buy one of the products, they click on the link and are actually taken back to your Web site to complete the transaction. By using an affiliate program, this "click-through" is tracked, and the affiliate is given "credit" for the sale. Typically, affiliates earn 8 to 15 percent of the total sale—for doing nothing more than allowing the merchant's products to be sold on their Web site. In some cases, the merchant pays commission to their affiliates for these product sales, sales leads, or some other defined sales-related activity that is of value to a merchant, but typically, commissions are only based on sales. One of the largest affiliate programs that is in place on the Internet is with Amazon.com, which has over 600,000 affiliate Web sites in place at this time. Since selling products as an affiliate of Amazon costs nothing and you can earn a monthly income, there are few reasons not to become an affiliate. Obviously, if you want to expand your online business, your goal is to have others become affiliates of your Web site.

In most cases, the arrangement between affiliate Web sites is based on the total number of Web visitors that they send to your site, the number and total dollar value of sales that you get from the people sent to your site, or the number of clicks you get back to your site. When you use affiliates to send Web visitors to your site, you're taking advantage of a marketing technique that is extremely effective, while at the same time very affordable for even the smallest business Web sites.

When an affiliate program agreement is put into place, there are three separate entities that are involved with each of the actions that take place: 1) the Web site of the affiliate, 2) your business Web site, and 3) the Web visitor, or customer, who you are trying to attract to your Web site. Oftentimes, there is a middle-tier layer, which is an affiliate tracking application or server that actually records the "click-through" transaction.

Who Uses Affiliate Programs?

You may be wondering just what types of Web sites and businesses use an affiliate program. The answer is that almost any business can use this type of advertising program, although some plans place restrictions on language or Web content they consider offensive. Usually, the Web site is called a "merchant Web site," but this doesn't mean that a Web site needs to sell anything in order to use an affiliate program. There are many Web sites that have a high traffic volume on the Internet that make their money simply by the number of advertisers to which they sell space.

Once you do some research, you'll find that there are all sorts of affiliate Web sites on the Internet, which include some high-quality, popular Web sites all the way to the personal Web pages of some unknowns. Even small Web sites can make money when they become an affiliate for another Web site.

Affiliate Payment Process

Affiliate programs use different ways to determine payment. Each can be successful in its own way, but there are slight differences between each. The three most common methods of payment are as follows:

1. **Pay per click.** If you enter into this type of payment agreement, you'll be paying your affiliates a total price that is determined by the number of Web visitors that click on a link on the affiliate Web page to arrive at your business Web site. These Web visitors aren't required to buy anything; all they have to do is visit your Web site.

2. **Pay-per-lead.** If you're using this type of payment method, you'll be paying your affiliates an amount that is determined by the number of Web visitors who leave information at your Web site. All the Web visitor needs to do is fill out a form on your business Web site, which you can then use as a lead to further sales and communication with the Web visitor. Your goal is to make a sale and obtain the Web visitor as a repeat customer so that you can increase your client database.

3. **Pay-per-sale.** If you have this payment agreement with your affiliates, you pay a total that is determined by the number of sales you make from the Web visitors who are sent to your business Web site via the Web site of the affiliate. The amount you pay is based on either a predetermined amount that is fixed ahead of time for each sale or a certain percentage of each sale. Amazon. com's affiliate program is an example of a pay-per-sale program.

In this case, Amazon.com pays their affiliate when the affiliate sends them a customer who purchases something.

You'll find that there are types of payment agreements between you, the online merchant, and the affiliate as well. No matter what arrangement you come up with, you'll be paying your affiliates a certain amount of money each month that is based on the specified actions of the Web visitor. Two methods of affiliate payment that are becoming more popular are 1) residual payment programs and 2) two-tier payment programs.

RESIDUAL PAYMENT PROGRAM

With this type of affiliate payment program, your affiliates will be making a profit from the Web visitors that they send to your business Web site when these visitors continue to purchase your products or services. This is a great affiliate program if you're getting a constant and reliable payment from customers each and every month, since your affiliates know that they can count on your payment.

TWO-TIER PAYMENT PROGRAM

These affiliate programs have a structure similar to multilevel marketing organizations such as Amway or Avon, which profit through commission sales and sales recruitment. In addition to receiving commissions based on sales, clicks, or leads stemming from their own sites, affiliates in these programs also receive a commission based on the activity of affiliate sites they refer to the merchant site.

You may also, on occasion, run across some affiliate payment agreements that use the page view, or "pay-per-page-view (impression)," payment method. With this method you'll be paying your affiliates a total that is determined by the number of Web visitors who actually look at your banner ad. This type of payment agreement is really just an advertising technique that is linked to the use of your banner ads. There is one big difference between an affiliate program and an advertising program such as banner ad network programs: In an affiliate program, you only pay your affiliates when the action, such as a sale, a click, or a page view, is completed.

How Affiliate Programs Work

You'll find that affiliate programs work quite easily once they're correctly set up; however, there are many processes that run in the background of which you should be aware and that are necessary for the smooth operation of these programs. You'll need to have someone—yourself or someone you hire—keep a log of the actions that determine how your affiliates are paid. This means keeping track of the number of sales you generate from your affiliates and the number of page views that occur after Web visitors have linked to your business site via your affiliate. Most reputable affiliate software packages automate this task and simplify the process by keeping track of all affiliate sales, affiliate earnings, affiliate payments, and other critical information. Here are some of the items that need to be tracked:

- The total number of Web visitors who arrive at your business site after clicking on your link on your affiliate's Web site.

- The total number of Web visitors who notice your banner ad on your affiliate's Web site.

- The total number of Web visitors who generate an actual sale after arriving at your Web site via your affiliate.

You need to keep accurate numbers of the above actions so that your affiliates are paid accordingly. And although it may seem to be a lot of effort and time for you to closely administer your affiliate program by yourself, you'll find that the advantages outweigh the disadvantages. When you have complete control over your affiliate program, you'll be able to decide with which affiliates it is most beneficial for you to work.

Affiliate Program Networks

If you don't want to do all the administrative work yourself for your affiliate program, you can join what are called affiliate program networks, or "affiliate brokers." Affiliate networks act as the go-between for you and your affiliates. These network programs will keep track of all the activity that occurs on your Web site and your affiliate's Web site that has to do with the payment agreement that you've set up. Affiliate networks will take care of all the payment agreements and methods, keep a log of all the actions that take place between your Web site and the affiliate's Web site, manage and maintain all of the links and banner ads that need to be set up on your affiliate's Web site, and keep a list of your affiliate program within their network directory. An alternative to affiliate program networks is purchasing a stand-alone affiliate program, which you install on your Web server, such as ProTrack (**www.affiliatesoftware.net**).

One of the advantages of using an affiliate program network is that you'll have access to a number of different types of affiliate programs at one time so that you can mix and match your payment agreements. You'll be able to find just the right affiliate program that works best for you and your business. Of course, you'll have to pay a commission fee when you join an affiliate program network. Usually, the cost of hiring an affiliate network is about 15 to 25 percent of each transaction that occurs.

Becoming Part of an Affiliate Program

Becoming part of an affiliate program is a way that you can increase the success and profits of your Web site. Before you take part in an affiliate program, you need to decide what role you want to play in the process: the affiliate, the merchant Web site that affiliates, or a combination of both. If you have an online business Web site, you'll most likely want to have affiliates that are going to send potential customers to your site and increase the success and profits of your online or brick-and-mortar business. Those people who have a small Web site that offers content rather than sales may want to be an affiliate for a few business Web sites. The bottom line is that you need to decide how your Web site will best benefit and then take the steps to becoming an affiliate, having an affiliate, or being a little of both.

BEING AN AFFILIATE

The steps you need to take to be an affiliate for other Web sites are easy to implement. All you need to do is find an affiliate program network site on the Internet and join by filling out a simple application form that gathers the following information: 1) information that is personal, such as your name, address, and the type of payment plan that you prefer, including payment address, and 2) information about your Web site, such as your Web address (URL), the name of your Web site, and a description of your Web site. Once you've filled out the information form, you'll be asked to sign what is called a "service agreement" so that both you and the affiliate network are clear about the terms and conditions.

You may have to wait a few days to find out if your application to become an affiliate has been approved, at which time you can choose the type of affiliate programs that appeal to you the most and in which you would like to take part (most merchants have only one option). After you've chosen a few affiliate programs, it will be time for the "merchants" to view your Web site to see if they want to use you as an affiliate. Once you've been approved, the affiliate program network will help you in hosting the links and banner ads on your Web site that correspond with your chosen affiliate program. At this time you may be asked to work out the finer details of the payment side of things, such as which action you're going to be paid for and how much, such as pay-per-click, pay-per-lead, or pay-per-sale; however, this is typically set in advance. Most affiliate programs will only pay you once a certain minimum amount of earnings has been reached because the profit that you make as an affiliate doesn't amount to thousands. This is so that the affiliate network doesn't send out small amounts of money that add up to a small total. Additionally, most affiliates do not honor sales for purchases that you make through your own affiliate link. After you've been set up as an affiliate and understand for which actions you're being paid and how much, you can concentrate on the content and purpose of your Web site.

HAVING AFFILIATES

If you want to have affiliates that are going to advertise your business Web site, you can start your own affiliate program, as mentioned previously, with one of many programs available, or you can join an affiliate program network so that someone else can do the work for you. When you join an affiliate network, you'll have all the help that you need in setting up the program and choosing the right affiliates for your Web site. Most affiliate software packages offer free installation and setup.

When you first contact the affiliate network, you'll be asked to fill out an application form that defines your Web site and gives a general description of what products or services it promotes and sells. At this time you'll also sign an agreement for the conditions and terms of the program such as for which actions you want to pay (pay-per-click, pay-per-lead, or pay-per-sale). You'll also have to make a few deposits and pay a fee to become a member of the affiliate program. Many affiliate networks will charge you a one-time fee to join as well as a fee that you pay each year so that you can use the services that they provide.

The cost of joining an affiliate network will be anywhere from $500 to $6,000, depending on how successful the network is, which is a major factor in joining the network or in initiating your own affiliate program. Keep in mind that you'll also be paying each of your affiliates, and in addition, a portion of each payout will go back to the affiliate network. So just what do you get for all this money that you're paying for advertising? Your advertising budget will include complete setup of the affiliate program, accurate details of all actions that happen within your affiliate program, the sending of payments to your affiliates, and having your banner ad and links properly distributed to your chosen affiliates.

Most affiliate networks will allow you to choose your affiliates, or you can also choose to use any and all Web sites that are interested in linking to your Web site, which is a very common choice.

Joining an affiliate program network means that you won't have to do all the hard work necessary to running a successful affiliate program. When you run the show yourself, you need to find the right affiliates, buy software that is going to keep track of the affiliate actions so that you can pay accordingly, show your affiliates how to post your links and banner ads on their Web sites, manage all the accounting for your affiliate program, and be available at all times to help your affiliates and answer any questions that they have.

If you do decide to run the affiliate program yourself, you can buy software that is specific to keeping track of the action that takes place between your Web site and the Web sites of your affiliates. You can expect to pay from $150 to $600 for this type of software. The other alternative to buying tracking software is to join up with a Web site that will keep track of your affiliate action on their site, charging you a fee to release this information to you.

How Affiliates Link to Your Web Site

The next thing that you need to know about how an affiliate program works is how your affiliates are going to link back to your business Web site. There are several ways that this can be accomplished, depending on which method works best for you and your Web site. Here is a list of some of the more common methods of having your affiliates link to your Web site:

- **Banner ad links.** Banner ads use a combination of text and graphics to catch the attention of Web visitors so that they click on the link and end up on your Web site.

- **Text and content links.** Text links on your affiliate Web site are mixed in with the content of each Web page and usually appear as blue text so that Web visitors can click on the text and link to your Web site. Text links are a great form of advertising because they are less intrusive to the eye of a Web visitor than other advertisements that many Web visitors are trying to avoid. Using text links in the content of Web pages is becoming more popular as advertisers search for ways to make advertising on the Internet more subtle.

- **Links from a search box.** When Web visitors search through databases online, they can follow links back to your Web site. This method of advertising has yet to catch on in a big way when it comes to Internet advertising.

When Web visitors use the links that they find on Web sites, there are different ways that they can end up linking back to your Web site. The most common link is a jump to the home page of your Web site. When they arrive at your home page, Web visitors can find out general information about you and your business in a natural way without being forced to immediately look at the products or services that you're selling.

The second way that Web visitors can link to your Web site is by linking from an affiliate's Web site directly to a specific product or service that you're selling. Web visitors can easily find the products that you offer without searching through your Web site for the right Web page. This type of link is known as a "product-specific" link.

Another way that people can link back your Web site is through the use of storefronts. The storefront is a great way to let visitors to your Web site see a variety of the products or services that you're selling. You'll have the ability to change the way your storefront looks and the products that you're featuring whenever you want to try something new.

The fourth method of letting Web visitors link back to your Web site is called "co-branding." With this method, your affiliates can have their own separate identities on the Internet, while at the same time having visitors to their Web sites link to your business Web site. Your Web site will handle all of the sales for your business, but you'll have some appearance on your Web site of your affiliates so that, many times, Web visitors won't even know that they have been on two different Web sites.

The final way that Web visitors can link back to your Web site is by clicking a link and ending up on a registration page on your Web page. Using the registration link method, people need to register before they can browse through your Web pages. This is the least preferred method, as many site visitors will go elsewhere when presented with yet another request for information or personal data.

The Success of Affiliate Programs

Just what makes an affiliate program a successful and profitable choice? The main reason is that when you use an affiliate program, you have the ability to use links to encourage people to visit your Web site, browse your content, browse through your products and services, and potentially become customers in your database.

Essentially, by using an affiliate program, you're replicating your Web site and products to hundreds or thousands of other Web sites throughout the world, dramatically increasing the exposure and potential sales for your profits—all at little or no cost.

For the most part, affiliate programs work best when the affiliate, the merchant, and the links all have something in common with the product or service that is being sold. When you, as a merchant, make wise choices about which affiliates you want to host your Web links, you have a better chance of catching the interest of customers and potential customers. You come out ahead because you get those customers that you might not otherwise get, while at the same time your affiliates come out ahead because they can be linked to products that have something to do with their Web site without ever having to run an e-commerce Web site of their own. If you're using an affiliate network program, the network also comes out ahead because they earn a profit by bringing you and your affiliate together and taking care of the finer details of managing the affiliate program for you.

Affiliate Marketing Definitions and Terms

Source for terms and definitions:
www.marketingterms.com/dictionary/9/

Affiliate: The publisher/salesperson in an affiliate marketing relationship.

Affiliate directory: A categorized listing of affiliate programs.

Affiliate forum: An online community where visitors may read and post topics related to affiliate marketing.

Affiliate fraud: Bogus activity generated by an affiliate in an attempt to generate illegitimate, unearned revenue.

Affiliate marketing: Revenue sharing between online advertisers/ merchants and online publishers/salespeople, whereby compensation is based on performance measures, typically in the form of sales, clicks, registrations, or a hybrid model.

Affiliate merchant: The advertiser in an affiliate marketing relationship.

Affiliate network: A value-added intermediary providing services, including aggregation, for affiliate merchants and affiliates.

Affiliate software: Software that, at a minimum, provides tracking and reporting of commission-triggering actions (sales, registrations, or clicks) from affiliate links.

Exclusivity: Contract term in which one party grants another party sole rights with regard to a particular business function.

Payment threshold: The minimum accumulated commission an affiliate must earn to trigger payment from an affiliate program.

Return days: The number of days an affiliate can earn commission on a conversion (sale or lead) by a referred visitor.

Super affiliate: An affiliate capable of generating a significant percentage of an affiliate program's activity.

Two-tier affiliate program: Affiliate program structure whereby affiliates earn commissions on their conversions as well as conversions of Webmasters they refer to the program.

CHAPTER 15

Promoting Your Business Offline

While this book is certainly geared toward no- and low-cost advertising techniques for your online business, there is another benefit to consider: publicity campaigns, as well as other promotional and advertising opportunities, which can apply to both your online or traditional brick-and-mortar business. Your goal is to increase profits and expand your business, without spending a significant portion of your budget in the process

Publicity can earn you a reputation as the expert in your specialty or target market and can help you gain public trust, recognition, and respect, which ultimately lead to new customers and increased profits for your business. Your goal is to attain this without spending thousands of dollars on traditional, and often risky, methods of marketing and advertising. One way you can help achieve this is by developing your own media kits. When you "make" your own media kit, you'll develop techniques that work for you and your company and at minimal cost. A media kit be can comprise of written text as well as online or office videos, CD-ROMs, DVDs, or other distributable media. It is common to convert large media files to Adobe Acrobat PDFs to distribute easily on the Web.

Many times, potential customers will only buy from a business that they trust or that has been recommended to them by a satisfied customer or friend. Building a media kit or press release kit can reveal significant amounts of information about your business and will satisfy potential customers, distributors, and even public media outlets. By developing your own media kits, you can implement advertising and publicity campaigns that will affirm your position in the marketplace. It's certainly possible for you to get advertising exposure offline without spending $5,000 per month or more on Internet advertising, hiring a PR agency, or advertising offline.

Mass media is another potential outlet for you to consider, although this is often a costly venture. Mass media includes radio, TV, and print (magazines and newspapers). Mass media will allow you to quickly create your own advertising exposure so that you build up the creditability that wins new customers and keeps these customers as repeat customers. When you gain that level of trust, you get increased customer confidence, more sales, and higher profits. Here are some ideas for increasing publicity and promotion offline, which are typically no cost and may even generate revenue for your business:`

- **Offer to be a speaker** at a seminar or lecture. You can also lead workshops that have a direct correlation to the products and services that your business is selling. This is a great way to gain the public exposure that you need to appear positive and confident about your business. This exposure will add to your trust and credibility for potential customers. Make sure that you hand out business cards that include your Web site URL so that people can find your Web site on the Internet.

- **Write opinions and articles** for online publications. Make sure that you upload any articles that you write to your Web site. These online publications will provide what are called "hotlinks" back to your own Web site, which is a great way to further promote your online business Web site. Make sure that you include your e-mail in the byline of any articles and opinions that you write.

- **Radio (including streamed radio) is a valuable resource** for what is called "re-used" media. Make sure that you always get the most leverage out of anything you write or develop for any type of media. Make sure that you're prepared for any media opportunity that comes your way. Try to have several articles or press releases ready ahead of time so that you can read your article on the radio and promote your business offline.

Writing for print media, such as newspapers and magazines, allows you to add your business byline at the end of a column that has to do with the products or services that you're selling. Write an article that describes new products or reviews successful ones. You want to optimize your print exposure in any way that you can. The possibilities are endless when it comes to where you can submit your articles and subtly promote your business, as some quick research on the Internet will show you. Consider submitting articles to newspapers, trade publications, and any other possible outlets. Eventually, you will triumph, and once you are in print, it is easier to have subsequent articles published.

Increasing Your Public Exposure and Profile, Both Offline and Online

You want people to know that you are capable, upbeat, confident, and credible. You want to increase your business reputation and profile by taking advantage of any media exposure opportunities that allow you and your business to present your products and services, and thus your knowledge, in a variety of venues that highlight your business as the best in the market. Why spend thousands of dollars when you can gain market awareness for free?

Brand Recognition and How You Achieve It

Brand recognition assists you as you establish and expand your online presence. It's easier when you use a media kit to help secure your positioning in the marketplace. By creating your own media, you have the control over all the aspects of marketing, and you will have achieved a major milestone in promoting your business. The aim of successful brand recognition is that your customers will recognize your name and will be willing to buy, and even pay more for, your products and services because of your commitment to value and quality. You need to remind your customers often that their decision to buy from you was the right decision. You let your customers know this by sending links or e-mail newsletters that highlight the media exposure that you have developed. You can never stop promoting your company—it's a continuous circle of advertising, promotion, and publicity.

By building your business profile, along with your brand recognition, you greatly improve your trustworthiness and credibility within the offline and online marketplace. This stops the high exit-and-drop rates that are often experienced by many Web sites as Web visitors come and go when they are not familiar with your company or its products and services.

Be an Expert About Your Products and Services

Knowing you're an expert in the marketplace isn't going to be enough; you need to let the public and your customers know that you are an expert. Successful marketing is one of several things that will determine the prosperity or failure of your online business. Here are some tactics and tips that you can use for the successful marketing of your business:

- **Be creative and look outside of the box.** You need to establish new ways of marketing your products and services. Take time to examine your competitors so that you know what they're doing and what you have to do better. Visit niche product sites online, and then model their promotions.

- **Brand recognition and continuity.** This is an important, although many times overlooked, tactic in establishing the credibility of your company and the quality of the products that you provide. Put your company logo at the top of your online order forms to encourage brand recognition. People will get to know your business, and familiarity with your products and services will lead to success. Make your guarantees clear to customers, and honor them.

- **Take the occasional risk.** Taking a stand and voicing an opinion in a respectful debate will win you attention and respect for your leadership in the marketplace.

- **Build an advertising campaign** not only around your product or services, but around current events, community support, and unique marketing campaigns.

Positioning yourself as an expert in your target market takes patience, time, and confidence. Just knowing the advantages of effective marketing is half the battle in getting there. Remember, it's the combination of advertising online and offline that really communicates the benefits and unique aspects of your business, and that will drive potential customers to your Web site.

Publish Your Market Knowledge

Take any opportunity to publish your knowledge about your products and services since there are several advantages that will aid your online marketing strategy. Foremost, publishing your knowledge puts you in the position of expert in your product market, which draws traffic to your Web site and contributes to your brand recognition.

Your goal when it comes to publishing your expert knowledge is to publish for free. There are ways that you can publish a full page of promoting yourself and your business without spending a dime. Contact editors of trade and other publications and offer them your press releases or articles for their next publication. Many editors are looking for useful and relevant content so that they can meet deadlines. You need to take advantage of this opportunity and create the perfect article for publication. Make sure that you target newspapers, magazines, newsletters, Web sites, and Web magazines as ideal opportunities for displaying your article. Keep in mind that magazines that have both an offline and an online image are excellent for increased exposure for driving customers to your Web site and increasing the public awareness of your company and its products or services.

CHAPTER 16

Unlocking the Secrets of EBay

Don't make the mistake of overlooking the potential of eBay sales and how they can dramatically improve the visibility and sales of your products. There are many advantages to advertising and selling products on eBay, and the low cost is one of the main reasons. eBay is one advertising opportunity that you might not want to miss so that you can maximize your business exposure on the Internet through a variety of targeted and auction-style sales. When you open and operate an eBay storefront (or eBay store), you can connect with millions of people every day who shop on eBay.

By opening an eBay store, you can promote your products online through eBay. To assist you with the process, eBay provides you with an array of tools and wizards to facilitate the process. You can typically have your storefront operating in less than an hour. eBay provides you with a wide range of management tools and, most importantly, provides you with the eBay turbo loader software, which manages your inventory, controls pricing, and allows you to easily list any or all products on eBay with just few simple mouse clicks.

It costs very little for you to open an eBay store. For as little as $15.95 per month, you can start to boost your Internet presence, increase your sales, and add to your customer database. When you start an eBay store, you'll have these tools at your disposal:

- An online storefront that is completely yours to develop and create to fit your business needs.

- Easy tools to manage the running of your eBay store.

- Tracking methods and a way to analyze how your business is doing within the eBay community.

- Tools at hand for marketing and merchandising your product.

Benefits of an EBay Storefront

When you open an eBay storefront, you'll find that there are many benefits to you and your business. An eBay storefront gives you the opportunity to reach thousands of people each day and increase the exposure that you need to obtain more customers. One of the big benefits of having an eBay storefront is that it gives your Web site a look of professionalism that is going to give you the credibility that you need to reach customers who are looking for a particular product or service on the Internet. It takes only a few minutes to start your eBay store, which means that you'll be up and running in no time and ready for customers to find you. Many business that already have a their own Web site still use eBay storefronts as a tool to reach even more customers on a daily basis.

You are able to customize your storefront to the exact design that you feel best stylizes the products that you're selling. There are over twenty different design categories from which you can choose when you sign up for an eBay storefront, or you can simply design your own (even based on your current Web site design). One of the most overlooked benefits, aside from the increased visibility and generated Web sales, is that when you operate an eBay storefront, you are given a unique Web site address or URL on the Internet so that customers can find you quickly and easily, bookmarking your storefront Web site so that they can return again later for repeat sales and to find out what's new in your store. Of even more significance is the fact that this Web site URL can be submitted to all search engines, dramatically increasing your overall sales visibility within the search engines and on the World Wide Web.

Each month, you'll have access to a variety of reports that will let you know exactly how your product sales are doing. Some of the data information that you'll receive each month includes a traffic report so that you know how many Web visitors are stopping by your eBay storefront, sales reports to let you know how many sales your storefront has generated, and accounting information that you can use to export your PayPal and eBay sales transactions into accounting software programs such as QuickBooks or your own Excel spreadsheet.

EBay Storefront Promotion

When it comes to the promotion of your eBay storefront, you won't be left in the cold since eBay will give you all the help that you need to bring customers to your eBay store. EBay will list your storefront on all the appropriate listings within their Web site pages and will send out marketing correspondence to your customers.

When you sign up with eBay storefront, you'll have a search engine in the content of your store. This means that your customers will be able to use this search tool to find the products or services that you're selling. You'll save a lot of time using the eBay storefront to sell your products and spend more time concentrating on your business and other marketing strategies. When you sign up with eBay storefront, you'll see a definite increase in your sales and profits and you will watch your customer database grow and turn into repeat sales. You should consider linking your main Web site to your eBay storefront, offering the opportunity for customers to shop in the auction-style storefront setting of eBay as an alternative to fixed prices.

How to Get Started with EBay Sales

You need some basic equipment to establish an eBay storefront. In addition, you must complete some financial documents to establish your store's online identity and payment method. You will need a good, dependable computer. We recommend a standard Pentium III or higher and 20 to 40GB of free hard disk space with an available USB 2.0 or Firewire port to connect to your digital camera. A digital camera is a must because, as you will read in the hints section, digital imagery of products greatly increases your product sales. You must have a good e-mail address, and we highly recommend you create one just for your eBay sales traffic. You will need a bank account or PayPal (or both). We recommend you establish a PayPal account and make this your preferred method of payment since payment is instantaneous and secure. You will need some photo editing software to crop, resize, and touch up your digital photographs. We recommend Corel Paint Shop Pro X (**www.corel .com**) for this purpose. Although not required, it is highly recommended that you design your storefront and product descriptions using HTML code. Purchase Microsoft FrontPage 2002 or higher, which simplifies the HTML process by creating Web sites in a GUI environment, which automatically creates the required HTML code. If you want to display more than one photograph of your product (eBay lets you display one image at no cost), then you will need to have access to a Web server to import your digital images and then insert the HTML links to those images into your eBay storefront.

EBay Tips, Tricks, and Secrets to Generate Sales

- EBay sales are predominantly auction based, and therefore the more bids you receive, the more likely your product will sell at a higher price. Start your listings at a low price to encourage interest and bids. Products with multiple bids tend to sell more frequently and at a higher cost than similar items with a high initial listing price.

- It's all about feedback. This is what your customers say about their shopping experience with you. Feedback can be given on any transaction, and savvy eBay shoppers check the feedback quality of the prospective seller before they bid. Positive feedback of 100 percent is simple to attain: just follow through with sales and quickly package and ship the products and you will always have satisfied customers. As your number of positive feedback grows, so does your status as a reputable seller within the eBay community.

- To create listings from your eBay storefront, here are some simple rules to follow. Again, we recommend you use one of the eBay templates or use Microsoft FrontPage (**www.microsoft.com**) to develop your HTML code.

  — **Don't use ALL CAPITAL LETTERS.**

  — **Be descriptive, and provide lots of detail** on your products. You can expand to include much more than just the product details. This is a great opportunity to tell the prospective bidders why they should have the product, benefits, etc.

  — **Always include one or more digital images.** You get one free with eBay, but we recommend more for certain products where multiple-angle views may enhance sales.

  — **Use HTML code to create your descriptions.** If you just type into the eBay description block, your paragraphs will not be broken up properly and will be difficult to read. Create your description in FrontPage, go to the HTML view, and cut and paste the HTML code into the description block in eBay. Although this is not readable, when displayed in the browser, the HTML code is interpreted and displayed with proper formatting, coloring, tables, etc. Keep your coding simple and classy. Don't overdo it with flashing icons, images, and text that distracts the viewer. A clean, simple interface is best to sell your products. We also recommend you only use white backgrounds for any descriptions or Web pages.

  — **Include shipping costs and methods** (first class, media mail, priority mail, etc.). We recommend you only include flat-rate shipping, which covers your costs for the packaging and shipping costs. You can also pay for shipping and print USPS shipping labels directly from PayPal after the completion of the sale. Shipping estimates or unknown shipping costs will lose potential bidders who are wary of unknown shipping costs. You should figure high for shipping costs, but be reasonable. Twenty dollars to ship a 1 pound book is not reasonable, but $5 may be reasonable. As a side bonus, you can ship books media mail for under $3, making a profit off the excess shipping costs. This is a great way to offset the costs for your eBay and PayPal fees. You should also give some thought to packing materials, which can be expensive. By using USPS priority mail services, you can get free boxes and packing tape. Don't forget about USPS flat-rate boxes and envelopes, which are also free packing material plus have the benefit of flat-fee shipping costs, regardless of the envelope or box weight.

— **Ensure that your description and title are relevant** to what the user will be searching for.

— **If you have multiple items to sell, space them out over time**; don't list one after the other. TurboLister from eBay simplifies this process, and you can also use delayed listings to specific auction listing start times.

— **Highlight the unique features of your products in the title.** Instead of just listing your brand-new product as ASUS K8N-E Deluxe Socket 754 Athlon 64 Motherboard, list it as ASUS K8N-E Deluxe Socket 754 Athlon 64 Motherboard **BRAND-NEW** to emphasize the fact that it is a brand-new product.

— You can list items for three, five, seven, or ten days. You do pay a $0.10 premium per listing for ten-day listings. There is much debate about what length of time items should be listed and when the best time of day is to start a listing. **Seven-day auctions are the standard, and this is what we recommend**, unless you must sell products quickly and opt for the three- or five-day options. As an experienced eBay seller, **you will soon discover that the last 60 seconds of all auctions are when most of the bidding action takes place.**

— **Auctions should start at the lowest amount possible.** Bidders are looking for bargains, and starting bids of a few dollars or less are more likely to attract interest than bids that start at or near full retail value. In most cases, bids for low starting amounts produce significantly more interest (and thus more bids) and typically sell above the expected final bid amount.

— As discussed earlier, **the flat shipping fee should cover your shipping costs (including packaging)** and, potentially, some of your eBay and PayPal fees. Under no circumstances should you ever have a case where the shipping charges do not cover the actual shipping costs.

— **Do not use a reserve price.** The main reason is that people are looking for a deal, and they know that if you have a reserve price, you are not willing to part with the item at a lower price and let them get a great deal. Most bidders will ignore anyone who puts a reserve price. You do take a risk that they may sell for less than your desired profit.

— **Make sure you follow up with the winning bidder via e-mail.** Typically, there is no reason to use the telephone as all eBay communication is Web/e-mail based. EBay accounts should be checked daily at a minimum, or more often for storefronts. You should review the "My Messages" folder for any questions or comments from sellers. We highly recommend you create template e-mails that are generated by eBay when an item you are selling has been won. These e-mails validate the sale, confirm payment information, act as an invoice, and tell the auction winner that you value and appreciate their business and will ensure that they are satisfied with the transaction.

— **Send out a template e-mail when an auction is paid for.** This confirms that payment was received and the order will be processed, and you can tell the customers how the item will ship.

— **We highly recommend using PayPal to generate shipping**

labels for all your products. In addition to being very simple, it also includes free delivery confirmation from the U.S. Postal Service and automatically notifies the winner that their item has been shipped; it will also provide the date and delivery tracking information via e-mail.

If you are interested in learning more about eBay, check out the following books:

- *eBay Income: How ANYONE of Any Age, Location, and/or Background Can Build a Highly Profitable Online Business with eBay.* This title is a complete overview of how eBay works. It also guides you through the whole process of creating the auction and auction strategies. It is available from Atlantic Publishing for $24.95 (Item # EBY-01). Visit **www.atlantic-pub .com** or call 1-800-814-1132 to order.

- *The eBay Success Chronicles: Secrets and Techniques eBay PowerSellers Use Every Day to Make Millions.* PowerSeller experts who make their living on eBay every day share their secrets and proven successful ideas. It is available from Atlantic Publishing for $21.95 (Item # ESC-02). Visit **www.atlantic-pub.com** or call 1-800-814-1132 to order.

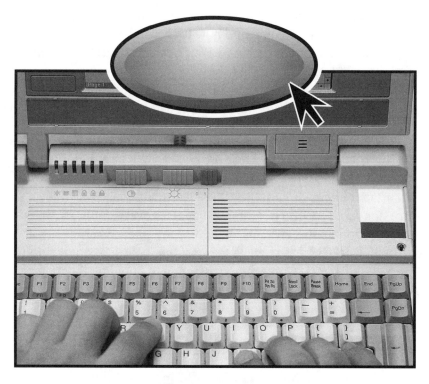

Summary

Using the Internet to advertise for your online or traditional brick-and-mortar business is all about technique, confidence, and planning for success. Set clear, definitive goals, and strive to reach them. Promote your business through any avenue possible—most of them are free. Develop affiliate programs and e-zines, and write professional articles to distribute through a variety of media channels. Market yourself as an expert in
your field.

The advantage of an e-commerce or online business is that you can easily change marketing techniques and implement multiple campaigns through a variety of techniques simultaneously—all at little or no cost. What could be more satisfying than having your customers searching for your products or Web site on the Internet 24/7 to conduct business with YOU? We have presented the best Web design techniques, tips, and hints to optimize your Web site for maximum search engine effectiveness and discussed Web site automation and how to increase the amount of traffic that your Web site receives each day. We discussed basics on establishing your Web site, selecting the right hosting company, implementing an e-commerce solution, and using a variety of marketing and advertising techniques designed to dramatically increase your profit margin.

Create a checklist of items to complete, and work your way through them. This checklist may quickly grow and seem to be a daunting and overwhelming task; however, you don't have to do everything at once, and you can implement various techniques and monitor how they perform for you. Not every solution is ideal for every online business. Enlist your kids, spouse, friends, or significant other to help you with the "grunt" work (ALT tags, meta tags, writing Web site content, doing research, etc.). There is significant satisfaction in knowing that your family and friends helped make your online business a success.

Top Ten Reasons to Follow the Guidelines in This Book

1. You support other forms of advertising promotions that **work hand-in-hand with the advertising on your own Web site**. You can leave your Web site URL in the most unlikely places on the Internet where it will be seen, noticed, and acted upon.

2. The Internet can be called a "stand alone" advertising portal that allows you to advertise your business to **reach millions of potential customers each day**.

3. **Your business image improves** when you advertise on the Internet. Studies show that when customers can link to your Web site, they consider you to be a legitimate business. These same studies show that when you have a Web site, your business is taken more seriously than when you don't.

4. Advertising on the Internet is **one of most cost-effective methods of advertising** that is available. This is because all the advertising is done "electronically," and therefore you don't have the added expenses of postage, printing, and duplication.

5. **The Internet is interactive and allows you to make changes to**

your Web site that are implemented immediately. This means that you can see results instantly when you make changes to your Web site, or you can change your advertising techniques just as quickly.

6. **The Internet is becoming more and more expandable** when it comes to the types and methods of advertising that can take place on the Web.

7. **The Internet is available and accessible at all times,** which means that you can reach potential customers 24/7.

8. You can **specifically target the marketing areas** that you want to target with little or no expense to your business.

9. Advertising on the Internet **allows you and your business to do market testing on the Internet**. This is because you can test different products or services with very few risks to your investment.

10. Advertising on the Internet means that you'll be able to **stay one step ahead of your competition**.

Here are some other hot tips and other tidbits of information that are sure to help propel your Web site to success:

- Good Web site content is critical.

- Invest in e-zines and e-mail campaigns: they are cheap, easy, and reach many customers instantly.

- Avoid spam at all costs.

- Target your market.

- Learn how to design and maintain your Web site yourself. You can save thousands annually!

- Automate your site. Let it do the work for you!

- Use a robust shopping cart.

- Establish an affiliate program.

- Implement Google and Yahoo! marketing campaigns.

- Do promotions, and do them often!

- Give away free items as an incentive.

- Collect as many leads as possible.

- Communicate effectively.

- Start an eBay storefront.

- Establish a banner advertising program.

- Establish an up-sell or cross-promotion program.

Take the time to follow the guidelines we have provided on search engine optimization, Web site design, e-commerce integration, Web site automation, branding, and online business promotion to keep your site on the competitive edge. No business should miss out on the nearly unlimited free or no-cost advertising, marketing, and promotional potential of the Internet. There are no guarantees on how to achieve top ranking across the major search engines, but the techniques we have provided, along with hard work, determination, and self-promotion, will put you well on your way to achieving top ranking—with the satisfaction that you did it on your own, without hiring "experts," and saving countless thousands of dollars along the way!

Glossary of Terms

Source for terms and definitions: **www.marketingterms.com**

Linking Strategy

Link checker: Tool used to check for broken hyperlinks.

Deep linking: Linking to a Web page other than a site's home page.

Inbound link: A link from a site outside of your site.

Outbound link: A link to a site outside of your site.

Reciprocal links: Links between two sites, often based on an agreement by the site owners to exchange links.

Internet Advertising Definitions and Terms

The following definitions about Internet advertising terms and definitions will give you a better understanding of some of the many Web advertising concepts you need to learn so that you can successfully advertise on the Internet.

Source for terms and definitions:
**http://searchcio.techtarget.com/sDefinition/
0,,sid19_gci211535,00.html**

Ad rotation: Ads are often rotated into ad spaces from a list. This is usually done automatically by software on the Web site or at a central site administered by an ad broker or server facility for a network of Web sites.

Ad space: An ad space is a space on a Web page that is reserved for ads. An ad space group is a group of spaces within a Web site that share the same characteristics so that an ad purchase can be made for the group of spaces.

Ad view: An ad view, synonymous with ad impression, is a single ad that appears on a Web page when the page arrives at the viewer's display. Ad views are what most Web sites sell or prefer to sell. A Web page may offer space for a number of ad views. In general, the term impression is more commonly used.

Ad: For Web advertising, an ad is almost always a banner, a graphic image, or set of animated images (in a file called an animated GIF) of a designated pixel size and byte size limit. An ad or set of ads for a campaign is often referred to as "the creative." Banners and other special advertising that include an interactive or visual element beyond the usual are known as rich media.

Advertising network: A network representing many Web sites in selling advertising, allowing advertising buyers to reach broad audiences relatively easily through run-of-category and run-of-network buys.

Affiliate marketing: Affiliate marketing is the use by a Web site that sells products of other Web sites, called affiliates, to help market the products. Amazon.com, the book seller, created the first large-scale affiliate program and hundreds of other companies have followed since.

Banner: A banner is an advertisement in the form of a graphic image that typically runs across a Web page or is positioned in a margin or other space reserved for ads. Banner ads are usually Graphics Interchange Format (GIF) images. In addition to adhering to size, many Web sites limit the size of the file to a certain number of bytes so that the file will display quickly. Most ads are animated GIFs since animation has been shown to attract a larger percentage of user clicks. The most common larger banner ad is 468 pixels wide by 60 pixels high. Smaller sizes include 125 by 125 and 120 by 90 pixels. These and other banner sizes have been established as standard sizes by the Internet Advertising Bureau.

Beyond the banner: This is the idea that, in addition to banner ads, there are other ways to use the Internet to communicate a marketing message. These include sponsoring a Web site or a particular feature on it; advertising in e-mail newsletters; co-branding with another company and its Web site; contest promotion; and, in general, finding new ways to engage and interact with the desired audience. "Beyond the banner" approaches can also include the interstitial and streaming video infomercial. The banner itself can be transformed into a small rich media event.

Booked space: This is the number of ad views for an ad space that are currently sold out.

Brand, brand name, and branding: A brand is a product, service, or concept that is publicly distinguished from other products, services, or concepts so that it can be easily communicated and usually marketed. A brand name is the name of the distinctive product, service, or concept. Branding is the process of creating and disseminating the brand name. Branding can be applied to the entire corporate identity as well as to individual product and service names. In Web and other media advertising, it is recognized that there is usually some kind of branding value whether or not an immediate, direct response can be measured from an ad or campaign. Companies like Proctor and Gamble have made a science out of creating and evaluating the success of their brand name products.

Caching: The storage of Web files for later re-use at a point more quickly accessed by the end user.

Cache server: In Internet advertising, the caching of pages in a cache server or the user's computer means that some ad views won't be known by the ad counting programs and is a source of concern. There are several techniques for telling the browser not to cache particular pages. On the other hand, specifying no caching for all pages may mean that users will find your site to be slower than you would like.

Click rate: The click rate is the percentage of ad views that resulted in click-throughs. Although there is visibility and branding value in ad views that don't result in a click-through, this value is difficult to measure. A click-through has several values: it's an indication of the ad's effectiveness, and it results in the viewer getting to the advertiser's Web site where other messages can be provided. A new approach is for a click to result not in a link to another site but to an immediate product order window. What a successful click rate is depends on a number of factors, such as the campaign objectives, how enticing the banner message is, how explicit the message is (a message that is complete within the banner may be less apt to be clicked), audience/message matching, how new the banner is, how often it is displayed to the same user, and so forth. In general, click rates for high-repeat, branding banners vary from 0.15 to 1 percent. Ads with provocative, mysterious, or other compelling content can induce click rates ranging from 1 to 5 percent and sometimes higher. The click rate for a given ad tends to diminish with repeated exposure.

Click stream: A click stream is a recorded path of the pages a user requested in going through one or more Web sites. Click stream information can help Web site owners understand how visitors are using their site and which pages are getting the most use. It can help advertisers understand how users get to the client's pages, what pages they look at, and how they go about ordering a product.

Click: According to ad industry recommended guidelines from FAST, a click is "when a visitor interacts with an advertisement." This does not apparently mean simply interacting with a rich media ad, but actually clicking on it so that the visitor is headed toward the advertiser's destination. It also does not mean that the visitor actually waits to fully arrive at the destination, but just that the visitor started going there.

Click-through: A click-through is what is counted by the sponsoring site as a result of an ad click. In practice, click and click-through tend to be used interchangeably. A click-through, however, seems to imply that the user actually received the page. A few advertisers are willing to pay only for click-throughs rather than for ad impressions.

Co-branding: Co-branding on the Web often means two Web sites or Web site sections or features displaying their logos (and thus their brands) together so that the viewer considers the site or feature to be a joint enterprise. Co-branding is often associated with cross-linking between the sites, although it isn't necessary.

Cookie: A cookie is a file on a Web user's hard drive (it's kept in one of the subdirectories under the browser file directory) that is used by Web sites to record data about the user. Some ad rotation software uses cookies to see which ad the user has just seen so that a different ad will be rotated into the next page view.

Cost-per-action: Cost-per-action is what an advertiser pays for each visitor that takes some specifically defined action in response to an ad beyond simply clicking on it. For example, a visitor might visit an advertiser's site and request to be subscribe to its newsletter.

Cost-per-lead: This is a more specific form of cost-per-action in which a visitor provides enough information at the advertiser's site, or in interaction with a rich media ad, to be used as a sales lead. Note that you can estimate cost-per-lead regardless of how you pay for the ad. In other words, buying on a pay-per-lead basis is not required to calculate the cost-per-lead.

Cost-per-sale: Sites that sell products directly from their Web site or can otherwise determine sales generated as the result of an advertising sales lead can calculate the cost-per-sale of Web advertising.

CPA: See cost-per-action.

CPC: See cost-per-click.

CPM: CPM is "cost per thousand" ad impressions, an industry standard measure for selling ads on Web sites. This measure is taken from print advertising. The "M" has nothing to do with "mega" or million. It's taken from the Roman numeral for "thousand."

CPS: See cost-per-sale.

CPTM: CPTM is "cost per thousand targeted" ad impressions, apparently implying that the audience you're selling is targeted to particular demographics.

CTR: See click-through rate.

Demographics: Demographics is data about the size and characteristics of a population or audience, for example, gender, age group, income group, purchasing history, personal preferences, and so forth.

FAST: FAST is a coalition of the Internet Advertising Bureau, the ANA, and the ARF that has recommended or is working on guidelines for consumer privacy, ad models and creative formats, audience and ad impression measurement, and a standard reporting template together with a standard insertion order. FAST originated with Proctor and Gamble's Future of Advertising Stakeholders Summit in August 1998. FAST's first guideline, available in March 1999, was a guideline on "Basic Advertising Measures." Our definitions in this list include the FAST definitions for impression and click.

Filtering: Filtering is the immediate analysis by a program of a user Web page request in order to determine which ad or ads to return in the requested page. A Web page request can tell a Web site or its ad server whether it fits a certain characteristic such as coming from a particular company's address or that the user is using a particular level of browser. The Web ad server can respond accordingly.

Fold: "Above the fold," a term borrowed from print media, refers to an ad that is viewable as soon as the Web page arrives. You don't have to scroll down (or sideways) to see it. Since screen resolution can affect what is immediately viewable, it's good to know whether the Web site's audience tends to set their resolution at 640 by 480 pixels or at 800 by 600 (or higher).

Frequency cap: Restriction on the amount of times a specific visitor is shown a particular advertisement.

Hit: A hit is the sending of a single file whether an HTML file, an image, an audio file, or other file type. Since a single Web page request can bring with it a number of individual files, the number of hits from a site is a not a good indication of its actual use (number of visitors). It does have meaning for the Web site space provider, however, as an indicator of traffic flow.

House ad: Self-promotional ad a company runs on its media outlets to put unsold inventory to use.

Impression: According to the "Basic Advertising Measures," from FAST, an ad industry group, an impression is "The count of a delivered basic advertising unit from an ad distribution point." Impressions are how most Web advertising is sold and the cost is quoted in terms of the cost per thousand impressions (CPM).

Insertion order: An insertion order is a formal, printed order to run an ad campaign. Typically, the insertion order identifies the campaign name, the Web site receiving the order and the planner or buyer giving the order, the individual ads to be run (or who will provide them), the ad sizes, the campaign beginning and end dates, the CPM, the total cost, discounts to be applied, and reporting requirements and possible penalties or stipulations relative to the failure to deliver the impressions.

Inventory: Inventory is the total number of ad views or impressions that a Web site has to sell over a given period of time (usually, inventory is figured by the month).

IO: See insertion order.

Keyword marketing: Putting your message in front of people who are searching using particular keywords and key phrases.

Media broker: Since it's often not efficient for an advertiser to select every Web site it wants to put ads on, media brokers aggregate sites for advertisers and their media planners and buyers, based on demographics and other factors.

Media buyer: A media buyer, usually at an advertising agency, works with a media planner to allocate the money provided for an advertising campaign among specific print or online media (magazines, TV, Web sites, and so forth), and then calls and places the advertising orders. On the Web, placing the order often includes requesting proposals and negotiating the final cost.

Opt-in e-mail: Opt-in e-mail is e-mail containing information or advertising that users explicitly request (opt) to receive. Typically, a Web site invites its visitors to fill out forms identifying subject or product categories that interest them and about which they are willing to receive e-mail from anyone who might send it. The Web site sells the names (with explicit or implicit permission from their visitors) to a company that specializes in collecting mailing lists that represent different interests. Whenever the mailing list company sells its lists to advertisers, the Web site is paid a small amount for each name that it generated for the list. You can sometimes identify opt-in e-mail because it starts with a statement that tells you that you have previously agreed to receive such messages.

Pay-per-click: In pay-per-click advertising, the advertiser pays a certain amount for each click-through to the advertiser's Web site. The amount paid per click-through is arranged at the time of the insertion order and varies considerably. Higher pay-per-click rates recognize that there may be some "no-click" branding value as well as click-through value provided.

Pay-per-lead: In pay-per-lead advertising, the advertiser pays for each sales lead generated. For example, an advertiser might pay for every visitor that clicked on a site and then filled out a form.

Pay-per-sale: Pay-per-sale is not customarily used for ad buys. It is, however, the customary way to pay Web sites that participate in affiliate programs, such as those of Amazon.com and Beyond.com.

Pay-per-view: Since this is the prevalent type of ad buying arrangement at larger Web sites, this term tends to be used only when comparing this most prevalent method with pay-per-click and other methods.

Proof of performance: Some advertisers may want proof that the ads they've bought have actually run and that click-through figures are accurate. In print media, tear sheets taken from a publication prove that an ad was run. On the Web, there is no industry-wide practice for proof of performance. Some buyers rely on the integrity of the media broker and the Web site. The ad buyer usually checks the Web site to determine the ads are actually running. Most buyers require weekly figures during a campaign. A few want to look directly at the figures, viewing the ad server or Web site reporting tool.

Psychographic characteristics: This is a term for personal interest information that is gathered by Web sites by requesting it from users. For example, a Web site could ask users to list the Web sites that they visit most often. Advertisers could use this data to help create a demographic profile for that site.

Rate card: Document detailing prices for various ad placement options.

Rep firm: Ad sales partner specializing primarily in single-site sales.

Reporting template: Although the media have to report data to ad agencies and media planners and buyers during and at the end of each campaign, no standard report is yet available. FAST, the ad industry coalition, is working on a proposed standard reporting template that would enable reporting to be consistent.

Rich media: Rich media is advertising that contains perceptual or interactive elements more elaborate than the usual banner ad. Today, the term is often used for banner ads with popup menus that let the visitor select a particular page to link to on the advertiser's site. Rich media ads are generally more challenging to create and to serve. Some early studies have shown that rich media ads tend to be more effective than ordinary animated banner ads.

ROI: ROI (return on investment) is "the bottom line" on how successful an ad or campaign was in terms of what the returns, generally sales revenue, were for the money expended (invested).

RON: See run-of-network.

ROS: See run-of-site.

Run-of-network: A run-of-network ad is one that is placed to run on all sites within a given network of sites. Ad sales firms handle run-of-network insertion orders in such a way as to optimize results for the buyer consistent with higher priority ad commitments.

Run-of-site: A run-of-site ad is one that is placed to rotate on all nonfeatured ad spaces on a site. CPM rates for run-of-site ads are usually less than for rates for specially-placed ads or sponsorships.

Self-serve advertising: Advertising that can be purchased without the assistance of a sales representative.

Splash page: A splash page (also known as an interstitial) is a preliminary page that precedes the regular home page of a Web site and usually promotes a particular site feature or provides advertising. A splash page is timed to move on to the home page after a short period of time.

Sponsor: Depending on the context, a sponsor simply means an advertiser who has sponsored an ad and, by doing so, has also helped sponsor or sustain the Web site itself. It can also mean an advertiser that has a special relationship with the Web site and supports a special feature of a Web site, such as a writer's column, a Flower-of-the-Day, or a collection of articles on a particular subject.

Sponsorship: Sponsorship is an association with a Web site in some way that gives an advertiser some particular visibility and advantage above that of run-of-site advertising. When associated with specific content, sponsorship can provide a more targeted audience than run-of-site ad buys. Sponsorship also implies a "synergy and resonance" between the Web site and the advertiser. Some sponsorships are available as value-added opportunities for advertisers who buy a certain minimum amount of advertising.

Targeting: Targeting is purchasing ad space on Web sites that match audience and campaign objective requirements. Techtarget.com, with over 20 Web sites targeted to special information technology audiences, is an example of an online publishing business built to enable advertising targeting.

Underdelivery: Delivery of fewer impressions, visitors, or conversions than contracted for a specified period of time.

Unique visitor: A unique visitor is someone with a unique address who is entering a Web site for the first time that day (or some other specified period). Thus, a visitor that returns within the same day is not counted twice. A unique visitors count tells you how many different people there are in your audience during the time period, but not how much they used the site during the period.

User session: A user session is someone with a unique address that enters or reenters a Web site each day (or some other specified period). A user session is sometimes determined by counting only those users that haven't reentered the site within the past 20 minutes or a similar period. User session figures are sometimes used, somewhat incorrectly, to indicate "visits" or "visitors" per day. User sessions are a better indicator of total site activity than "unique visitors" since they indicate frequency of use.

View: A view is, depending on what's meant, either an ad view or a page view. Usually an ad view is what's meant. There can be multiple ad views per page views. View counting should consider that a small percentage of users choose to turn the graphics off (not display the images) in their browser.

Visit: A visit is a Web user with a unique address entering a Web site at some page for the first time that day (or for the first time in a lesser time period). The number of visits is roughly equivalent to the number of different people that visit a site. This term is ambiguous unless the user defines it, since it could mean a user session or it could mean a unique visitor that day.

Search Engine Marketing

Description tag: An HTML tag used by Web page authors to provide a description for search engine listings.

Doorway domain: A domain used specifically to rank well in search engines for particular keywords, serving as an entry point through which visitors pass to the main domain.

Doorway page: A page made specifically to rank well in search engines for particular keywords, serving as an entry point through which visitors pass to the main content.

Invisible Web: The portion of the Web not accessible through Web search engines.

Keyword: A word used in a performing a search.

Keyword density: Keywords as a percentage of indexable text words.

Keyword research: The search for keywords related to your Web site, and the analysis of which ones yield the highest return on investment (ROI).

Keywords tag: META tag used to help define the primary keywords of a Web page.

Link popularity: A measure of the quantity and quality of sites that link to your site.

Link text: The text contained in (and sometimes near) a hyperlink.

Log file: File that records the activity on a Web server.

Manual submission: Adding a URL to the search engines individually by hand.

Meta tag generator: Tool that will output META tags based on input page information.

Meta tags: Tags to describe various aspects about a Web page.

Pay-per-click search engine: Search engine where results are ranked according to the bid amount, and advertisers are charged when a searcher clicks on the search listing.

Search engine optimization: The process of choosing targeted keyword phrases related to a site, and ensuring that the site places well when those keyword phrases are part of a Web search.

Search engine submission: The act of supplying a URL to a search engine in an attempt to make a search engine aware of a site or page.

Search spy: A perpetually refreshing page that provides a real-time view of actual Web searches.

Title tag: HTML tag used to define the text in the top line of a Web browser, also used by many search engines as the title of search listings.

Top 10: The top ten search engine results for a particular search term.

URL: Location of a resource on the Internet.

Volunteer directory: A Web directory staffed primarily by unpaid volunteer editors.

Search Engines and Web Directories

Search engine: A program that indexes documents, then attempts to match documents relevant to the users' search requests.

Metasearch engine: A search engine that displays results from multiple search engines.

Portal: A site featuring a suite of commonly used services, serving as a starting point and frequent gateway to the Web (Web portal) or a niche topic (vertical portal).

Web directory: Organized, categorized listings of Web sites.

AltaVista: Search engine located at **www.altavista.com**.

Ask Jeeves: Metasearch engine located at **www.askjeeves.com**.

DogPile: Metasearch engine located at **www.dogpile.com**.

Excite: Portal located at **www.excite.com**.

Fast Search: Search syndication company located at **www.fastsearch .com** and **www.fast.no** — also powers the search engine located at **www.alltheweb.com**.

Go Network: Defunct portal located at **www.go.com**.

Google: Search engine located at **www.google.com**.

Goto: Pay-per-click search engine that changed names and is now located at **www.overture.com**.

Inktomi: Search syndication company located at **www.inktomi.com**.

Ixquick: Metasearch engine located at **www.ixquick.com**.

Looksmart: Web directory located at **www.looksmart.com**.

Mamma: metasearch engine located at **www.mamma.com**.

MSN Search: Search destination at **search.msn.com**.

Northern Light Search: Search engine located at **www.northernlight.com**.

Raging Search: Search engine located at **www.raging.com**.

Yahoo!: Portal located at **www.yahoo.com**.

Zworks: Metasearch engine located at **www.zworks.com**.

Web Design and Marketing

Ad space: The space on a Web page available for advertisements.

ALT text: HTML attribute that provides alternative text when non-textual elements, typically images, cannot be displayed.

Animated GIF: A graphic in the GIF89a file format that creates the effect of animation by rotating through a series of static images.

Bookmark: A link stored in a Web browser for future reference.

Cascading style sheets (CSS): A data format used to separate style from structure on Web pages.

Favico: A small icon that is used by some browsers to identify a bookmarked Web site.

Flash: multimedia technology developed by Macromedia to allow much interactivity to fit in a relatively small file size.

Frames: A structure that allows for the dividing of a Web page into two or more independent parts.

Home page: The main page of a Web site.

JavaScript: A scripting language developed by Netscape and used to create interactive Web sites.

Linkrot: When Web pages previously accessible at a particular URL are no longer reachable at that URL due to movement or deletion of the pages.

Navigation: That which facilitates movement from one Web page to another Web page.

Shopping cart: Software used to make a site's product catalogue available for online ordering, whereby visitors may select, view, add, delete, and purchase merchandise.

Site search: Search functionality specific to one site.

Splash page: A branding page before the home page of a Web site.

Web browser: A software application that allows for the browsing of the World Wide Web.

Web design: The selection and coordination of available components to create the layout and structure of a Web page.

Web site usability: The ease with which visitors are able to use a Web site.

Additional Case Studies

Case Study for Advertising on the Internet – Banners

The following case study signifies the success that can be achieved by implementing successful Internet advertising techniques to an online business.

Source:**www.martech–intl.com/best2/cybergold.htm**

SUCCESSFUL STRATEGIES FOR YES.COM.HK – A CASE STUDY FOR INTERNET ADVERTISING BUSINESS

Yes.com.hk, a spin-off company of the publisher of the teen magazine *YES!*, started its operation in mid-1996 as a vertical portal for teenagers in Hong Kong. The company has gone through several different business models from subscription-based to B2C and has decided to stay with the pure advertising-based model after the failures of previous business models. Nonetheless, the advertising model has suffered many setbacks after the recent dotcom crash, and yes.com.hk's revenues have decreased since mid-2000. In this paper, we investigate several methods to improve revenue for yes.com.hk by considering the advertising strategies of yes.com.hk. Finally, we make several suggestions based on the results of our analysis.

INTRODUCTION

Traditional media companies—newspapers, magazines, TV, and radio broadcasters—are looking for new ways to obtain more revenue out of the Internet. They are also particularly keen on developing Internet advertising business since their brands are already well known in local communities, and they have plenty of content that can be used on their Web pages to attract viewers. "Everyone in the broadcasting business is experimenting with the Internet to enhance their audience and explore new sources of improving their bottom lines," said Dennis Wharton, spokesman for the National Association of Broadcasters, which represents radio and television broadcasters.

Nevertheless, one of the main challenges is finding the right approach with advertising. "Click-through" rates, or CTR in short, which measure the number of times viewers click onto a particular ad, have plummeted to an average of 0.30 percent from around 8 to 10 percent in 1996, according to industry sources.

BACKGROUND OF YES.COM.HK

In Hong Kong, the management of Yes Communication Ltd., the publisher of the popular teenager magazine *YES!*, realized that the Internet was an attractive medium of information disclosure and a potential lucrative market on its own. For that reason, the company launched a subsidiary named yes.com.hk in 1996, responsible for development of a companion Web site of the magazine.

TEENAGERS – A PROFITABLE MARKET

The success and popularity of the *YES!* magazine, which had a weekly circulation of about 92,000 in the first half of 2000, according to HKABC, is certainly a sound proof that the market dedicated to teenagers is real and profitable.

Teens are often described as being heavy users of media and greatly influenced by images in the media, and thus comprise an appealing market to advertisers and marketers. However, selection of any particular medium by teens varies as a function of the limitations of each medium and the gratifications that are sought by youth. Both traditional and Internet advertising have its limitations of each medium. They make active choices about the media they use according to their personalities, socialization needs, and personal identification needs. In fact, teens already use the Internet as a conduit for social stimulation (Arnett, 2000).

The growing number of single parent families among our society leads to a side effect where teens tend to purchase household goods. In spite of this, special care must be taken to tackle this market because research has shown that teens are skeptical toward advertising and they are more apt at recognizing emotional advertising than previous generation (Manglebury, 2000).

TEENAGERS ON THE INTERNET – PREVIOUS RESEARCH

The interactivity of the Internet provides teens an opportunity to communicate directly with advertisers. The Internet is able to combine several unique qualities of each medium (that is, print, sound, and visual), which was not possible before. Chat rooms and newsgroups are replacing the traditional conversation among young people.

The ability of the Internet to deliver and obtain information in a flexible, effective manner at relatively low costs is very attractive. However, not many research projects have focused on how teens use the Internet and the effects on the time spent with other media activities, as well as its ability to fulfill interpersonal communication needs. Advertisers are not sure about the impact of Internet and its relationship with teens. Logically, what are the most effective advertising strategies for advertisers, to communicate with teens?

PREVIOUS BUSINESS MODELS OF YES.COM.HK

Yes.com.hk's Web site went online in August 1996 and began as a subscription-only content site. The response was not positive, with less than 1,000 subscribers. Therefore, the company abandoned this model in 1998 and provided the content free of charge to all Internet users, with some parts accessible only to registered users, which is also free.

The company has also tried B2C commerce in 1997 by selling online some of the magazines published by the parent company and artist-related items. As local people could buy these directly in the nearby news stands, the customers were mainly from overseas, but the business was plagued by high delivery costs, usually 40 to 200 percent of the items being sold. Realizing that the online business was not likely to be profitable in the near future, in 1999, the management decided to refocus its attention to the advertising business model and, at the same time, keeping the spending under control because it simply makes no sense to spend millions and millions per month without any clear or confident way of making profits, whether it is e-business or not. The cash burn rate of yes.com.hk is less than half a million per month, which is relatively low when we consider the fact that, in February 2001, the average daily hit rate of the Web site was 2 million, and this figure is comparable to large portals like hongkong.com.

CURRENT PRICING SCHEME

Yes.com.hk currently charges advertisers a fixed monthly rate to display banner ads. The fee is negotiable, but usually it is related to the number of impressions.

All the banners at yes.com.hk are random banners, independent of the section of the Web site (ROS or run-of-site banners). Sometimes, yes.com.hk provides editorials that cover certain products at the advertiser's request. The company also offers a special package that combines both the offline print ads of *YES!* magazine with online banner ads, targeted for skeptics of Internet advertising.

Registered Users

As of February 2001, the number of active registered users at yes.com.hk was about 288,000, with a male-to-female ratio of 55:45.

Year 2001—the future of advertising model looks grim—yes.com.hk, upon the decision of focusing mainly in Internet advertising, is facing many challenges ahead. The dotcom bubble outburst, combined with the slowdown of the global economy (Starling, 2000) has forced many companies to reduce their expenses, including ad spending. The average rate (of placing ROS banners) for yes.com.hk has decreased from HK$10,000 per month in early 2000 to HK$8,000 in 2001, a 20 percent decrease.

The hope is not lost, however. Hong Kong was found to have the highest CTR in the world (Lai, 2001). According to a survey in 2000 (Lai, 2000), the industry average CTR in Hong Kong was 0.35 percent and the average CTR of vertical portals in Hong Kong: 0.79 percent Comparing these figures to the average CTR of 1.23 percent of yes.com.hk in 2000, we can see that the company is way ahead of many portals in Hong Kong and the potential to earn profits is still very high.

POTENTIAL COMPETITORS

In the offline world, the magazine *YES!* has so far enjoyed a virtual monopoly in the market. Yes Communication Ltd. possesses a large library of copyrighted photos of famous artists and celebrities of Hong Kong, Taiwan, and Japan that constitutes one of its major strengths and at the same time a tough barrier to entry of other potential players as well.

In the online world, as the cost of switching from one site to another is almost nil, any Web site that appeals to teenagers in Hong Kong is a competitor. This fact has made the advertising business model not profitable up to now.

RESEARCH GOALS

Our research goal is very simple, yet difficult to have an immediate and definite answer: How to make Internet advertising business of yes.com.hk more attractive?

RESEARCH METHODOLOGY

The adoption of successful advertising strategies will very likely help the company to reach profitability. We believe that a good strategy should lead to one of the following:

- Increase in the value of the advertising service so that yes.com.hk can charge more for its services.

- Reduction of the seasonal factors that affect the revenues.

- Attract more people to the Web site, making it more appealing to potential advertisers.

The methodology we describe here to increase the brand value of yes. com.hk is by studying the success factors of the advertising campaigns that the company has helped advertisers in the past. By pushing an ad strategy that encompasses these success factors to potential advertisers, it is likely to increase the probability of success of the campaign. The raise of success rate leads to a better brand name, allowing yes.com.hk to distinguish itself from other Internet Web sites in Hong Kong.

WHY CLICK-THROUGH RATES?

Jakob Nielsen (Nielsen, 1997) believes that only loyal customers will provide revenue for the site and the majority of visitors (site tourists) will not contribute any revenue at all. Therefore, dotcoms should refuse to pay for eyeball measurements like cost per thousand (CPM).

Although many advertisers have found measuring the branding effects of banner ads difficult (Zaret, 2000), a banner click represents an active and positive acknowledgment of having viewed an ad and at least a momentary desire to further investigate the marketing message.

It is of our opinion that click-through rates (CTR) is one step beyond simple eyeball measurements and can be easily traced. As such, CTR is used in this paper as an objective measurement of banner ad effectiveness.

ANALYSIS OF "SUCCESS FACTORS"

Yes.com.hk, being targeted mainly at teenagers, suffers from seasonal fluctuations in traffic due to exam periods and summer vacation. The measurement of success by direct comparison of the click-through rates in different periods would be unfair. As such, a seasonal compensation factor is introduced to make the comparisons more meaningful.

After calculating the success degree values, we have fed the values, along with chosen factors, to a data-mining tool called Clementine for analysis. By using the "Rule Induction" tool, many rules have been extracted. Most of them were irrelevant (confidence level too low), and the two most relevant rules are shown below:

Rule 1. Free gifts = Yes & Celebrities = No & Banner Design = Good => Success = Yes

Rule 2. Game = Yes => Success = Yes

The results (as shown in rule 2) imply that the presence of a small online game is important to the success of the ad campaign. In other words, interactivity of a banner ad is a key factor #1. The success of the Wrigley's chewing gum promotion (Head, 2000) with the use of online games further highlights the importance of interactivity. The research firm KPE has coined the term advergaming for the mix of a small online game with ads (Olsen, 2001a).

Offering free gifts is the next important factor. However, to be effective, the free gifts must be of some value to users. Take the case of Red Earth, for example. Although it has offered 10 percent discount and free make-up products, the overall end result was not satisfactory, because most customers have 20 percent discount with their Esprit cards and the free make-up products were not up to the most current trend. In other words, the need of vertical integration should not be ignored in marketing campaigns.

Banner design is also essential to attract visitors to click. Even when a user does not click on an attractive banner, anything that can capture attention contributes to the brand awareness.

The use of celebrities is not recommended due to the high costs and uncertainty in their effectiveness, unless the product being promoted is somehow related to the person/group (the case of Netvigator.com and Warner Music). Yes.com.hk should, therefore, make recommendations to new advertisers based on the above-mentioned factors.

ADDRESSING THE NEEDS OF TEENAGERS

A study conducted in the United States by Ferle in fall 1997 (Ferle et al, 2000) has found that teenagers used the Internet to fulfill various needs shown in the following list (sorted by decreasing order of importance):

1. Fun and games

2. College/Universities and homework

3. Music

4. Socialization (travel, making friends)

5. Health

6. Shopping

The "New GenerAsians" youth survey in 2000 by AcNielsen has found that ICQ was voted as the most popular tool by HK teenagers, which means that the socialization needs of teenagers in HK are ranked in a relatively high position. Yes.com.hk until now addresses mostly the first point ("fun and games"). Internet music broadcasting was once attempted, but the high costs of licensing music have deterred the company from continuing this activity.

The Web site has currently a section for making friends called "Love Matching." However, the scope is rather limited.

There is still a large room for improvement to fill the gaps for points 2, 4, 5, and 6 above. Therefore, we recommend the addition of chat rooms and private e-mail boxes with online advisers that respond to questions of health and school related problems. As the Internet has a distinctive advantage of allowing anonymity, it is easier for teens to ask embarrassing questions. We believe that incorporating such features will increase the attractiveness of the Web site and the user loyalty.

Since the inclusion of shopping requires a new infrastructure that includes payment gateways, new pricing schemes, and a redesign of the user interface, we suggest the postponement of this problem to a later stage.

Yes.com.hk should also incorporates new types of banner ads, such as rich media banner ads. Yahoo!, the giant Web portal, has recently pushed a new type of rich media ad that provides greater interactivity and better screen effects than simple animated GIFs (Olsen, 2001b). In addition, new banner ad sizes should be tested according to the new rules that the Internet Advertising Bureau has recently issued to build a better "emotional" element into an Internet (Olsen, 2001c).

Almost all of the banner ads hosted by yes.com.hk are random. New packages that offer targeted ads based on the gender, sex, or other preferences of registered members should be provided. By addressing the needs of different advertisers, yes.com.hk may be able to increase its customer base.

Conclusion

As stated in the beginning, the objective of this research was to identify the most effective Internet advertising strategy through banner advertisement for yes.com.hk. An effective strategy can proceed from different perspectives:

- Focus on the users' needs—diversify the content to improve the loyalty of users.

- Focus on the advertisers' needs—provide more flexibility and variety in advertising packages and introduce new pricing schemes.

- Minimize revenue fluctuations—different strategies should be employed for peak and non-peak seasons.

- Increase the success rate of ad campaigns at yes.com.hk.

For the last point, several critical attributes have been identified, which include games, free gifts, celebrities, and banner design, and they were carefully studied. These attributes were selected out from the top 10 banners from January 2000 until May 2001. Data extracted from the existing Web log was processed by the data-mining tool Clementine for analysis.

The research was important because it sought to determine the important attributes that can increase the time spent by teenagers with the ads. The success of banner advertising will prove the legitimacy of the advertising model of yes.com.hk.

Based upon the findings, it was concluded that:

- Small interactive games and free gifts can provide the highest brand impression after normalization of the banner click-through rate.

- The revenue of yes.com.hk was influenced by the seasonal factors such as exam periods and summer vacations.

- Media-rich banner design is important to attract teenagers to click on the banner. It has to include elements such as video, visual, and graphic.

RECOMMENDATIONS

Based on the conclusions, the following recommendations are made:

- Although the attributes that can attract teenagers to yes.com.hk have been identified, ongoing monitoring of user behavior on yes.com.hk is required to understand their navigational behaviors.

- The use of gaming and free gifts is encouraged because they have been proven to be effective in terms of impression and click-through rates.

- The pricing scheme for yes.com.hk should shift from a fixed monthly rate to an adjusted monthly rate according to the level of customization, banner ad size, interactivity, and season. For example, for non-exam periods, yes.com.hk should charge for a higher price due to a higher traffic volume.

Case Study for Advertising on the Internet— Generate More Traffic

The following case study signifies the success that can be achieved by implementing successful Internet advertising techniques to an online business.

Source: **www.martech-intl.com/best2/cybergold.htm**

Web advertising, like the Web itself, is new. When the Web first began, traditional, mainstream companies had no use for advertising in this medium. The birth of advertising on the Web began with "link trades," whereby two Web sites would provide hyperlinks to the other parties' sites.

As the Web grew, link trades proliferated to include commercial advertisers. As the Web's original population was chiefly avid computer enthusiasts, computer companies were the main commercial presence. Computer companies could place links anywhere and be assured of a targeted audience-computer enthusiasts.

The Web soon reached a wider audience. Advertisers from other industries entered the Web advertising fray, paying real money in exchange for hyperlinks. Furthermore, advertising became more formal, with highly designed banner ads replacing simple linked text.

Cybergold, a new Internet advertising company, wants to establish a new paradigm for the Web. Cybergold expects to profit by becoming a primary brokerage of new advertising and by selling its enabling pioneering technologies to other potential Internet partners. Cybergold faces vast challenges since it must demonstrate the viability of both its advertising concept and its enabling technology in order to survive.

THE PROBLEM

Widespread Web advertising has spawned the need for effectiveness and pricing measures. How much does it cost to reach an appropriate and interested audience? How can an advertiser be certain the audience has been reached?

Today's dominant pricing model is measured in CPM, a standard advertising industry measure for cost per thousand. This figure attempts to describe the cost of exposing an advertisement to 1,000 people through traditional media such as newspapers, television, and radio spots. On the Web, the CPM paradigm is less well understood and explained; however, it is an industry standard that advertisers are used to, so CPM on the Internet will not disappear quickly, if at all.

At the present, Web CPMs range from around $10 up to $150 for popular sites like HotWired. This fee per 1000 consumers is not small — a CPM of $15 translates to $15,000 for a four-week placement. Lower CPMs generally indicate high-volume, untargeted traffic. Sites with a higher CPM generally have a more loyal following and let advertisers target a more specific audience, such as those reading *The Wall Street Journal* online.

OTHER QUANTITATIVE MEASURES

Transfer rates measure the number of clicks on an ad, indicating how many viewers are paying attention to that ad. Through the act of clicking on the ad, impressions — where the number of users who call up a page with an ad banner on the ad — are counted.

Impressions may also be referred to as page views.

Click-throughs – Where the number of users who click on an ad banner are counted. Click-through rates range from 1 to 10 percent of page views.

Keyword searches – Where search engines sell banner ads for particular, popular searches on their site. Whenever anyone searches for "apartments" on any of the major search engines, for instance, a RentNet banner will appear.

Sponsorships – Where sponsors generally obtain prominence or exclusivity in particular areas on a Web site. This category includes entitlements — getting a sponsor's brand into an area's title.

Joint developments – Where an advertiser's brand and products are integrated into the content of the site itself, often in a game or narrative, blurring distinctions between advertising and editorial.

THE OUTCOME

Cybergold was founded by Nat Goldhaber in 1995 and based on the attention theory work of his philosopher cousin. Nat's cousin believes our global society is turning into an attention society where the largest payment anyone can give is his or her attention. Cybergold matches this concept of attention as a valuable commodity with the interactive, multimedia, and user tracking capabilities of the World Wide Web.

Cybergold is a group of very well-known experts with an unproven concept. Whether Cybergold can live up to the brand equity built on its board's reputation and unique idea remains to be seen. However, this strategically created entity is sure to draw both immense publicity and speculators by the droves.

The basic Cybergold concept is to have advertisers pay potential consumers to focus on product information. The concept seems foreign and unworkable based on today's understanding of advertising as unwanted, broadcast noise. Cybergold hopes to propagate this "payment for attention" advertising concept by changing all the rules of the current game.

Cybergold members fill out an initial questionnaire to specify their profile and areas of interest.

Every time consumers log onto Cybergold, they allow the system to glean more information about them. Cybergold tracks information such as time spent within an ad, which ads are chosen and in what order, where the consumer chose to click within ads, what time of day the consumer logged in, and whether the consumer answered the ad questions and/or participatory information correctly, and tracks the evolving preferences of this consumer through the life of the relationship.

Second, Cybergold will harness the interactive and multimedia capabilities of the Web to make the advertising entertaining. Cybergold will provide members with three minutes of information, games, and a quiz about the content of the site they just viewed. This means that consumers will consider Web advertisements to be a fun activity worthy of their effort and attention.

Third, Cybergold will only charge advertisers for consumers who actually view and participate in their Web advertisements. A member must complete an activity or quiz within the Web advertisement to be paid for his or her attention.

Finally, Cybergold will pay members for their attention in "Cybergold" via cash, airline miles, or charitable donations. They are looking to change this payment scheme in the near future when a better, more global e-cash payment scheme emerges as the Internet standard.

CYBERGOLD

If the concept works, Cybergold will open up a whole new concept in advertising with many potential avenues of growth for the company.

Case Study for Advertising on the Internet— Putting It All Together

The following case study signifies the success that can be achieved by implementing successful Internet advertising techniques to an online business.

Source: **www.martech-intl.com/best2/marshall.htm**

Marshall Industries was one of the first companies in its sector — distribution of electronic components — to recognise and take advantage of the opportunities offered by information systems, computer networking, collaborative tools, Intranets, and the Internet. These new technologies play a key role in helping Marshall differentiate its offering from that of its competitors and establish a competitive advantage in what is basically a commodities market.

Marshall Industries is the fifth largest domestic U.S. distributor of industrial electronic components and production supplies. Sales growth really took off in 1993, when total sales grew at 13.5 percent, followed by 26 percent in 1994 and 22.7 percent in 1995. Most of Marshall's customers are OEM manufacturers in computer mainframes, office equipment, communication, etc. Marshall distributes semiconductors, connectors, passive components, computer systems and peripherals, production supplies, tool kits, instrumentation, and workstations from 150 suppliers, mainly brand names. The products fall into over 170,000 individual parts numbers.

THE PROBLEM

Marshall faces two challenges today. It needs to maintain the first-mover advantage it gained through using the new technologies to improve and optimise its relationship with its constituents, as its competitors follow in its footsteps and start offering similar services; this will be achieved through constant innovation. In addition, it needs to learn how to compete in a new market, the interactive and entertainment services industry; this will mean developing new skills beyond technological competencies.

Rob Rodin, the CEO, clearly wanted his company to be seen as an innovator, ahead of its competitors. These objectives, of course, were subject to the need that the changes generate revenues and new customers, although Marshall does not focus as much as its competitors on financial targets at the micro, individual activity levels. Instead, it is more interested in the global effects of the company. This means that projects such as the redesign of information systems and the introduction of groupware, Intranets, and Internet were not implemented on the basis of a predicted fixed ROI. Top management was, however, convinced (and remains convinced) that electronic-based applications would significantly contribute to the company's financial results.

Before implementing electronic-based applications, Marshall did carry out some basic market research. It organized focus groups with customers (who would be the future users of the systems) and employees (who were the most familiar with the legacy systems). Many engineers declared that they did not see a use for electronics-based applications. However, Marshall believed that these results were due to generational differences among engineers, since a 25 year-old engineer is completely different from a 50 year-old engineer.

In the beginning, therefore, Marshall made the decisions for its constituents — customers, suppliers, and employees, believing that customers do not always know what they want in advance.

Marshall distinguishes between two different kinds of customers:

- **Design engineers**, who constitute its core customers. These people are looking for technological specs and want to know what's out there and how it all compares. Although they had declared that they would not use the billboard advertising on the Web during the original focus groups, in reality they make extensive use of these and advertising has become a major source of revenues for Marshall. Purchasing is almost spontaneous. The Internet has given these customers a vehicle facilitating their purchases. They are given information concerning price, availability, and product characteristics. Marshall was actually forced to create sites for more than fifty of its suppliers, which did not have a Web presence.

Suppliers provided the content and Marshall converted this content into a harmonized site. Some suppliers showed strong resistance and invoked all kinds of reasons for not wanting to prepare such sites, such as legal reasons (what if there is a mistake in the specifications?). Marshall convinced them by proving to them that there was little difference between information on the Internet and information on paper, that the problems in the real world were the same as the problems in the virtual world.

- **Purchasing departments of manufacturing companies**, who are negotiating long-term, high-volume, high-price contracts with Marshall. They care more about prices, lead times, ordering forms, out-of-stocks, etc. Their relationship with Marshall continues to be mainly based on direct, telephone or face-to-face interactions.

THE OUTCOME

Marshall's Internet solution contains password/SSL-protected areas with customised information for specific classes of users. A new service specificly for design engineers should soon be introduced. It is used by suppliers to find information about sales volumes, design registration activity, pending sales opportunities, and quotations. Customers use it to find information about backlog, credit limit, work in progress, purchases to date, pricing, and inventory.

The nature of Marshall's relationships with its suppliers depended on the sophistication of these suppliers. The least sophisticated waited for monthly paper reports on the state of business. However, suppliers realised that they could not afford to wait 30 days to get the information and that constant, up-to-date information was necessary. Marshall undertook an aggressive campaign to move over its suppliers to electronic-based solutions. It organized interactive multimedia seminars over the Internet, in which over 100 suppliers participated. Suppliers understood that they needed to follow in order to remain competitive.

Marshall is currently running a pilot program to test the potential for doing EDI over the Internet. As there is too little demand yet from suppliers, Marshall prefers to wait until suppliers integrate this technology into their workflow before it starts pushing this feature.

ASSESSMENT

The company also claims that the Web site has produced 125,000 new customers since 1994 and that 10,000 new addresses are logged on each month from 67 countries. A reliable cost-benefit analysis is difficult to carry out. On the cost side, the company says it has invested $1 million in development costs of the Web site since 1994. During the last three years, employment decreased 16 percent while sales doubled.

Resources

The following resources and their URLs have been compiled to point you in the right direction for tips, advice, software, and other information that you will find useful for your business. This is certainly not an all-encompassing list; however, it is our list of preferred companies.

DOMAIN NAME REGISTRATION

GoDaddy.com
 www.godaddy.com

WEB HOSTING COMPANIES

Readyhosting
 www.readyhosting.com

Verio
 www.verio.com

Rackspace
 www.rackspace.com

WEB SITE DESIGN

Gizmo Graphics Web Design
 www.gizwebs.com

Secure Server Certificates

GoDaddy
www.godaddyssl.com

Geotrust
www.thawte.com

VeriSign
www.verisign.com

E-commerce Software

Monster Commerce
www.monstercommerce.com

PDG Software
www.pdgsoft.com

PayPal
www.paypal.com

Rich Media Technologies
www.justaddcommerce.com

E-Commerce Templates
www.ecommercetemplates.com/

DemandWare
www.demandware.com/solution2.html

Search Engine Optimization

Google
www.google.com/webmasters/seo.html

Intelligent Web Marketing
www.i-web-marketing.com

CPM (clicks per impression) Calculator
   www.clickz.com/resources/adres/cpm_calculator/

Logo Design

Logo Twister
   www.logotwister.com

LogoWorks
   www.logoworks.com

Permission-Based E-Mail/E-Zine Management

Topica.com
   www.topica.com

Marketing Definitions—An Exhaustive Review

Marketing Terms
   www.marketingterms.com

Index

meta tag 47, 146, 170

Microsoft FrontPage 99

N

network 184, 199, 215

newsletters 49, 120

O

opt-in 117, 126

opt-out 126

Overture 206

P

page views 180

pay-per-click 176, 213

payment 99

PayPal 18

penalties 136

pixels 178

postcards 120

press release 66

privacy 160

proxies 138

Q

quantity discounts 21

Quickbooks 24

R

repeat customers 48

S

sales tax 24

search 72, 206, 219

search engines 47, 143

security 44

server 137, 139

Shockwave 179

shopping cart 19, 26, 109

spam 134, 170

storefront 23

T

tag 148

target market 88

testimonials 71

title tag 170

About the Author

Bruce Brown has been an officer in the United States Coast Guard for more than 22 years and is currently stationed as Comptroller at the Coast Guard Air Station in Clearwater, Florida. Prior to this assignment, he was heavily involved in designing document imaging applications and Web-based financial application systems design and deployment for the Coast Guard Finance Center in Chesapeake, Virginia. For the past eight years, he has owned and operated of a small Web design and consulting firm. He currently resides in Land O' Lakes, Florida, with his wife, Vonda, and youngest son, Colton. His oldest son, Dalton, is currently attending the University of South Florida and his other son, Jordan, is attending the University of Florida.

Here's What Experts Say About

How to Use the Internet to Advertise, Promote, and Market Your Business or Web Site—With Little or No Money

"This book is one of most complete Internet business how-to guides I have ever seen."

> — **Chris Nelson, CEO**
> Capital Merchant Solutions Inc
> www.FreeAuthNet.com

"This book has it all! With so many how-to-build-your-own-Web-business books on the market, this book exceeds all with up-to-date information, legitimate, low-cost, and effective Internet marketing strategies."

> — **Jennifer Somogyi**
> Founder - The Professional Women's Outreach
> Organization - www.pwoo.org
> Developer - Search Engine Marketing
> Discussion - www.search-engine-marketing-discussion.com

"Once upon a time, Web entrepreneurs were sold the idea that simply having a Web site would enable them to reach a whole new world of customers, day or night. In all the hype, they forgot that the same thing is true of owning a telephone. In his book, How to Use the Internet to Advertise, Promote, and Market Your Business or Web Site, *Bruce Brown offers practical advice on the real work -- and opportunity -- involved in building a successful Web business. Anyone considering a Web business will find this book valuable reading."*

> — **Michael Warren, President**
> USA4SALE Networks, Inc.
> publisher of several free classified sites based
> in Florida, including www.ocala4sale.com

"The internet offers almost unlimited promotional opportunities for just about every business. Many of these possibilities are free or inexpensive. Are you a business person who is looking for a new and innovative way to promote your business to a large audience for a reasonable price? Then you need to learn more about internet advertising techniques.

This book is for the business person who has a Web site and wants to utilize it more effectively. Do you understand SEO (search engine optimization)? Effective use of search engines and keywords is critical for strangers to find your site. Have you considered pay-per-click or AdSense possibilities for your Web site?

In addition to your Web site, you can do many things to draw new customers to your site and encourage them to visit often. Newsletters, articles, specials, and more are wonderful tips to attract and keep visitors. Would an affiliate program help you? It's a very effective promotional tool, and ways to optimize the exposure are discussed in this book.

You will find many tips and suggestions to help you learn to promote your online or brick-and-mortar business more effectively. The possibilities are only limited by your imagination."

— **Nikki Leigh, Author**
www.nikkileigh.com
Moderator, www.affcommunity.com
Contributing Editor, www.affiliatemarketing

"If terms like affiliate, e-zines, auto-responders, search engine optimization, and banner advertising leave you confused and unsure where to begin your online marketing and promotions strategy, take heart. How to Use the Internet to Advertise, Promote, and Market Your Business or Web Site offers up clear explanations and concrete ideas you can put to work today."

— **Terry Rilling, Retired marketing professional**

Learn to take advantage of the INTERNET

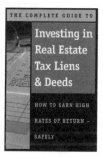